PENGUI

JUST LIKE THAT

Osho defies categorization, reflecting everything from the individual quest for meaning to the most urgent social and political issues facing society today. His books are not written but are transcribed from recordings of extemporaneous talks given over a period of thirty-five years. Osho has been described by the *Sunday Times* in London as one of the '1000 Makers of the 20th Century' and by *Sunday Mid-Day* in India as one of the ten people—along with Gandhi, Nehru and Buddha—who have changed the destiny of India.

Osho has a stated aim of helping to create the conditions for the birth of a new kind of human being, characterized as 'Zorba the Buddha'—one whose feet are firmly on the ground, yet whose hands can touch the stars. Running like a thread through all aspects of Osho is a vision that encompasses both the timeless wisdom of the East and the highest potential of Western science and technology.

He is synonymous with a revolutionary contribution to the science of inner transformation and an approach to meditation which specifically addresses the accelerated pace of contemporary life. The unique Osho Active Meditations™ are designed to allow the release of accumulated stress in the body and mind so that it is easier to be still and experience the thought-free state of meditation.

OTHER BOOKS BY OSHO IN PENGUIN

- *The Book of Man*
- *The Book of Woman*
- *Yoga: The Science of Living*
- *The Essence of Yoga*
- *Little Book of Relationships*
- *Little Book of Osho*
- *Osho: New Man for the New Millennium*
- *The Inner Journey: Spontaneous Talks Given by Osho to Disciples and Friends at a Meditation Camp in Ajol, Gujarat, in India*
- *Life's Mysteries: An Introduction to the Teaching of Osho*

OSHO

Just Like That
Talks on Sufi Stories

PENGUIN BOOKS

PENGUIN BOOKS

Published by the Penguin Group

Penguin Books India Pvt. Ltd, 11 Community Centre, Panchsheel Park, New Delhi 110 017, India

Penguin Group (USA) Inc., 375 Hudson Street, New York, New York 10014, USA

Penguin Group (Canada), 90 Eglinton Avenue East, Suite 700, Toronto, Ontario, M4P 2Y3, Canada (a division of Pearson Penguin Canada Inc.)

Penguin Books Ltd, 80 Strand, London WC2R 0RL, England

Penguin Ireland, 25 St Stephen's Green, Dublin 2, Ireland (a division of Penguin Books Ltd)

Penguin Group (Australia), 250 Camberwell Road, Camberwell, Victoria 3124, Australia (a division of Pearson Australia Group Pty Ltd)

Penguin Group (NZ), 67 Apollo Drive, Rosedale, North Shore 0632, New Zealand (a division of Pearson New Zealand Ltd)

Penguin Group (South Africa) (Pty) Ltd, 24 Sturdee Avenue, Rosebank, Johannesburg 2196, South Africa

Penguin Books Ltd, Registered Offices: 80 Strand, London WC2R 0RL, England

Published by Penguin Books India 2008

10 9 8 7 6 5

ISBN 13: 978-0-14306-315-5

This edition is for sale in South Asia only.

Edited by Krishna Prabhu

Osho comments on excerpts from:
The Way Of The Sufi by Idries Shah © 1968 Idries Shah, first published 1968: Jonathan Cape Ltd., 30 Bedford Square, London WC 1, U.K., and *The Sufis* by Idries Shah with introduction by Robert Graves © 1964 Idries Shah, first published 1964 by W.H. Allen, London, UK.

Typeset in Sabon by Mantra Virtual Services, New Delhi
Printed at De-Unique Printers, New Delhi

Contents

Introduction   *vii*

1.   The Unteachable Teaching   1
2.   Why Have You Come?   28
3.   An Open and Shut Case   59
4.   Asking the Experts   85
5.   Mind Games   114
6.   Blind Man's Buff   139
7.   A Man who Loved Seagulls   165
8.   Beyond Mother's Knees   188
9.   When Shibli is Absent   215
10.   Just a Small Coin   240

Introduction

It seems important to me
that Osho be known to an audience
wider than his beautiful community,
and that this book in particular
find new readers.
I am very grateful for his amazing talking,
his daring experiments
with community and transformation,
his enlightenment, and his jokes!
(Did you get the satire
of American consumerism
with the ninety seven Rolls Royces?
Some people missed that.)
The humour always bubbles close,
no matter what's being discussed.

The lack of a 13th floor in American hotels,
the responsibilities of being awake,
a dog jumping in a river,
Gurdjieff's nonidentification,
the prodigal son,
meditation,
the aggression of science,
Shibli and his three teachers –
there's great generosity of detail here,
and His joy is primary.
It's all one thing, really, these morning talks.
Reading them, you'll taste
a fresh springwater from those days.
The catalyst for each is part
of a Sufi story, brilliantly interpreted.
But don't come with your intellectual
acumen drawn.
Or do – He will meet you
however you approach.
This is a profound form of play.
Osho improvises the jazz discourses
of the century.
Better than Gurdjieff.
What am I doing in the front of this book?
I got asked because of my work on Rumi,
and also perhaps because I visited
the commune in Pune in October 1988
and felt very at home there.
Maybe I'm what he called in the early 80's
a *shravakar.*
Here's a Sufi story
that he doesn't discuss in this book:

Ibn Khafif Shirazi once said,
'I heard that there were two great masters in Egypt
So I hurried to reach their presence.
When I arrived I saw
two magnificent teachers meditating.
I greeted them three times,
but they did not answer.
I meditated with them for four days.
Each day I would beg them to talk with me,
since I had come such a long way.
Finally the younger one opened his eyes.
"Ibn Khafif, life is short.
Use the portion that's left
to deepen yourself.
Don't waste time greeting people!"
I asked him to give me some advice.
"Stay in the presence of those
who remind you of your lord,
who not only speak wisdom, but *are* that."
Then he went back into meditation.'

I feel like that man, Ibn Khafif.
At Osho's level of being,
introductions are unnecessary
and serve mostly as puffery
for the introducer.
Let the music begin.

—Coleman Barks, author of translated versions from
Jelaluddin Rumi's Methnawi: *Open Secret*, *We Are Three*,
Delicious Laughter, *Feeling the Shoulder of the Lion*, and
others.

One

The Unteachable Teaching

A MAN CAME to Libnani, a Sufi teacher, and this interchange took place.

Man: I wish to learn. Will you teach me?
Libnani: I do not feel that you know how to learn.

Man: Can you teach me how to learn?
Libnani: Can you learn how to let me teach?

Truth cannot be taught...but it can be learned. And between these two sentences is the key of all understanding. So let me repeat: truth cannot be taught, but it can be learned—because truth is not a teaching, not a doctrine, not a theory, a philosophy, or something like that. Truth is existence. Truth is *being*. Nothing can be said about it.

If you start saying something about it you will go round and round. You will beat around the bush, but you will never reach the centre of it. Once you ask a question *about* you are already on the path of missing it. It can be encountered directly, but not through about. There is no *via media*. Truth is here and now. Only truth is. Nothing else exists. So the moment you raise a question about it the mind has already moved away. You are somewhere else, not here and now.

Truth cannot be taught because words cannot convey it.

Words are impotent. Truth is vast, tremendously vast, infinite. Words are very very narrow. You cannot force truth into words, it is impossible. And how is one going to teach without words?

Silence can be a message. It can convey, it can become the vehicle. But then the question is not of the master's concern to teach it. The question is of the disciple's to learn it.

If it was a question of teaching, then the master would do something.

But words are useless—nothing can be done with them. The master can remain silent and can give the message from every pore of his being—but now the disciple has to understand it. Unaided, without any help from the master, the disciple has to receive it.

That's why in the world of religion teachers don't exist, only masters. A teacher is one who teaches, a master is one who IS. A teacher is one who talks about the truth, a master is truth himself. You can learn, but he cannot teach.

He can be there, open, available—you have to drink him, and you have to eat him. You have to imbibe him. You have to become pregnant with him. You have to absorb.

A master is one who has become the truth and is available for all those who are ready to absorb him; hence Jesus says to his disciples: Eat me. Truth can be eaten; it cannot be taught. You can allow it to reach you, but it cannot be forced on you.

Truth is absolutely nonviolent, it will not even knock at your door—even that much will be too much aggression.

If you allow, if you are receptive, it is all there. If you are closed, if you are not receptive, for millions of lives you may search for it and you will go on missing it. And it has always been there, it has always been the case. Not even a single step was needed. Not even the opening of the eyes was needed. Not even a single movement towards it was needed. It was already there: you had to be receptive.

Truth cannot be taught, but still, you can learn it. So the whole art depends on how to become a disciple.

Humanity is divided in three parts. One part, the major part, almost ninety-nine percent, never bothers about truth. It remains oblivious. It is completely asleep. It has no inquiry. It lives a somnambulistic life. The question of, What is truth? never arises. This is the greater part of humanity.

They live in ignorance, completely unaware that they are ignorant, not only unaware that they are ignorant—they may be thinking and dreaming that they know.

In fact this is part of their sleep, that they think they know. And what is the need to learn? To *destroy* the need to learn, this is the best thing to do: to go on feeling that you already know. Then there is no question of learning, no need to become a disciple. You are satisfied, in your grave. You are dead.

This is the greater part of humanity. Even if you approach people of this fragment and tell them about truth, they will laugh. They will say you are talking nonsense. Not only that, they will deny that there is anything like truth or God or nirvana. If you give them the message of an enlightened being they will say there never existed such a being, and he cannot exist: 'We are the whole of humanity.'

Somebody asked Voltaire about the origin of religion, and Voltaire is reported to have said, 'Religion was born when the first charlatan met the first fool on the earth.' In the encounter of the charlatan and the fool, religion was born. This has an element of truth in it. It is true in a sense, but it is true not about religion, but about pseudo-religion.

Religion is born, not between a charlatan and a fool—pseudo-religions are born that way—religion is born between a master and a disciple. Religion is born between a being who has attained and a being who is authentically in search to attain it. Religion is born between truth and a disciple.

But the first part of humanity remains completely unaware, blissfully unaware, because when there is no inquiry, no search, they live a comfortable life of no effort. They go on falling down. They never rise high, they never reach the peaks. And they don't know. They not only don't know, they never dream that there are peaks of experience, heights of ecstasies.

They remain almost like animals: eating, sleeping—and confined to such things. A life of routine, moving like a wheel; they are born, they live, they give birth to others, and they die. And the wheel goes on moving: they are born again, the same thing is repeated again and again, ad nauseam.

Then there is the second part of humanity: a few, who inquire. But they don't know how to learn. They search, but they don't understand that this search needs an inner transformation, only then it becomes possible. An inner mutation is needed.

In this dimension, learning is not like other learnings. You can learn chemistry, physics, mathematics, without any change in your consciousness. There is no need to change your consciousness; as you are, you can learn. But religion is a learning in which a basic requirement is: First change your consciousness.

Even before the learning starts you have to be prepared for it. A long preparation is needed, otherwise learning cannot start.

The second part inquires, but is not ready, so it goes on round and round in theories, hypotheses, human mental projections, inventions of articulate people, verbalizations, philosophies, metaphysics—there are thousands of theories available for this type of person.

He can choose—the market is vast, and he can go on changing from one theory to another, because no theory can give you the right thing. Theories can't give, so you get fed up with one theory, then you choose another; you get fed up with one teacher, then you move to another teacher—and people go on, they become wanderers.

I come across the second type of people every day. They have been to this ashram, they have been to that, they have been to this teacher and to that, and they have been moving from one to another: nothing satisfies. But they are not aware that it is not a question of the teacher, it is the basic preparation that they are lacking. They are not yet ready to be disciples, and if you are not ready to be a disciple, how can you find the master? Tradition has it that when the disciple is ready the master appears on his own accord. You need not even search for him, he will come. Whenever a disciple is ready, the master will appear immediately. You go on searching for him, and he never appears. Something is wrong within you. Something within you frustrates the whole effort. You are not ready.

You cannot meet a master on your conditions, you have to fulfil *his* conditions. And they are eternal, they have never changed, they remain the same. One has to learn how to be a disciple.

This second part of humanity becomes a wandering mass of inquirers. They never gain much. They become rolling stones, which never gather any moss. They move on...rolling.

Then there is a third part—very rare human beings, exceptions, the cream of humanity.

That third part is those who seek, who inquire; but the inquiry is not intellectual, the inquiry is total. The inquiry is not like learning any other subject; the inquiry is so total that they are ready to die for it, they are ready to change their whole being for it. They are ready to fulfil all conditions. Even if death is a condition, they are ready to die. But they want to learn what truth is, they want to be in the world of truth; they don't want to live in the world of lies and illusions and dreams and projections.

This third type can become a disciple. And only this third type, when they have attained, can become masters.

That's why I say truth cannot be taught but it can be learned. But then the whole thing depends on you.

A master exists—you have to be in the presence of the master completely empty of yourself. That is the meaning of death. A disciple comes and dies before the master. That's what surrender means.

He comes and leaves himself outside the door. Where he leaves his shoes, he leaves himself there also. He comes to the master completely empty. In that very emptiness, truth is possible. In that very emptiness the master starts flowing. The master becomes like a tremendous waterfall, falling into the valley of the disciple. From his peaks of being he reaches to the bottommost depth of the being of the disciple. And remember, he is not doing anything, it simply happens. When the valley is ready the waterfall happens of its own accord. The being of the master starts flowing towards the disciple.

It is not something that the master is doing, it is not something the disciple is doing—nobody is doing anything. The master is present to the disciple, and the disciple is present to the master, and the phenomenon happens of its own accord. It is a jump of the flame of the master into the heart of the disciple. But that needs to remain open, and the disciple needs to remain empty—just the receiving end.

That's why I say again and again that the art of disciplehood is the art of being a feminine consciousness: receptive, allowing, not creating barriers, not closing doors, not trying to be safe and secure. Trusting.

Trust is the word. And in trust, truth happens. To trust is to be ready to learn. Yes, trust is the word. To trust is to be a disciple.

If you are still thinking, then you are still in control. You have not surrendered. If you are still saying this is right and that is not right, then your mind is there, then you belong to the second part of humanity, not to the third.

Now, let me divide these three parts again from a different direction. The first part of humanity has doubt as its soul, and the doubt is so strong that it is almost like a trust in doubt, believing in disbelief. It is so strong because the first part of humanity—the greater part—the major part, never doubts its own doubt. It trusts doubt.

If you are so much in doubt, so certain in doubt, you will be completely closed. Not even a single window will be open. To be a disciple is very very far away; even to become a student is difficult then. Even the idea that somebody knows more than you is impossible for you to entertain.

This part remains foolish, stupid. It is a stonelike part, dead, with no life, because unless energy is moving continuously into the unknown, you can't have life.

When every day you move into the unknown, only then you are alive, throbbing. Your heart is beating. You are growing. Growth is always from the known into the unknown.

The second part of humanity inquires; its doubt is shaken. But its trust is not yet grounded. No more is it part of the greater humanity, it has moved away from them a little bit— even that little bit is too much to allow them to go back— but it is still in limbo, just hanging in the middle. It has no trust.

The first part trusts too much in doubt, the second part has come to doubt its doubt, but a trust is not born. The third part is trusting in trust. The trust is absolute. The people of the second part will call you blind. Your *shraddha*, your trust in trust, will appear to them as blindness. The first part of humanity will call you mad. Your trust will look just like madness. How can a person who thinks believe so totally? It is impossible. But to the third part, to whom trust has happened, the blindness will be the only capacity to see. And madness will be the only sanity.

These three different humanities have different languages. They don't communicate with each other—it is almost impossible. It is just like when you are talking to somebody who does not know your language, and you don't know his language—at the most through gestures a little communication is possible, but not much.

Sufis say that only the third part of humanity can learn. Sufi masters are very choosy. It is very difficult to be accepted by a Sufi master, very very difficult. They create all sorts of obstacles around them.

First, they live in such an ordinary way that you cannot suspect that here is a master. They live in absolutely ordinary ways. For example, the master may be a blacksmith or a shoemaker or a carpet maker or a butcher or a carpenter— just the very ordinary world. You cannot suspect that the man who makes your shoes and repairs your shoes is a master. He won't allow any suspicion; that is the way he protects himself from those who are not ready but think themselves ready. From intruders he protects himself in this way.

You will never see a Sufi master going to the mosque or the temple—to any public place—to pray. No, he prays when everybody is fast asleep, at midnight. Even his wife may not suspect what this man has attained. No, this is part of the Sufi method—not to allow anybody to know.

Jesus must have lived with some Sufis in Egypt. He carries a few of their teachings in the Bible. One of them is: Whatsoever you do with your right hand, don't allow your left hand to know about it. This is a Sufi tradition: Live completely in the dark, so nobody knows and intruders don't come, pseudo-seekers don't knock, and foolish people don't trespass on your time and your energy.

Then second, if somehow you come to know about a Sufi master, years you will have to wait with him—as an apprentice, not for meditation. If he is a shoemaker, you will have to learn shoemaking for years. And they are hard taskmasters. Sometimes ten, twelve years will pass and you will be simply working on shoes and preparing shoes, and the question should never be raised, unless the master himself asks, 'What have you come for? What do you want?'

He will watch you. He will be with you. In that togetherness something will grow, by and by, through very indirect methodology—for example, shoemaking. It is a meditation because the disciple is told to do only the thing that is given to be done; no thinking is allowed.

And remember this, if you work with your hands there is much possibility for the mind to remain vacant. If you work with the mind, then there is less possibility of course because the mind will have to think.

Sufis work with their hands—carpet making, shoemaking, carpentry, or anything whatsoever, but with their hands. Hand and head are the two poles, and if your energy is moving through the hands, the head by and by subsides. And if for years, twelve years—such a long time!—you are simply working with the hands, you completely forget the head. There is no need of it. The head becomes nonfunctioning, and that is what is needed for a disciple: the head must be in a nonfunctioning state. Thinking should stop. The mind should become like a no-mind. Not filled with thoughts, dreams, ideas. Completely empty.

While the disciple is an apprentice, working on shoemaking, the master goes on watching what is happening in his head. Is the energy completely moving into the hands?

Now physiologists agree that if you work with the hands, the same energy moves from the head. The energy is the same. Your right hand is joined with your left brain, your left hand is joined with your right brain. Try this: whenever you feel that there is too much thinking, and you cannot stop it, rub both your hands fast, make them hot by rubbing, and suddenly you will feel the head has stopped, the energy is moving in the hands.

People who cannot sleep—this is the best medicine for them yet known, better than any tranquilizer. Just close your eyes and rub your hands, and feel them getting warmer and warmer and warmer—and through rubbing they will get warmer—and you put into your imagination also that they are getting warmer. When the hands are warm, the head becomes cool. These are the two polarities.

Hands should be warm, and the head should be cool. But when there is too much thinking, the head will be warm and the hands will be cool. That is unhealthy. You are going towards madness. A moment will come when the head starts functioning on its own, unconnected with the whole body. That is what madness means: a part has become autonomous, a part has become dictatorial.

Zen masters in Japan always go on working with the hands. Sufi masters in Mohammedan countries always go on working with the hands. Doing something with the hands is always beautiful. It brings your head energy down into the body.

If you continue for years to work with the hands you become head*less*. The physical part of the head remains, but the energy part, the thinking part, disappears; you become headless.

For years a disciple has to be with the master. Difficult unless you trust, because who knows whether this man is a master or not? Who knows whether he has attained or not? How to judge? But if you trust, by and by an inner affinity with the master happens, an inner affinity, just as it happens sometimes with lovers, but rarely, because lovers never surrender. They talk about it, they say they have surrendered, but they never surrender. In fact through surrender they may be trying to manipulate the other, the surrender may be just a trick. The fight continues in lovers.

Rarely, but sometimes it happens, if two lovers are really in love, an affinity happens. Somewhere they become one. A bridge comes into existence. The bodies remain two, but their inner flames come so close that they become one. Rarely it happens in love; and only for moments—again the flames go apart, come again together, go apart. It continues to be so. But between a disciple and a master, when this closeness happens it goes on growing closer and closer and closer, and a moment comes when only two bodies exist: somewhere in the inner world the beings are no more two. The jump, the leap of the flame has happened.

To learn from a master is to learn how to be with him. To learn from a master is to learn how *not* to be with yourself.

Religious learning is a totally different dimension from other learnings, other disciplines. In other disciplines you remain the same. And you start accumulating information. You want to learn about geography—you go to a teacher and you learn. You remain the same, only information goes on increasing. You become more and more knowledgeable, but your being, your quality of being, your state of being remains the same.

When you come to learn religion, or truth, then it is different: it is not accumulation of information, it is not an increase in your knowledge; it is a growth in your being. Not that you will know more, but that you will *be* more. Not that your memory will be more disciplined, no, but your being, your very being will become more still and silent, blissful.

Religion is the learning of being. And all other learnings are just training for memories. All other disciplines give you knowledge. Religion gives you *knowing*, not knowledge; knowing, the capacity to see, the tremendous energy to be. This difference has to be understood, then you will be able to understand this small dialogue—but very potent.

A man came to Libnani, a Sufi teacher, and this interchange took place.

Man: I wish to learn. Will you teach me?

The man emphasizes his wish. That is necessary, but not enough. You may wish, that doesn't show that you are ready. Your wish may be just a dream, your wish may be founded on wrong reasons, your wish may have no willpower behind it, it may be impotent. Your wish may be the wish of a beggar—and truth is not possible for a beggar. Your wish may be just childish. By accident you may have come upon the idea that one needs truth, that one needs to know God.

A wish is very feeble unless it becomes a burning desire— what Sri Aurobindo calls *abheepsa*. *Abheepsa* means such an intense burning desire that you are completely absorbed by it. Nothing of you is left behind. It is not a part of you that desires, it is the whole of you that desires. The desire has become your being. Then it is *abheepsa*. It is a total desire in which everything is surrendered.

A wish is just a ripple on the surface of the mind. You are passing on the road and a beautiful Rolls Royce passes by: a wish comes in the mind that you also would like to have a Rolls Royce. You see a beautiful woman—and a wish arises. A wish is just a ripple on the surface—and truth is not open for those who come to it in such a feeble way. Truth demands you in your totality.

Truth is like a woman: it wants to possess you totally. Truth won't tolerate any competitor, it is jealous. If you think that you have a hundred wishes, and one wish is for truth, then you are not ready for truth. When the hundred wishes disappear and only one wish remains, when all the wishes disappear in one wish, it becomes *abheepsa*.

It becomes a burning desire, a total desire—your whole being aflame, afire—and you are ready to risk anything and everything.

The man said: *I wish to learn.*

Learning is not possible if you simply wish. It happens every day that people come to me, they talk about god and meditation and this and that, and if I don't answer them immediately they ask something, if I go on talking about something else, within seconds they have forgotten that they had come to ask about god. It is just a wish, a whim in the mind, not rooted. Otherwise, if you are thirsty and you come and you ask about water, and I talk about other things, those other things won't quench your thirst; rather, on the contrary, your thirst will grow while I am talking about other things. Whenever I start you will say again, 'Give me a glass of water, I am thirsty.' And if I go on talking about other things your thirst will grow meanwhile. When I stop again you will say, 'I will die! Give me a glass of water!'

But you come and you talk about god, and you say you would like to know about god, and I ask about your health and how is your wife, and how are your children?—and you have forgotten about god. Then you remain with me for one hour and you never mention anything about god again.

It was not a thirst, just a vagrant wish, just a vagabond wish with no roots in you. Just a ripple on the surface, a breeze passed. You were passing on the road and you saw a sannyasin. The orange robe—and a wish came into the mind: you would also like to know what this sannyas is. You had never thought about it before, never dreamed about it before, it has never been a desire—just, you saw a sannyasin and suddenly the orange robe created a wish in you. A breeze passed and created a ripple, and you would also like to do what these mad orange people are doing.

And what is meditation? You come to me, and you ask about meditation. But you don't mean it. You ask and you don't mean it. You think it is as if I can give you meditation and you will carry it home just like any other commodity from the market.

Meditation will need long preparation. Meditation will change you completely.

One woman came to me—she belongs to one of the richest families in India—and she said she would like to meditate, but she wants to know, if she meditates, is it going to create some trouble in her life?

I asked, 'What type of trouble do you mean?'

She said she had a husband and children and a big family. If she meditated, would it create a rift?—because the husband was not interested in meditation at all. Not only not interested, he was against it: 'And I have come to you without his knowledge. I can secretly meditate, but I want to be certain that it will not disturb my family life in any way.'

Another woman was with her who had followed her. She said, 'What are you saying…because meditation will make you better! You will be more silent, more happy—how is that going to disturb your life? Your life will become better!'

I listened. Then the woman said, 'Yes, if this is going to be so, I am ready.'

I told her, 'This is not going to be so, because whether you become good or bad it makes no difference: you change, and the relationship will be in disturbance.'

Sometimes I have watched: if you become bad it doesn't affect your relationship so much as when you become good, because when you become better the other ego is hurt more.

If a husband starts meditating, the wife's ego is hurt more—her husband is going beyond her, and he is moving away from her. He may become more silent, so that when his wife is angry he may not react—but that will create more anger. The wife will think, 'What does he think of himself?

Has he become a saint?'

She will try to bring you down, back where you were before. Your anger is known to her but your silence is unfamiliar, you look strange. You don't look like her husband. You are a totally different man, and if you go on rising higher in meditation, you become more and more independent—the wife feels she is being left behind. That cannot be tolerated.

If a husband becomes a drunkard it is okay, nothing much is wrong. On the contrary, deep down the wife may feel good because she appears better than the husband, and she can teach and preach and moralize, and whenever the husband comes she can create guilt in him, that he is a drunkard—'and you are killing me and the children and the whole family! What are you doing?' She feels good if you are bad, because it is always a comparative feeling. A drunkard can be tolerated. If a husband starts going to prostitutes, that can be tolerated. But if the husband starts meditating, becomes religious, that is intolerable, that is impossible to tolerate. It hurts, it hurts deeply.

I told the woman, 'As far as I know, if you meditate it is going to create trouble. You will become silent, you will become happy, more blissful, more contented, but your husband will feel left behind. A gap will arise between you. The planes will become different. You will move farther away.'

Then the wife said, 'Then wait. Then I don't want any meditation, any silence, any prayer, no. I am happy in my life, I don't want to disturb it.'

This is a wish. You would like to have something without disturbing your life in any way. You cannot have anything valuable without disturbing your life in any way, that is

.impossible. In fact, the greater the phenomenon, the more is going to be the disturbance, the more is the risk. If you want God you will be ready to lose all. If you want to become a disciple you will have to surrender all that you have. In that surrender is the only possibility, the possibility of a transfer of being.

I have been telling you again and again the story of Buddha and Mahakashyapa, but it has multidimensional meanings. It is said Buddha sat one morning under the tree, with a flower in his hand. He was going to give a sermon, and the monks waited—ten thousand *bhikkhus* waiting and waiting, and it was getting hotter, and the sun had risen high, and Buddha was silent and looking at the flower. Then suddenly one disciple by the name of Mahakashyapa started laughing loudly, a good belly laugh.

Everybody looked at Mahakashyapa: Has he gone mad? This morning seems to be strange; Buddha has never done this—he has always come and talked. Today he has come with a flower and he is sitting and looking at the flower as if he has forgotten all the ten thousand disciples who are there.

And then, look! Now this Mahakashyapa was laughing—and nobody had ever heard him laugh, he was such a silent man. In fact nobody had ever *known* him. This was the first time that he had done something publicly. He was so silent, unassuming; he lived like a shadow. Nobody ever felt his presence even. He was absolutely nonaggressive, because when you try to let your presence be felt, that is violence. You are trying to attract attention. This man nobody knew. What has happened to him? He has gone mad!

Buddha looked, called Mahakashyapa near him, gave him the flower, and told him, 'Whatsoever I could give through words I have given to others, and that which cannot be given through words—I give it to you, Mahakashyapa.'

In Zen they call it a transfer beyond scriptures, a transfer beyond words.

What was given to Mahakashyapa? Still they go on asking in Zen monasteries, still Buddhists go on pondering over it. Twenty-five centuries have passed since that morning, and great philosophers have pondered over it: What happened that morning? What was transferred? It was not a transfer of a flower, a flower is just a symbol. It was a transfer of the whole being of Buddha to Mahakashyapa. Not that Buddha entered into Mahakashyapa; he remained himself. It is just— you bring one lighted lamp near another which is not lighted; suddenly the flame jumps from the lighted lamp to the unlighted lamp. The lighted lamp remains the same, nothing has been lost, not even a bit, but a new light has come into being. It is a leap, a jump of truth—*that* had happened that morning.

Buddha gave the flower as a symbol. The flower has remained a symbol in India of the absolute flowering of consciousness. A lotus flower means when the consciousness has flowered absolutely, and the fragrance has been released into the cosmos. That morning Buddha jumped, the flame of Buddha jumped into Mahakashyapa. This is how truth is transferred.

Just wishing for it cannot be of much help. You have to desire it, you have to desire it so deeply that you become the desire, just a fire, a desire, a burning flame of desire. Be near a master and be a burning flame of desire to *know*, and suddenly one day it happens: a transfer beyond scriptures, a transfer beyond words, a transfer from being to being, not from mind to mind. That's what Buddha said: 'Whatsoever can be said through words, I have given it to others, a transfer from mind to mind, and that which cannot be said, I give it to you, Mahakashyapa'—a transfer from being to being. Others were students, Mahakashyapa was a disciple. Mahakashyapa became the second buddha.

The man said: *I wish to learn...*

This is a very feeble thing. You can learn geography, chemistry, and other such nonsense, by wishing to learn. People learn even without wishing, people learn even against their wish. Look at the children; they are forced to go to school against their wish, they never wish to go, they have been forced—even they can learn. They come out of the universities with Ph.Ds and they never had any wish to learn. Now they have become doctors, Ph.Ds, D.Litts, they will become professors and they will teach others who have no wish to learn.

As far as worldly knowledge is concerned even without a wish it can be learned, but as far as religious knowing is concerned even with wishing it is not possible. The wish has to become a burning desire, *abheepsa*.

In English there is no word like *abheepsa*. It means when only the desire is left, nothing else. Even the one who desires is no more there, he is also part of the desire. When the desire is not part of you but you have become part of the desire, then it is *abheepsa*.

I wish to learn, said the man. *Will you teach me?*

A master cannot be asked in this way. It is not a question of the master's will to teach; he is always ready to teach. It is not a question of his willing or not willing; he *is* the teaching. Even while he is sitting silently, he is teaching. He is breathing silently—he is teaching. He is moving—he is teaching. He is eating his food—he is teaching. He is asleep—he is teaching. A master is a continuum of the message. He is teaching.

Once it happened: A man came to a Zen master and asked to be taught. The master said, 'Okay. You be here, and I will teach you.' The man remained for one, two, three hours, then his patience came to an end.

Many people were coming and going. Many people were asking many questions—the master had many disciples, a great monastery, and he was talking to people, teaching people, giving them methods, solving their problems—and the man was sitting in the corner. He became very impatient, almost feverish.

When he could get a time he said, 'Wait. I have been here for three hours and you have not taught me anything!'

The master looked at him and said, 'What have I been doing the whole time? People came, they asked me questions, I answered. There was teaching in it—not in the answer but in the answering. You should have watched how I answered. People came, they greeted me, I responded. There was teaching. And sometimes people came and they simply sat by my side in silence, and I was silent, they were silent—there was teaching for you. What have I been doing for these three hours, you fool! I have been teaching you.' But the man was at a loss. He couldn't understand what type of teaching this was.

A master does not teach, he *is* the teaching. His whole being is a message, a continuous message. The way he moves his eyes, the way he gestures, the way he looks at you—something is there continuously being conveyed. And if you cannot see you are blind.

It is not a question to ask a master: Will you teach me? That is what he exists for. His own work is fulfilled, his own work done. As far as he himself is concerned now there is no need to breathe anymore, everything is finished. If he lingers a little while on the shore, it is for you; otherwise his ship has arrived. In fact, the ship has been waiting long. If he lingers a little while more on the shore it is for you. It is to teach. It is to share that which he has attained. It is not a question of asking a master, 'Will you teach me?' Rather, on the contrary, one has to ask, 'Am I ready to be taught?'

Libnani said:

I do not feel that you know how to learn.

When you come to a master it is not a question of what you say. He does not bother to listen to you, what you say. He feels what you are. You may say, 'I wish to learn,' or you may say, 'I desire to learn,' or you may say, 'I am burning with desire and I am ready to surrender....'

This happens. People come to me and they say, 'Accept us, we are totally at your disposal. Whatsoever you want to make of us, make. We are surrendered.' They touch my feet. And if I say to them, 'Then become a sannyasin, be initiated,' they say, 'That is difficult. It will be very very difficult to move in orange robes in the market.' And just a moment before the man was saying, 'I am at your disposal, surrendered, and whatsoever you want to make of me you can.' He is not ready even to change his dress, and he was saying that he allows me to change his being!

He is not aware of what he has said just a moment before. People are talking in their sleep, drunk. They don't know what they are saying. They may be touching my feet, but they don't know what they are doing—because if it is just a gesture, a polite gesture, it is meaningless. If it is just a mannerism, it carries no significance. But if it is real, authentic, then it can become a transforming force.

But if immediately I say, 'Change your clothes,' they are afraid. And if I say, 'Change your being,' how will it be possible for them?...because if just changing the clothes creates trouble in the market, when you change your being you will be constantly in trouble. Wherever you go you will be constantly in trouble because you will be an outsider. You will belong to a different world, and nobody will feel familiar to you. Even your own people will become separate and fall apart, they will not be able to understand you, you will become a foreigner in your own home. You will be an outsider and people will avoid you, they will not come near you. They will be afraid, because your disease can be infectious.

One need not ask a master; one has to be just in the presence of the master. In India we use the word *darshan*. That means just to be in the presence of the master. Don't say anything—he can know without your saying, and whatsoever you say may not be true about you because you are so fragmentary. One fragment says something, another fragment says something else—you are a crowd, you are not one. This moment you say something, the next moment you change. You are a confusion, a chaos.

When you are near a master, you just put yourself in his presence and leave it to him to decide what type of man you are and what is possible for you. Let the master decide—don't say anything.

Libnani said: *I do not feel...*You say that you wish but I can feel you—*I do not feel that you know how to learn.* You are incapable. You don't have the receptivity. You don't have that feminine being which can learn. You are not open. I can see—you are closed from everywhere, not even a keyhole from where something can enter...all windows closed, all doors closed.

When you are closed you have different vibrations around you. Even from miles away a master can feel whether the man who is coming is closed or open. An open being has a different quality: weightlessness, as if he doesn't walk; he flies, as if gravitation has no effect on him. He is no more part of the earth.

An open being is totally different. When you come to a master, and if you are open, you are ready to learn.

This man must have been closed. He had come to learn but he was not ready to open. How can you learn if you are not open? A mind filled with prejudices, concepts, theories, scriptures, knowledge, is not capable of learning. To learn one has to unlearn first. Unlearning is the way of learning.

Whatsoever you know, you have to drop it; a clean slate is needed. You are filled too much; too much knowledge you carry already in your head. This man must have been a scholar or something, a pundit. He may have known the Koran, may have crammed it completely, could have repeated it by memory.

The master said, 'I feel that you don't know how to learn. You have come to me but you have not come to me. You have carried all your luggage—rubbish, rot, inside the mind. Throw it out!' Only then is there the possibility that you can learn something.

A man came to Ramana Maharshi and said, 'I have come from very far, somewhere in Germany, and I have come to learn from you.' Ramana said, 'Then you go elsewhere, because here we teach unlearning. Learning is not our way. You go elsewhere.'

He may have been a German scholar, he may have known the Vedas, Upanishads, it may have been because of his learning that he became interested in Ramana. Reading the

Upanishads, the desire arises to find a man who knows. Moving through the pages of the Vedas one becomes enchanted, charmed, magnetized, hypnotized. One starts seeking a man who is a seer of whom the Vedas talk, a man of the calibre of the seers of the Upanishads—a man who knows. He may have come because of the scriptures.

But you don't know the man who knows. He is always against scriptures. Scriptures may lead to him, but he will tell you to drop all scriptures. The ladder through which you have come—he will say, 'Throw it! Now that you have reached me there is no need for Vedas and Upanishads and Korans; you drop them! Now I am here, alive.'

Jesus says: I am truth, no need to bring scriptures here. Ramana said, 'Then you go elsewhere, because here we teach unlearning. If you are ready to unlearn, be here. If you have come to learn more, then this is not the right place. Then go somewhere else—universities exist for learning. When you come to me, come to unlearn. This is a university for unlearning, a university to create no-mind, a university where whatsoever you know will be taken away.'

All your knowledge has to be dropped so that you become knowing, so you get a perfection, a clarity, so that your eyes are not filled with theses, or theories, with prejudices, concepts; so your eyes have a clarity, an absolute clarity and transparency, so that you can see. The truth is already there. It has always been there.

Said Libnani: *I do not feel that you know how to learn.*

Man: *Can you teach me how to learn?*

Must have been a very logical man. He reacts logically. He says, 'Okay, if you think I am not ready to learn, then teach me how to learn.' *Can you teach me how to learn?*

With logic this is the problem: the problem remains the same. Libnani says: *I do not feel that you know how to learn.* The man gives a logical reply. If he had been a man of understanding, not of logic, he would have closed his eyes. He would have looked within, he would have watched around his own being and self: 'What does Libnani say? He says he feels that I do not know how to learn'—he should have observed his own being.

If he was a man of understanding then he would have meditated on it. He would have said to Libnani, 'I will go and meditate over it, what you have said. You have said a great truth. Already you have started teaching me. I have already learned something—that I don't know how to learn! I already know at least this much. This can become a good beginning. I will go and I will meditate over it. It is such a potent truth that you have said to me. You have felt rightly. Let me now watch myself to understand whatsoever you have said to me.'

But no, the man must have been a logical man; not a man of understanding but a man who knows, knowledgeable. He argues the point like a lawyer. He says, 'This is an argument.' He says, 'Okay, if you feel that I don't know how to learn, can you teach me how to learn?' Again the emphasis is on the master: 'Can *you* teach me?' The emphasis has not shifted a single bit.

He goes on thinking that truth is something to be taught, and Libnani is emphasizing the fact that truth is something to be learned. And that is their polarity. Very subtle. He has missed the point. He again says the same thing: *Can you teach me how to learn?*

Libnani: Can you learn how to let me teach?

The emphasis remains the same on both sides. Again Libnani says: *Can you learn how to let me teach?*

Truth cannot be taught. But it can be learned. And if you think that it can be taught you will go on wandering and wandering and wandering. You may meet many teachers and masters, but you will not meet truth because from the very beginning you have taken a wrong step. The emphasis should be that truth can be learned. The emphasis is on the disciple, and if the disciple is ready, the master appears.

And what is disciplehood? It is openness. It is receptivity. It is a welcoming attitude. It is trust.

Have you ever watched a roseflower? In the evening when the sun is setting and the day is over and the roseflower has had its day and now it is time to dissolve, the petals of the roseflower start falling, slowly, towards the ground, with no hesitation. A rose petal, so delicate, but so strong, doesn't hesitate about where it is falling, where it is going, whether there is any earth to find, to rest, to go to sleep, to die—or is it falling in a bottomless abyss? Who knows? But no hesitation. So soft, so delicate, but so strong, not any uncertainty, not any clinging to the flower anymore. The time has come. It simply leaves the flower and falls to the ground.

A Sufi master used to say to his disciples: Simply trust. Do not the petals flutter down just like that?

When you come to a master be like a rose petal. Fall into the master, fall unto the master just like that—as a rose petal falls towards the earth unhesitating, absolutely in trust that the earth must be there—to rest, to die, with no effort of its own. The very gravitation of the earth does the work—it has just to trust. If it trusts, it doesn't cling to the plant, it just trusts and flutters down.

Simply trust! That is what disciplehood is. Do not the petals flutter down just like that?

Enough for today.

Two

Why Have You Come?

BAHAUDDIN EL-SHAH was sitting with a number of disciples *when a number of followers came into the meeting hall. El-Shah asked each of them, one by one, to say why he was there.*

The first said: You are the greatest man on earth. I gave him a potion when he was ill, so he thinks I am the greatest man on earth, said El-Shah.

The second said: My spiritual life has opened up since I have been allowed to visit you.

He was uncertain and ill at ease and none would listen to him. I sat with him, and the resultant serenity is called by him his spiritual life, said El-Shah.

The third said: You understand me, and all I ask is that you allow me to hear your discourses for the good of my soul.

He needs attention and wished to have notice paid to him even if it is criticism, said El-Shah. This he calls the good of his soul.

The fourth said: I went from one to another practising what they taught. It was not until you gave me a wazifa exercise that I truly felt the illumination of contact with you.

The exercise I gave this man was a concocted one

not related to his spiritual life at all, said El-Shah.
I had to demonstrate his illusion of spirituality
before I could arrive at the part of this man which
is really spiritual, not sentimental.

The search depends on the seeker. Masters can only show
the way. The search depends on the seeker—what quality of
being, what quality of inquiry the seeker brings to the search.
Everything will depend on it, on why he is in search, what
the reason is, because the reason of the search will become
the cause of his growth. If the reason is wrong, from the very
beginning he has taken a wrong step, and the right end cannot
follow a wrong beginning. The first step is the last step also,
because the first step implies in it, has in it already, the last
step as a potentiality.

The seed is the tree because the seed will become the tree.
The end will come out of the growth of the seeker, and if
from the very beginning a wrong reason exists to seek and
search, then everything is going to be in vain.

The masters can only show the way, they can only indicate.
Everything else has to be done by you, by the disciple. The
discipline is not going to be imposed; no master ever imposes
a discipline on anybody. He helps you to find your
discipline—that is the difference between a pseudo-master
and a real master.

A pseudo-master is one who has already a ready-made
formula, a pattern. He imposes that pattern on each and
everybody, whosoever comes to him. The man who comes is
irrelevant to a pseudo-master. The man who comes is just a
number, not a person, just something on which he can project,
impose his discipline—which is a ready-made phenomenon.
He has already the blueprint in his mind. A pseudo-master

kills many people, destroys many people, because everybody has his own blueprint of growth within him. No outer discipline is needed.

A real master, a master like Bahauddin, does not impose anything on you. He simply helps you to find your discipline, he helps you to seek your way. He helps you to grow, not according to him but according to your own being—because you are the seed and the tree is going to come out of you. The master can at the most be a loving gardener, a compassion which goes on showering on you. It nurses you, but it does not impose anything upon you.

With a real master also you will die. But there will be a resurrection. With a pseudo-master you are simply destroyed with no possibility of any creation out of it.

This has to be remembered by you all. You are here with me. I am not giving you any forced discipline. That doesn't mean that I am against discipline. No, I am all for it. But the discipline should come out of you. Your discipline will be your discipline, nobody else's. Your flower will be your flower, nobody else's, and that is going to be unique. That is the beauty—that whenever truth is attained it is always unique because everybody attains in his own way. Everybody flowers into it as an individual. You become more and more authentically individual.

This is the meaning of resurrection—the false within you will die. But you carry the real. You are already pregnant with it, it has to be helped.

A real master is what Socrates used to say about himself—that he is a midwife. A real master is a midwife. He does not give you anything, he simply helps you, your own being, to be brought to light, to be brought to birth. But if you have come with a wrong reason then the master cannot help you because you will frustrate all his efforts.

Just a few days ago a man came to see me from South America. He had travelled long just to see me, but then could not see me. He himself frustrated his own effort.

He is a sort of guru in his own right. He has many followers in Latin America. And that created the trouble. He thinks himself somebody special so he wanted a special interview with me, not with anybody else present. He was not ready to come at seven in the evening when I usually see people. With others, it was hurtful to his ego. He wanted a special interview, only for him. I could have given it, but that would have been wrong. There was no trouble in it, he could have been given a separate time, but that would have been very very dangerous to his own growth, because then I am yielding to a wrong reason.

He thinks himself special; hence he needs a special interview. This egoistic standpoint will not be of any use. From the very beginning something is wrong. The very first step is going to be wrong. So I didn't give him a special interview. I insisted: You come at seven o'clock tomorrow evening. He must have felt frustrated. He wrote a letter, and he wrote, 'I will be waiting for you at Hotel Amir tomorrow at four o'clock in the afternoon.' He wrote it in such a way that it can either mean that he wants me physically to go to the Hotel Amir, or it may mean that he simply wants my spiritual presence to be there. That too is tricky, clever and cunning.

At four o'clock I really tried. I really tried to make contact with him because the man *has* potential. The man has a potentiality, and can be helped tremendously. He can grow and become a beautiful flower. But the ego is also very great.

I made an attempt to be there spiritually at four o'clock

but he was not even waiting for me. When I reached his room it was filled with tobacco smoke, and he was smoking, surrounded by smoke, not even waiting for me, because this is no way to wait. He should have been in meditation. He should have closed his room and become silent, as silent as possible, because physical contact is possible without any special preparation by you, but spiritual contact needs preparation. It needs a receptivity. It needs a subtle awareness, because the phenomenon is very very subtle. It is like such a small breeze coming in that if you are not aware you will not be able to feel it. It is not like a storm that, even if you are fast asleep, you will be awakened by.

I reached, I stood by his side. On the outside he was surrounded by the smoke of his cigarette, and inside, even a deeper smoke of the ego. And in his mind were racing many thoughts, and not even a single thought of me.

Of course, at seven o'clock he didn't turn up to see me. Again a message: 'Because you didn't contact me at four o'clock I am not going to come to see you.'

And then he had to go back. He had come a long way, but something in him frustrates his whole effort: the ego. He must have come for some wrong reason. He must have come to be recognized by me, that he is something special. And I tell you, he *is* special, but the very effort that he wanted recognition frustrates the whole journey from the very beginning. The first step goes wrong.

I could have yielded if he was an ordinary man. I could have even gone to the Amir Hotel. There was no trouble. Physically I could have gone because then there would be nothing much at stake. This man has potential, a great possibility lies deep in him, but he himself is frustrating it. He needs to be humble, only then can he rightly begin. But he is already a guru. That creates trouble. He has followers. You can always find followers, the world is so stupid and you can always find more stupid people than you. They become your followers. There is nothing difficult in it.

When you come to me, why you have come is going to play a great part in the whole drama that is going to follow. And I have to watch that I do not help a wrong beginning, because once started it will be more and more difficult to change it. It will become stronger and stronger. It has to be stopped from the very beginning. The seed has to be burned if it is wrong. Once I start and the sprouts come out of the earth, the seed is already gaining roots, becoming stronger. And once the tree has become very big, then it will be difficult...very very difficult.

A seed can be burned very easily, but to cut a tree and burn a tree is going to be very difficult. And you are the tree! So when you have many branches, many leaves, many fruits—maybe wrong, bitter, poisonous, but still then you will resist: nothing should be cut. When you resist even when the tree is not there, just the seed is there, you can imagine how much resistance you will create, how much you will fight when the tree is there and you feel you have grown—and you can grow wrongly. Remember this, growth in itself does not mean much. One can grow in a wrong way.

Growth in itself is not the goal. There is a right growth and there is a wrong growth. In the West now there is much work going on around the concept of growth, but I have not come across anybody in the growth movement who is aware that growth in itself is not the goal and cannot be the goal. You can grow wrongly, you can grow rightly.

So growth in itself is not the goal—but right growth. And once you grow wrongly it becomes more and more difficult at each step, at each level of growth.... The further you have gone the more difficult it is to move back, because growth becomes a rigid pattern. Right growth is a totally different thing. From the very beginning one has to be aware; hence the need of a master, because from the very beginning how can you be aware? You will be aware at the end. From the very beginning, how can you be aware? You can only grope in the dark.

So if you move on your own, ninety-nine possibilities are there out of a hundred that you will grow wrongly, because who will say that this is not the way to grow? And every growth in the beginning feels good because you expand, you become bigger. Every growth, even wrong growth, feels good. And wrong growth does not need much effort. It is like weeds in the garden—they don't need much care, just a little water now and then and they will grow. But if you are trying to grow roses, they need care, they need a gardener. Weeds don't need a gardener, but roses do need one.

In the West the growth movement is moving in many dimensions, but is completely oblivious of the fact that you can help people to grow wrongly—and then there will be difficulty. Then you have created something which will be more and more difficult every day to destroy. A master is needed, who can see the wrong seed from the very beginning, and can help you to destroy it, so that the right seed can be found within you. You carry the right seed also.

You are a confusion of right and wrong. You are a confusion of good and bad. You are a confusion of weeds and roses. Somebody has to be there to sort it out for you, because you cannot do this at this moment of your consciousness. Your whole being is a confusion.

When a disciple comes to a master, the first thing that

arises in the master is: Why has he come to me? He starts looking into the disciple: Why? for what reason? what has brought him to me?

I must have watched thousands of people coming to me. Rarely it happens that a person has come for a right reason—rarely. Humanity seems to be in such a bad shape; rarely it happens that a man comes with a right reason. He may think he has come for a right reason. That is not the point. His thinking is not of much value because the reason is hidden deeper in the unconscious, not on the surface. He cannot think about it.

The first thing that comes to a master is: Why?—why has this man come to me? And he cannot listen and believe in you. Whatsoever you say is not of much worth because next moment you will change it. Tomorrow you will change it, you are a flux. You don't have a crystallized centre in you which can reply. The master has to go deeper into your unconscious, to the very roots of your being, and see why you have come here. He cannot listen and believe in you, you are not yet believable. You are so deceptive that you don't know, you may be deceiving yourself. Once your why is known then something can be done. Then it has to be brought to your consciousness. And only on the right reason can your future growth be founded and based.

This small incident in Bahauddin El-Shah's life is very beautiful and will help you to understand many things.

Bahauddin El-Shah was sitting with a number of disciples when a number of followers came into the meeting hall.

There is a distinction between disciples and followers. A

follower is one who is not yet a disciple, attracted but not yet fallen into the trap of the master. He cannot leave him, but also cannot trust him. A follower is somebody who hangs around undecided whether to go away from the master or to come closer. He is afraid to come close because a master is a death; he is also afraid to go away because a master is a resurrection.

A follower is just either on the way to become a disciple or on the way to become an enemy. Either a follower will come closer and will become a disciple, or he will have to find excuses to go away and will become an enemy. Whenever a follower goes away he has to become an enemy; otherwise what rationalization does he have to go away? How will he satisfy himself as to why he has come away from such a great man as Bahauddin, such a pure soul that he is known as the emperor of masters? Hence El-Shah. Bahauddin is his name. *El-Shah* his disciples call him, the master of masters, the emperor of all masters—and he was...one of the greatest magnetic forces in the history of the Sufis.

When you come near a man like Bahauddin you have to decide either to be a friend or to be an enemy. You cannot remain indifferent. You cannot afford to be indifferent. A decision has to be taken because such a man as Bahauddin creates decisiveness even in you, who are absolutely indecisive, who live in indecision, who are born in indecision.

You live in indecision and die in indecision, never knowing what you are doing, why you are doing it, whether you really wanted to do it or not...just drifting with the crowd.

When you come near a master you have to decide, because it is no ordinary affair. It is a great risk, your whole life is at risk. So if you move around in India you will find either my friends or my enemies, those who are madly in love with me or those who are madly in hate with me. That is bound to happen. The reason is simple. Those who are madly in love with me and those who are madly in hate with me—they both had to decide.

A firm decision is needed. You have to decide that you are the enemy and you have to go on talking about me and against me because that is your only protection; otherwise you will be pulled in, you will be trapped. You can protect yourself only if you are constantly talking against me—not that you are spreading hatred against me, that may be a byproduct, but in fact you are simply protecting yourself by your attitude of hatred, continuously feeding it. You are afraid that if you stop feeding hatred you may come closer. And the fear is there that if you come closer death happens.

A follower is one who is just in the middle, on the fence, not yet decided whether to jump inside the house or jump outside the house and run away. On the fence is the follower. A disciple is one who has decided to jump into the house, who has become a part of the house of the master.

There are many who live on the fence their whole lives. They are the most foolish people in the world because sitting on the fence is not a comfortable position, and sitting on the fence gives nothing. It is wasting your life and time. Either come in or go out. Don't sit on the fence too long because it may become a habit, and then nothing will be the only outcome of it.

Bahauddin El-Shah was sitting with a number of disciples when a number of followers came into the meeting hall.

Followers, still thinking, trying to decide what to do,

what not to do, still afraid of the commitment and yet not decided to leave....

El-Shah asked each of them, one by one, to say why he was there.

He asked the followers, not the disciples. When you have become an initiate it is not only that you have chosen the master. In fact just the reverse is the case: the master has chosen you.

You may be given the impression that you are free to choose. That has to be given because you are so egoistic, you feel good that you are free to choose. But the real thing is that before you choose a master, the master has already chosen you. You choose him because he has chosen you already; otherwise you cannot choose him, he will create situations in which he will not allow you to choose. He may even force you to go away.

Always remember, when a master has chosen you, only then can you choose him. His very acceptance of you creates a desire in you to choose him. If he is not accepting you the desire to choose him will not arise in you, or it may be just a feeble wish and soon it will disappear like a small ripple on the surface of an ocean. It cannot persist.

As you are, nothing persists in you for long. When I ask you, 'Would you like to be initiated into sannyas?' I have already initiated you. Now it is just a game. You can play around and fool around a little. You can say, 'I will think about it.' You can say, 'Wait, as yet the right moment has not come for me, as yet I cannot be wholeheartedly in it, as yet I am just fifty-fifty, divided.'

And I tell you, 'Yes, decide, meditate, think about it,

and when you decide, come to me.' But I have already come to you. And the decision will sooner or later erupt into your consciousness. You can delay a little, that is all. You postpone it a little, that's all.

And it has to be so. How can a disciple choose a master? By what criterion? How to judge? A disciple is not in any position to penetrate the master. He can judge from the outside, but a master is not on the outside. The master is the inside of all things. The master is the *very* inside.

On the outside he may be playing tricks. He has to, because he has to avoid a few people, in fact many—the first part of humanity, the major part, which is not in any inquiry. They also come to a master, not to seek God or truth, just curious, with childish curiosity. A master has to avoid them. He has to create some situation around him so that they are not attracted. He may spread rumours about himself. He may show different faces to different people. He may be very hard, cruel, to certain groups. He may try to prove himself a madman to certain people so that once and for all they decide that this man is not for them, and forget the man and leave him.

On the outside there is no possibility to decide what type of man is inside. And you have not been to the inside of your own existence; how can you penetrate into the inside of a master, which is like a vast abyss? One goes on falling and falling and falling into it. That's why a master creates fear. You start trembling as if he is the brink of a deep abyss. If you look into him you will feel dizzy. Fear may take you over, you may start trembling and perspiring. No, there is no way for a disciple to decide.

For a disciple, to trust a master is just like falling in love. It happens. But for a master it is not a happening. For a master it is a very very alert, conscious phenomenon. Once he sees that the right man is there he opens his door. Once he sees that the right man is there for the right reason, he accepts him, and that very acceptance creates something in you, a decision, a will, a burning desire, *abheepsa*, to be closer and closer to this man. Even if it means death, you are not afraid. And it *means* death, because resurrection is possible only when death has happened.

The master was sitting with the disciples; there came a few followers into the meeting hall.

El-Shah asked each of them, one by one, to say why he was there.

It was a demonstration for the disciples. He was showing something to the disciples, and Sufi masters always do this— they demonstrate things. They don't believe in teaching directly, they create a situation and they demonstrate.

The disciples watched. He asked the followers one by one, why they were there, what has led them to be there, what reason, what urge, what search.

The first said: You are the greatest man on earth. That's why I am here.

How can you know that this man Bahauddin is the greatest man on earth? What criterion do you have? What touchstone? Who is great? And who is the greatest? And how do you come to the conclusion?

Said El-Shah,

I gave him a potion when he was ill, so he thinks I am the greatest man on earth.

That is the reason, the criterion, the touchstone: he was ill and I gave him some medicine that helped, so I am the greatest man on earth. And if the potion had failed he would not have looked at me again. Then he would have found some other man who was the greatest on earth, whose potion works.

How you judge! By such small things! Illness and a medicine. Even if you are cured it is not much of a point to be near Bahauddin. It would have been better if you had gone to a doctor or a physician.

Many people come to me because of illnesses. They have tried doctors, physicians, this and that 'pathy'; they have tried many things and nothing happens. Then they come, then they talk about God. And I can see they are not interested in God at all; they are ill, physically, mentally, and they are in search of a miracle, some miracle medicine. They are talking about meditation, they are talking about God, they are even ready to take sannyas, but their search is wrong. They should not be near me, they should go to a physician, because they are not even aware of the spiritual urge in them. It is something physical, or something mental—which is the same, because your mind and body are not two things. They are two poles of the same phenomenon.

And even if you are cured, nothing is cured in you. Even if you have a healthy body it makes no difference to your inner growth. Maybe, as you are, health may not prove a blessing. It may even prove a curse to you.

I remember one anecdote in Jesus' life. It is not related in Christian books, it is not in the Bible, but Sufis have that story about Jesus.

The story is that once Jesus entered a small town. He saw a man running after a prostitute, completely magnetized, hypnotized. He stopped the man and asked, 'What are you doing? Why are you wasting your life in such foolish things?'

The man looked at Jesus and said, 'You don't recognize me, my lord, but I recognize you—how can I forget you? I was blind and you touched my eyes, and now I can see. But what better can I do with my eyes than be charmed by a beautiful body? What more can I do with my eyes than cherish the beauty of form! What else is there to see? And I was blind, my lord, and you are so great, you blessed me. Now I can see and enjoy.'

Jesus felt very sad because he had never thought that eyes could become a curse. But as man is, as you are, you will turn all blessings into curses.

He entered the town, he saw another man completely drunk, lying in the gutter, crying and weeping and shouting and screaming. He went near the man and asked, 'What are you doing? Why are you wasting your life like a drunkard? This life is a great opportunity to know and realize the divine. There is only one life—and once missed, missed forever! And time never returns, you cannot reclaim it again. Be awake!'

Listening to this man the drunkard opened his eyes and said, 'My lord, have you forgotten me? I was ill and I was bedridden for ten years, then you touched me and you cured me. Now I am healthy. But what else can one do with the body? I am enjoying! Eat, drink and be merry! I am following that rule. And now I am healthy because of you. You are so great!'

Jesus became very sad. He had never imagined that health could be turned into a curse. He turned back. He was so sad that he didn't want to go into the town.

When he was coming out of the town he saw a man who was trying to hang himself from a tree, to commit suicide.

Jesus reached him in time, stopped the man and said, 'What are you doing? Life is precious, every single moment of it—and God has given you such a gift, and you are destroying it! What are you doing?'

The man looked at Jesus and said, 'If I have not forgotten, you are the same man who created the trouble. I was dead. You touched me and you revived me. Now what can I do? Life is meaningless. And I must tell you—don't touch me again. Enough is enough. I was dead and you revived me, but don't do this again to anybody else! I am fed up with life and death was a blessing, and you revived me, and for three years continuously I had to suffer again. Now I am going to commit suicide—you please go away from here! Who knows, you may touch me again.'

Health, life, strength, youth—everything you turn into a curse, because everything depends on your consciousness. There are people who have turned their illness into a blessing, who have turned their blindness into an inner insight, who have turned their death into a new life. It depends.

Said Bahauddin: *I gave him a potion when he was ill, so he thinks I am the greatest man on earth.*

And that's why he is here. Not because of me, not because of any inner search, but because of the potion that I gave him. In fact, I am not great, the potion was great. And he is hanging around me just in case he becomes ill again—I can give him a potion, a medicine. I am not more than a physician to him.

And what a waste! A Bahauddin, and you waste him. And the opportunity that he gives you—you waste that opportunity, and you take him as a physician.

But many people in the world go to the saints and sages

thinking that they can do miracles. These are the wrong people. That's why I say if you want to see the wrong humanity, the third category, the major part of humanity, you should go to Satya Sai Baba. There you will find all sorts of wrong people around him. Whenever there is somebody doing a miracle— it may not be a miracle, it may be just a magical trick, but if somebody is doing a 'miracle', wrong people are immediately attracted. The vast mob comes running. And they all think that they are spiritual seekers. They are going for health, for money, for something worldly.

If you are here for something worldly you are near a wrong person, because I am not going to do any miracle, because that is the way to attract the wrong people. I am not going to heal you. I am not going to do anything for any wrong reason.

The second said: My spiritual life has opened up since I have been allowed to visit you.

Said El-Shah:

He was uncertain and ill at ease and none would listen to him. I sat with him, and the resultant serenity is called by him his spiritual life.

This is what the whole of psychoanalysis in the West is all about. A psychoanalyst is not doing anything at all, particularly the Freudian psychoanalyst, the orthodox. He simply listens. The patient lies down on a couch, comfortably, and the psychoanalyst sits and listens, and the patient is allowed to say whatsoever he feels like, to move in free association. Whatsoever thoughts come he is allowed to express them. After a one-hour session one feels a certain serenity.

It is just the serenity that comes by talking. And then if you go on and on for three or four or five years of psychoanalysis, it costs a lot of money. That too helps, that too makes you calm down. Whenever a costly medicine is given to you it works better than a cheap medicine. The cheaper may have been better, but that doesn't matter. Cost matters. When you pay something you have to feel good; otherwise you will look foolish to yourself. Five years of psychoanalysis, thousands of dollars paid—of course one has to feel good! Otherwise you will look stupid. People will laugh: 'Then what were you doing there?' So one becomes very elated.

But talking helps. It is a catharsis, the mind goes on saying things. When you go on saying them again and again and again, they are released, they evaporate from the mind. And somebody listens, that is the whole trick, the whole business secret of psychoanalysis: somebody listens. In the world, in life, who listens to whom? Nobody pays any attention to what you are saying. In fact, the other is waiting for you to stop so he can say something.

I have heard, once it happened: There was a meeting in the town hall, and the speaker went on and on—an old politician—and he would not stop. People by and by left the hall. Only Mulla Nasruddin remained, the only one. The speaker was very happy and he thanked Nasruddin: 'I never thought that you loved me so much, or you loved my thoughts so much, or you so appreciated my philosophy.'

Nasruddin said, 'You don't understand me. I am the next speaker—I was waiting for you to stop!'

But this happens every day. Whenever you are talking to somebody you are interested in your talking. It is a catharsis.

It helps; it helps you to calm down a little from your tensions and anxieties. You have talked about them, you become a little aware about them, they are not so much of a burden. You can accept them.

But the other is not listening because he is in the same boat. He has his own anxieties, enough of his own. How can he listen to yours? Because if he really listens to yours he is gathering your anxieties also. So he listens with a closed mind. From one ear your talk enters, and from the other it goes out. It has to be so; otherwise your anxieties will be accumulating in his mind. And he is waiting for the opportunity, for when you stop, so that he can start.

I have heard that once it happened in a madhouse: A psychoanalyst was watching two madmen through the keyhole. He didn't want to disturb them and they were in such a great conversation. Both were professors of a university. Professors are more prone to become mad. Their very profession is a mad profession. They deal in thoughts, they deal in thinking, and when thinking and thoughts become too much, madness happens.

Those two professors were talking and the psychoanalyst was looking from the keyhole. He was surprised about only one thing. They were talking nonsense; nothing was relevant, consistent, not even one sentence was related to another. One was talking about something and the other was talking about something completely different, their talking was not related. That was not surprising, that's how mad people are. The surprising fact was this: when one would talk the other would listen. When he stopped the other would start, but the other would start not in any way related to the first; he would start from somewhere of his own, out of the blue.

This continued. Then the psychoanalyst knocked on the door. They opened the door. He said, 'I am very surprised about one thing, and have become very curious to know: why, when one talks does the other stop? And you are talking about such irrelevant things—one talks about the earth, the other talks about the sky, they are not related at all—then why do you stop when the other is talking?'

They both laughed and they said, 'Do you think we don't know the law of conversation?' This is the law of conversation: simply that you talk, then the other stops; when the other starts, you stop. This is a polite mannerism. But you are related to *your* inner talk, the other is related to *his* inner talk. You come nearer, but you remain parallel. Dialogue is not possible. Dialogue happens only when you really listen to the other, and while the other is talking, you are completely silent. Then only is dialogue possible. When the other is talking and you are talking within yourself, your inner talk continues, how is a dialogue possible? These are two parallel lines, like a railway track, parallel lines running for thousands of years, meeting nowhere.

People need catharses of their minds to throw things out. But now in a busy world, particularly in the West, nobody is there to listen; hence psychoanalysis. A professional listener— you pay for him just to listen to you. It helps. Psychoanalysis is nothing but a professional listening.

You pay attention because you are paid. Howsoever boring you listen with a smiling face, you show interest, you pay attention. The ego of the patient is consoled. Somebody listens and not an ordinary somebody—a Freud, a Jung, a very exceptional, extraordinary person—famous, great, known all over the world. The greater the psychoanalyst—I mean greater in the sense of more known—the more he helps the patients, because the patient feels so gratified. Somebody pays so much attention—he is so important! Even a Freud listens so attentively.

I have heard that one young psychoanalyst asked his teacher, an old man, 'This is really amazing. I get bored and tired after two or three patients because they talk such nonsense, and I have to listen and I cannot do anything, I cannot escape. I have to be attentive, I have to show interest.

I get so bored and tired after the third patient—but you are wonderful. You do it the whole day from morning to evening, and I never see you tired.'

The old man laughed and said, 'Who listens? That is just a face. Now I have become expert in showing attention without paying it, smiling without smiling, giving an ear but not listening at all. Who listens?'

But that is not the point, whether the other is listening or not. If he shows interest, that's enough. The patient feels good. He goes on talking rubbish, rot, but even to his rotten mind somebody is paying such keen attention, as if something very precious is being said. Ego feels gratified.

I see it happening every day. There are people who come to me, not to know anything from me, they come to me just to tell me something, and once they get warmed up through talking they forget what they are saying and why they are talking. They go on and on and on; it is difficult to stop them. And they feel very good....

Once a man came to me, and he was asking for many days, saying he would like to come because he has certain problems and he feels only I can solve those problems— nobody else can solve them so he has to come and I have to give him time.

I gave him time; he came. For one hour he didn't say

anything about his problems. And I had given him one solid hour. He talked and talked about meaningless things, about his wife and children, and this and that, and about his business. After one hour—and I had no way to say anything, he wouldn't give even a small gap for me to say yes or no, I simply nodded...after one hour he thanked me, he was very grateful. He touched my feet and said, 'You are such a wonderful man, you told me so many beautiful things'— and I had not said a single word!—'and you solved all my problems.' He had not talked about any problem and I had not solved any!

But that is not the point. I listened, I nodded, I showed interest, and he felt completely satisfied. That was the problem. He needed somebody, somebody he thinks is very great, who pays attention to him.

Bahauddin said:

He was uncertain and ill at ease and none would listen to him. I sat with him, and the resultant serenity is called by him his spiritual life.

It is nothing. It is just a gratification of the ego. And the man was saying, *My spiritual life has opened up since I have been allowed to visit you.*

The third said: You understand me, and all I ask is that you allow me to hear your discourses for the good of my soul.

He needs attention and wishes to have notice paid to him even if it is criticism, said El-Shah. This he calls the good of his soul.

Ego is so hungry. Attention is food for the ego. If somebody appreciates you—good, beautiful. If nobody pays attention to you and everybody is indifferent, that is hell. It will be better if they criticize you, but pay attention.

Three attitudes are possible: one, somebody pays attention to you; you feel groovy. One would think that criticism is not liked by people. You are wrong. That is the second alternative.

If you are not appreciated then the second alternative is, people should criticize you. You will act in such a way that people are *forced* to criticize you, because again, they have to pay attention.

The third is indifference. Nobody likes it. And unless you like indifference your ego will never die. In indifference, ego dies. Live in such a way that you don't ask anybody to pay attention; the ego will disappear. Indifference is poison for the ego.

So either appreciation—people should pay compliments to you; if not, then you will try at least for criticism. But indifference...indifference—the very word gives you fear. If nobody pays attention to you where will you be? Who will you be? Your identity will be broken.

There are two types of people in the world. Those who succeed in getting attention: politicians, artists, musicians, talented people in some dimension; they attract attention. If that is not possible—because success needs talents; if you want to be a musician just a hankering for attention won't help much, you have to be talented, and you have to work for it; it is a long discipline, a whole life has to be devoted to music. Success is a long-term affair. It is not easy, and everybody cannot be a musician, and only very rare people can rise to the height where attention is paid to them.

Then, if that is not possible—and it is not possible for millions of people—what should they do? They start the other way. They start becoming criminals, sinners, drunkards. No talent is needed for that. You can get drunk without any training; in fact training will not allow you to get drunk so soon. Untrained, even a small dose and you are drunk, and the whole town becomes aware of you. You walk on the streets shouting, screaming, doing things which you cannot do when you are in your saner moments. The whole town has to pay attention. You are lying in a gutter screaming and everybody who passes has to pay attention. You can become a criminal. The whole world has to pay attention.

I was just reading about a man who killed seven men in one day for no reason. He didn't know those people at all. They were strangers, not in any way related with him. One of them he killed from behind—he had not even seen the face, who the man is he was going to kill. And in the court he said, 'I wanted to see my picture in the newspaper.' Of course his picture was there. He made the headlines, front-page coverage. He wanted attention. People become criminals, people become antisocials, people become rebels, but it is attention that is needed.

As I have been observing, ninety percent of hippies are not really in rebellion. Now this is a new way to attract attention: the way you grow your hair, the dirt and dirtiness that you collect on the body, the smell that people can feel from far away—you have an aroma, a bad smell around you. Wherever you go people have to become alert; a hippie has come, tinkling his bells—what is he doing?

An easy way to attract attention. Very easy, simple; no talent, no training, no discipline is needed. You can become a hippie right now, immediately. Throw some dirt on the hair, find some dirty rags, a bell, smoke *charas*, and you are a hippie; wherever you go people will look at you as if you are the shah of Iran. Even if a hippie and the shah of Iran are standing together on the street, a hippie will be paid more attention.

Ninety percent of the young generation are trying to find easier ways, because in the West success has become a more and more difficult affair. Too much competition there! If you want a Ph.D it is a competition, a long affair—and then too there are thousands of Ph.Ds in the West, so it is not much of an attainment.

If in India you become a Ph.D it is something. Indians will always ask you what degree you have got. In the West degrees have become useless; in India they are still very very important because only a few are educated and millions are uneducated. To become a Ph.D is still precious. Somebody becomes a Ph.D—he has attained the very last, the ultimate of life. But in the West thousands of Ph.Ds are moving all around. Now it doesn't seem to matter much.

I was reading about the first Indian who became a matriculate, in Allahabad, somewhere in the beginning of this century. A great procession was arranged for him. He sat on an elephant like a king and eleven elephants followed him, and a great procession...the whole of Allahabad participated. It was a tremendous phenomenon, something miraculous had happened—a man had become a matriculate.

But now it is absolutely useless. You don't attain any attention through it. Nobody will bring an elephant, not even a donkey will be brought to you! If you try to sit on a donkey they will ask: Are you a Ph.D? Or just a matriculate trying to sit on a donkey? Get off it! Only a doctor, a man who holds a doctorate, will be allowed on the donkey.

No attention is paid. In the West, education now is universal; hence the dropping out of education, because there seems to be no fulfillment of the ego in it at all. And people have become so rich—Rockefellers, Rothschilds and Fords— you cannot imagine how to compete, and you cannot dream how to surpass them. It is almost impossible.

Then what to do? Purchase a bell, grow the hair, move in a way which is unorthodox, unconventional, and you simply get attention. But the whole search is for attention, whether through Ph.Ds or through a hippie style of life, whether by being a politician or by being a criminal, whether by being the president of a country, a Nixon, or a murderer, it makes no difference. The ego's ways are the same.

And I tell you, unless the ego is dropped, whatsoever you are you are a criminal. Your politics will be a politics of crime; your talent will be a talent for crime. Ego is the root cause of all crime, and if ego is there your success is also going to be criminal because you will succeed on the failures of many. You will succeed by destroying many. The competition will be cut-throat, it will be a murderous competition.

Wherever you move, if ego is there, whatsoever you do is going to be a crime. To me, ego is the criminal.

Don't ask for attention. Live in such a way that nobody becomes aware of you. Live in such a way that it is as if you never existed. Move in such a way that nobody comes to hear your movement, nobody even knows that you were here. Then only will you attain to the explosion which is spirituality. Otherwise the ego will be there, always like a hard rock on the possibility of the explosion. It will be destroying you within.

Why do you ask for attention?—because you are not

certain about yourself, who you are. But by attention how are you going to know who you are? You cannot know yourself by looking in the mirror, and you cannot know yourself by looking in the eyes of others—whether they appreciate or criticize, those eyes are not more than mirrors: friends, enemies—all are mirrors.

You have to know yourself directly, immediately.

You have to go withinwards.

Ego lives on attention. It is a false phenomenon. Understand it, and come out of it. Once you are out of it a different quality of serenity, a silence which surpasses understanding, a stillness—natural, spontaneous—and a bliss start bubbling within you, an inner dance. And that is the only dance there is, the only ecstasy there is. Unless you attain to that you are living a false, pseudo life, you are deceiving nobody but yourself.

The third said: You understand me and all I ask is that you allow me to hear your discourses for the good of my soul.

He needs attention and wished to have notice paid to him even if it is criticism, said El-Shah. This he calls the good of his soul.

Please, don't call this the good of your soul.

The fourth said: I went from one to another practising what they taught. It was not until you gave me a wazifa exercise that I truly felt the illumination of contact with you.

*The exercise I gave this man was a concocted one
not related to his spiritual life at all, said El-Shah.
I had to demonstrate his illusion of spirituality
before I could arrive at the part of this man which
is really spiritual, not sentimental.*

The fourth said, 'You gave me a Sufi exercise, a *wazifa*
exercise, and since then much has happened to me. I am
growing.'

And El-Shah said to his disciples, 'I have given him a
false exercise through which nobody can grow. It is not a
technique at all. But he says he is growing. He is not even
true to me. He is not only deceiving himself, he is trying to
deceive me that he is growing—and that exercise cannot help.
At the most that exercise can make him more sentimental,
not spiritual.'

But many people think that sentimentality is spirituality.
Emotions are as much mental as thoughts. And what you
call your heart is as much in your head as your head. You
can become emotional very easily. You can cry and weep
with tears falling down, big pearl-like tears—but nothing
spiritual. Tears are as physical as anything else.

The eyes are part of the body, and emotions are a
disturbance in the physical energy. You cry and weep—of
course you will feel relieved, you will feel relaxed after you
have had a good cry. You will feel relieved. All over the world
women know it. They know it well, that it helps. They cry
and they weep and then they are relieved. It is a catharsis,
but there is nothing spiritual in it. But people go on mistaking
things—things which are not spiritual they go on thinking
they are spiritual.

People come to me; they say that since they have come

their *kundalini* is arising. They have jerks in the body and they think they have become very very spiritual. There is nothing spiritual in kundalini; it is a physical force. Don't be befooled by it.

Then people come—they are seeing light. When they close their eyes they are seeing light...nothing but imagination. Good, you will have a good sleep if you can see light, because your mind is getting more concentrated. But it is *mind* still. Good as far as it goes, but nothing spiritual.

Then people come—they are seeing visions: Krishna playing on his flute, Jesus crucified, Buddha sitting under the bodhi tree. And they come to me so that I can certify, I can say, 'Yes, you have attained, you have realized, this is what spirituality is.' What more can you expect? Krishna playing the flute, what more? Such an extraordinary experience.

But it is nothing spiritual. Good dreams, beautiful dreams. Enjoy! But don't be befooled. Really a good dream—and after so many nightmares that you have lived through, Krishna playing the flute—nothing bad to enjoy for a while. You can also play the flute with him and dance around him, but don't be befooled. It is nothing spiritual.

Then what is spiritual? Spirituality is not an experience. You cannot experience it. If *you* experience it, it is something of the mind, something of the body—because how can you experience your*self*? Your being cannot be reduced to an object. You remain the subject. You are subjectivity. Everything else that you can see will not be you. You are the seer.

Spirituality is not an experience. It is not an object; you cannot watch and see it. *You are it,* the watcher, the seer. So then all experiences disappear. When there is nothing to be seen, when there is no object to be observed, but only awareness, vast, unobstructed awareness not obstructed by any experience, then you have become spiritual. You *become* spiritual; spirituality is not an experience.

Kundalini, lights, visions...all disappear. They are good indications that you are growing, but nothing of the spiritual. And the real master is not interested in the experiences on the way, he is interested only in the goal. The way has to be passed, transcended. He is interested only in *you*, in your absolute subjectivity, with no object, no experience, nothing; when your awareness burns like a flame in an empty sky—not even a breeze, nothing, no god....

In spirituality there is no god, that's why Buddhists, Jainas, never think of Christianity, Mohammedanism, the Jewish tradition as the last word in religion—because they go on talking about experiences: God, angels...they go on. Happiness, bliss—they go on talking about experiences. And spirituality is beyond all. It is the very beyondness. Only you remain, aware, fully aware, awakened, and all else has disappeared. In this total emptiness burns the flame of subjectivity, of absolute aloneness, awareness. Remember that.

I am not satisfied with your kundalini. I am not satisfied with your lights. I am not satisfied with your krishnas playing on the flute. All gods that you can see are your creations. Drop them all! Come to the point where nothing remains, *nothing* remains. Then only are you left in your total aloneness—and that has a beauty of its own. That is the hidden splendor. That is the spiritual.

Before that, everything is a game. There are games of the body—sex is the game of the body. There are games of the mind—love is the game of the mind. Spirituality is not a game. Everything finished, all games dropped, one comes back home, alone...sits in the home, no experience. All experiences are disturbances.

When only consciousness remains, only then a man like Bahauddin is satisfied with the disciple. Masters demand so much. They will not leave you with some foolish imagination, they will go on destroying all imaginations. When everything is destroyed, only that remains which cannot be destroyed— the deathless. You, in your fully awakened state.

Everything is a dream. There are layers and layers of dreams: beautiful dreams, ugly dreams, spiritual dreams, non-spiritual dreams. But spirituality is not a dream. Spirituality is the dreamer who has awakened out of all dreams. Then only the hidden splendour is revealed. The secret of all secrets becomes known.

Enough for today.

Three

An Open and Shut Case

Salih of Gazwin taught his disciples:
Whoever knocks at the door continually, it will
be opened to him.
Rabiya, hearing him one day, said: 'How long will
you say, "It will be opened"? The door has never
been shut.'

Nature, the whole of it, is a continuous ceremony—a marriage, a feast. Guests go on changing, but the feast continues; the feast never stops for a single moment. Singers change, but the song remains.

Except for man, nature is always in ecstasy. Man is a special case. If you look just at the present situation of man you will feel depressed, as if something has gone wrong. But if you can understand the future possibility of man then you will be happy, thankful. Nothing has gone wrong; only, with man, nature is trying to reach a higher ceremony.

Man has been sent on a journey. He looks to be without a home—because he has to attain a home in his being. He looks uprooted—because he has to find a richer soil for his roots. Man is nothing but a reaching of nature towards a higher harmony, a higher ceremony, a greater ecstasy.

But that is so if you look at the whole journey, and you can see the destiny. If you can't see the destiny, then man simply looks like a child gone astray. Then man looks like a disease. That's why for Sartre, or Camus, or Jaspers, man looks meaningless, a tale told by an idiot, full of fury and noise, signifying nothing.

The whole of human consciousness seems to be ill, ill at ease. But buddhas see deeper. They don't see just this moment. Hidden in this moment is the whole destiny of man. Man is the greatest experiment nature has yet made; but it is not yet a complete experiment, that is the trouble.

Man has lost the home that trees have, and he has not yet reached the end of his journey. Man has lost the moorings that birds have, and the stars and the sea have. He seems to be homeless, a stranger, an outsider. That is right! But a greater home, a better ecstasy, and a higher plenitude of being is waiting. You have to complete the journey.

Religion is nothing but the effort to make the journey complete. Nature has thrown you into a vast world, full of millions of possibilities, and you don't know who you are, where you are going. Nature has *pushed* you, and religion is to complete the journey, religion is to fill the gap; otherwise you will feel meaningless. You will feel depressed, you will live in anguish.

If you don't know the destiny, if you can't look into the seed—if you can look into the seed you can see the tree, the flowering, the possibility, the potentiality—but if you just look at the seed from the outside, it is nothing. No colours, just a dead thing, not even alive. Looks like a pebble.

What is the difference between a pebble and a seed? The pebble is just a pebble, with no future in it. The seed also looks like a pebble, but with a vast future in it, with life waiting to be released, flowers waiting to flower, fragrance waiting to be spread to the winds. A vast possibility, a potentiality.

If you think man now is the end product, then you will feel, like the existentialists, that man is meaningless, a tale told by an idiot. But if you can look into the potentiality, then suddenly, man is not diseased; rather, on the contrary, nature is trying to reach a higher point, a growth, the greatest yet attained—evolution working in man.

So this has to be understood: why nature is so harmonious, and man is in such a disharmony. Listen to the birds, constantly singing, humming, constantly enjoying; there seems to be no worry, no anxiety. Not that problems are not there, not that death doesn't exist for them—it exists, but it doesn't disturb their song. Birds, trees, oceans, rocks— they are unconscious, their ceremony is an unconscious ceremony...as if a man is singing while he is asleep, a man smiling while he is asleep. You can see the smile, but the man himself is not aware of what is happening—as if in a dream, drunk.

Nature *is* blissful, but absolutely unaware of it. And without awareness, what is bliss? It is meaningless. It has no significance, because the bird who is singing is not at all aware of what is happening. The song is just happening. There is nobody to listen to it, nobody to taste it, nobody to smell it, nobody to enjoy it. The song is just happening, part of an unconscious nature. Howsoever beautiful, it lacks something, something very essential.

It is *you* who listens to the sound of the bird. It is *you* who feels: How beautiful! The bird is completely unaware: the song is neither beautiful nor ugly—as if the song doesn't exist. If you are unaware, how can the song exist? It doesn't exist for you. It may exist for others, those who are aware.

Trees have flowers. Look at this *gulmohar* tree—complete, with flowers, more flowers than leaves...red, like a bride.

But not aware, not knowing what is happening! Nature is asleep, unconscious. Man has become a little conscious; hence the anxiety. A part of you has become conscious, a very small fragment of your being has become conscious, and the remaining whole remains unconscious. A division has happened, a conflict has arisen. You are no more one—you have become two. A split has happened, a gap between you and yourself, a duality. You are no more one. Something of you is different from the remaining whole. This creates anxiety. You cannot be as happy as the bird, and you cannot be as blissful as the sky. No, you cannot be, because you are aware. Awareness creates anxiety.

When you are happy you know it is not going to stay. You are aware that this happiness is just going to pass like everything else. This too will pass. A sadness settles. Even while you are in your happiest mood you cannot be absolutely happy. The awareness that this will pass makes you sad. Even in the happiest moment, misery enters—it has to be so, because now you are two, and whatsoever you do and whatsoever you are, you will always be dual, divided. The happiest moment will always carry the saddest possibility in it, and you will be aware of it. Alive, young, full of life and zest—but death is there, following you like a shadow.

The bird will go on singing, and die, and will not be aware even for a single moment that death is coming. But if you are not aware of death, how can you be aware of life? Awareness of life is at a cost; the cost has to be paid. That cost is the fear of death. If you are aware of life, you are bound to be aware of death. And how can you be at ease? Alive, something is dying, continuously. Alive, you are moving towards the grave. How can you celebrate and dance? How can one go dancing towards the grave?

With awareness humanity enters into the world. But with awareness enters anxiety and anguish. And this will be so unless you again become one. Duality is the anxiety. Hence Sufis, Vedantists, Zen people, all the mystics of all the ages, insist only on one thing, and that is: transcend duality, become *advait*, become non-dual. Become one again.

You *were* one, because you have been a tree, and you have been a river, and you have been a rock in the Himalayas, and you have been a million types of birds and animals, and you have lived all kinds of lives—vegetable lives, mineral lives, animal lives. You have passed through existence many many times, in many many forms. You have been one, but unconsciously one. Now, the duality has arisen. You have to be one again, this time *consciously* one.

Many times you will think: To become consciously one seems almost impossible. Rarely does a buddha happen. To a buddha, again the song comes, then again he is singing like a bird, he is flowering like a tree, he is open like the sky, he is rich like the earth, he is wild, like the wild ocean. Again he is one, but now this unity is a higher unity—the highest. He is consciously one. Oneness has been attained through consciousness. He is again nature, but in a totally different way. The quality of his being has changed. He is again back to nature, but he is no more the same. Consciousness has been attained.

But this happens rarely, so your mind will say: That seems to be impossible. It seems more possible to fall back into unconsciousness; hence the appeal of drugs, alcohol. Always, governments have been against drugs. Always, religions have been against drugs. Always, moralities have been against drugs. But still, for man they have a deep appeal. No law has been able to prohibit them from man.

What is the appeal? The appeal is this: alcohol and other drugs—now there are many in the market: marijuana, LSD, psilocybin…and many more will be coming—the appeal of drugs is that they give you the feeling of oneness without the effort of becoming a buddha. You fall back into nature. Through chemicals you force yourself back into unity with nature, where birds are singing and trees are flowering. You force yourself back.

This is a violence on the whole system of your being, and this is destroying the effort of nature to reach a higher harmony through you. This is against nature. For a few moments you can attain a forced oneness with nature, through drugs. But it cannot be a permanent achievement. It cannot become an integral part of your inner being. It can never become an integral part because to go back is not possible. You can only force yourself back.

It is like…. You cannot become a child again. You cannot step back. You cannot enter the womb of the mother again. There is no way back. Time doesn't move that way. It moves forward, it never moves backward. So you cannot go backward. The only way, the only going, is to go forward; there is no other going.

So drugs are a deception. They give you a feeling which is imaginary, hallucinatory, they give you a feeling that you are back, part of nature. People come to me; they say, 'I have been on a drug trip, and it was beautiful, and so many things happened.' Nothing happened!—because after it you are again the same, even worse. It only releases dreams in you, but you become so unconscious that you take the dreams to be real. You are not aware, so you cannot see whether this is a dream or a reality.

Under drugs you can think yourself a bird singing in the

trees, flying in the sky, but you remain all the time on the earth. You have not moved a single inch. And when the trip is over and you open your eyes, you are where you were. But in the meanwhile a dream was created, a vivid dream, a very real-looking dream, not even a suspicion that this was just a hallucination of the mind. You have done something with the cells of the mind, and they have started revolving, and they have created something—sometimes good, sometimes bad, sometimes hell, sometimes heaven. It depends on your mood, the physical condition of your body, the situation around, the whole milieu.

So sometimes you can visit hell, and sometimes you can visit heaven through chemicals, but you are not going anywhere, you remain where you are. But man is in such anguish that if even for moments he can escape from duality it feels like freedom.

All religions have been against drugs. The reason is this: if you become an addict then the whole possibility of your higher dimension, of your higher unity, of achieving buddhahood, of becoming a christ, is lost. They are not against drugs, in fact. They are not concerned with drugs, they are concerned with your higher unity. If you start falling backwards in your mind, and if you become attuned with the lower unity of nature, then who will evolve? Then you have frustrated the very effort of nature through you. It was going to achieve god—and you are satisfied with a drug.

It is a poor substitute, very very poor—but the appeal indicates something; it indicates that man can be at home in only two ways. Either he falls back into nature through chemicals, through sex, or through other means, or he rises above himself, and reaches a point where his whole consciousness has become conscious; nothing remains unconscious in him. The dark continent of unconsciousness is there no more. All corners of his being are lighted up. This is the meaning of becoming a buddha. A buddha means he who has no unconscious. A buddha means he whose whole being is transformed into light, awareness. Again—the celebration, the marriage, the feast, but on a totally different plane.

Jesus used to tell a parable—and his parables are multidimensional—the parable of the prodigal son. One man had two sons—the two brothers wanted to separate from each other. The father divided the property in two, and the elder son remained with the father; the younger left with all the riches that he had now got. The younger left, gambled, indulged, destroyed the whole property, became a beggar, went completely astray.

Then one day while he was begging, suddenly a thought arose: If I go to my father, he will forgive me. I know him— he has the heart of a father. Even though I have destroyed half of his property, his life's labour—I have not been good to him and I have not served him—still I know he loves me, and if I go back he will accept me.

He came back. The news reached the father that the son was coming back, so he arranged a great feast. The fattest lamb was killed, the oldest wine was brought up from the cellar. He asked friends to come and celebrate the coming of the son: 'My son is coming back home!'

The elder son was in the gardens, working in the field. When he was coming back a few people met him on the road and they said, 'Look—look at the injustice! You have been serving your father for all these years. You have been an absolutely obedient son, you never went against any of his wishes. But he never celebrated for you, a feast was never given, and now comes your younger brother, who went astray, gambled, indulged in sins, became a beggar. He was disobedient, a rebel. Now he comes and your father is giving a feast. This is injustice!'

Of course, the elder brother felt very angry, flew into a rage. He came running home and he asked his father, 'What is this? What is going on? For what? And for whom? This is injustice! I have been an obedient servant to you, and you never, never celebrated for *me*. And now comes your younger son, who has destroyed everything, your whole life's labour, and you are arranging a feast! I cannot believe my eyes! Don't you love me? It seems you only love your younger son.'

The father said, 'That is not the point. You misunderstand me. He has gone astray, and now he is coming back. You have never gone astray, you have always been with me: there was no point in celebrating.'

This parable is meaningful here, in the context of what I have said to you. Man is the prodigal son. Trees have always remained with the father, the birds always remain with the father. The rocks and the skies always remain with the father. They have never left home, they never went astray.

Man is the prodigal son. He went astray, he indulged, he destroyed much. But whenever a man comes back, there is a feast, because when somebody goes astray, becomes rebellious, he attains much experience. Whenever someone goes rebellious he is enriched. Whenever someone goes off singing, he knows life more than those saints who have never left home. He is enriched. Going astray is a way of knowing. Going wrong is a way of becoming more aware. Man is the prodigal son.

Whenever a prodigal son comes back, a Buddha, a Jesus, a Mahavira, the whole existence—the father—celebrates. The fattest lamb is to be killed then, and the oldest wine brought up from the cellar. There is going to be much dancing, singing, drinking. The whole existence celebrates a buddha: the son has come back. And the son has not come back the same, but enriched—enriched with a higher consciousness, enriched with a higher unity. He has attained to something which nature was seeking through him.

But if you remain in rebellion, if you remain on the road constantly going astray and astray and astray and never come back home, then there is going to be no celebration for you. Going astray is good, then so is coming back. One has to leave home to come back to it. In fact unless you leave it you will never be able to know what it is. You have to go astray in the wider world, only then when you come back will you realize what a home is. A buddha is nothing but a man come home.

You are buddhas still astray, still wandering here and there. Still you have not gathered the courage to come back to the father and ask his forgiveness. You don't trust. You don't trust the father that he will accept you. You don't accept yourself; how can you think that the father is going to accept you? You condemn yourself; how can you think that the whole is going to take you into its bosom, into its very heart?

Trust. Come back home. You have travelled enough, suffered enough—it was necessary, but don't prolong it too much. The problem is: if one remains in suffering too long one becomes attuned to it, it becomes a habit. One starts enjoying it, one starts clinging to it.

Religion is nothing but an effort to help you come back home. Nature has thrown you into the wider world. It has been the greatest experiment ever. A part of nature has been uprooted, has been made homeless. This is a great opportunity to learn, a great opportunity to grow, a great opportunity to become aware, and come back home. Become more and more aware, and you are coming back home. When you are perfectly aware, suddenly you are in, at home.

You know the Christian parable that Adam was thrown out of the garden of Eden. But my feeling is: Where can he be thrown out *to?*—because the whole *is* the garden of Eden. There is no outside to it. Existence has no outside. Existence is only *inside*, because the whole is implied in it, so where can the outside be? No, Adam has not been thrown out of the garden of Eden, only, his eyes are closed. He has always lived inside the garden, but he cannot see it because he is not aware.

Once you start seeing, suddenly you find you are in the garden—you have always been in the garden. In fact, you have never left home, it was only a dream. But it was needed to become aware. It was a hallucination, but it was needed. It was a nightmare, but it was needed. There was a need to be anxious, in anxiety, in anguish.

I would like to add one beatitude to Jesus' other beatitudes: Blessed are those who are in anguish, because they will attain to perfect consciousness.

Through anguish is the way. It passes through many hells, because without suffering nobody can become aware. That's why birds are not aware—they are not in suffering. Trees are not aware, they are not in suffering. Only man suffers; man is a special case. You should be proud of it. Man is an extraordinary phenomenon, man is not ordinary nature. Man is something new happening in nature, but it is so new that not even man is aware of what is happening to him. You have been thrown astray so that you have to seek and find where your home is. You have to make an effort to come back.

Now, this small anecdote:

Salih of Gazwin taught his disciples:
Whoever knocks at the door continually, it will
be opened to him.
Rabiya, hearing him one day, said: 'How long will
you say, 'It will be opened'? The door has never
been shut.'

It is something rare in the history of Sufis, this small anecdote. It is rare because both are enlightened: Salih, a master in his own right, and Rabiya, a rare woman, very rare, because very few women have become enlightened. Rabiya is one of them. Both are enlightened masters. Neither can be wrong, both have to be true, but they contradict each other.

Listen again. Salih taught his disciples: *Whoever knocks at the door continually, it will be opened to him.* He says, 'Go on knocking at the door. And be continuous—don't rest!' The door has to be knocked at continually. Just like Jesus says: Knock and it shall be opened unto you; ask and it shall be given, Salih used to say continuously: Knock and go on knocking! Don't rest. Don't go on holiday, because nobody knows when the doors will open—you go on knocking! And nobody knows how much knocking is needed—so go on knocking. At a certain point, at a certain degree, the door opens.

Salih can't be wrong. But *Rabiya, hearing him one day, said: 'How long will you say, 'It will be opened'?* Your whole life you have been saying: It will be opened, it will be opened.

Go on knocking. And I say unto you, Rabiya said: *'The door has never been shut.'* What foolishness to say: Knock! The door is already open—enter!

The problem is that both have to be right. Had Salih been a man of scholarship, knowledgeable, there would be no problem. The anecdote would be simple. He didn't know, he is not aware of what he is saying. He must have read in the scriptures, must have come across the saying of Jesus: Knock, and the door shall be opened to you. If he was a knowledgeable man, a pundit, there would be no problem: of course, Rabiya has to be right. But the problem is, Salih himself is a buddha! This man Salih is as enlightened as Rabiya—he cannot be wrong. And of course there is no possibility of Rabiya being wrong. Rabiya has to be right, and Salih has to be right. That is the puzzle.

Sufis have been thinking about this, how to solve it. It is always easy if one person has not attained; you can decide— he is wrong. The same type of problem has existed in the whole history of man. Mahavira contradicts Buddha, Buddha contradicts Mahavira, and the problem is, both have to be right. And people who cannot go so deep decide that only one can be right. A few have decided that Mahavira is right— they have become Jainas. A few have decided that only Buddha can be right, Mahavira has to be wrong—they have become Buddhists. And I tell you, those two persons, those two guys, Mahavira and Buddha, they are both right; anything else is not possible.

Then we have to go deeper. The matter cannot be settled so easily and on the surface. When Salih says, *Whoever knocks at the door continually, it will be opened to him*, he is not saying anything about the door, whether it is shut or open. He is not saying anything about the door, he is saying something to the seeker: Knock continuously. The question is not about the door; the door is not referred to at all, the door is not the context. The gestalt is different, the emphasis is different. The emphasis is on the seeker.

Salih is concerned with the disciple. He says, 'Go on knocking. Make every effort, knock continually.' When he is saying to the disciple, 'Make an effort, knock continually,' it is not a question of the door opening to him; by knocking continually the *disciple* will open. The door is not the point of reference. Salih is not concerned with that. He is saying, 'You go on knocking!'—because if you continually knock, *you* will open; otherwise you will remain closed. Salih also knows the door has never been shut. It is open, but *you* are shut.

And had the door been shut, even, Salih would have opened it for you. It would be easy! Salih would have opened the door and stood in the doorway, and allowed everybody who wanted to enter. The question is not of the door, the question is of your being. Your eyes are closed, your consciousness is closed, your being is closed, and unless you knock continually you are not going to open the door. And the door is not something outside; *you* are the door, and you are the one who has to enter by it.

Of course, Salih is right. But his statement is not about the door, his statement is about the disciple, the seeker, one who is on the path.

This is how Patanjali talks. Patanjali is like Salih, thinking continuously of the disciple, of the seeker, thinking continuously of those who are closed, blind. They don't understand the language of the final attainment. Salih has more compassion, and he knows that the door is open, it has never been shut.

You have always been in the garden of Eden; Adam has never been expelled. He may be hypnotized, and a suggestion may have been given to him that he is expelled, so that he thinks that he is expelled; but he has never been expelled. Where can he be expelled to? The whole is the garden of Eden. Wherever he is, he is in the garden.

You cannot be out of God, wherever you are. You may be a thief, a murderer, a robber, it makes no difference, you are in God. When you rob, God robs through you. When you rob, God is robbed by you. When you murder, God is murdered. And when you murder, God is murdering. You cannot be outside. You may think so, that may be your idea, but that idea closes your eyes, not the door.

Each individual has to open his own heart. That's why Salih says, 'Go on knocking continually; no holiday allowed, no rest. Don't be lazy, because if you work for a few days and then you stop, the whole work is undone; again you have to start from *abc*. If you stop again, then again the same will be repeated.' It is just like heating water: you heat the water up to fifty degrees, or eighty degrees, and then you take it off the fire, or you put the fire off and the water cools down; it comes down to room temperature. Next day, again you heat it; again you put the fire off.... Unless the water reaches a hundred-degree temperature it is not going to evaporate.

So go on knocking. A hundred-degree knocking is needed. Only then, suddenly, the door opens. Not that the door opens, suddenly *you* open. Your eyes open; suddenly you are closed no more. Your consciousness has become total. Unconsciousness has dissolved in it. No corner of your being is dark; everything is lit up.

Salih is right, and Salih is more helpful. He thinks of

those who have not yet reached. He has more compassion. He is not bothered about the right statement about truth. If even lies can help the travellers, he will use lies.

Buddha has defined truth as that which works. If a lie works, it is true. And if a truth cannot work, of what use is it? Throw it into the garbage can, it is of no use. Buddha's definition is really wonderful. He was the first pragmatist in the world. Now scientists agree with Buddha. But science took twenty-five centuries to learn the secret. Now, science doesn't talk about truth; it says everything is just a hypothesis. And what is a hypothesis?—something that works. We don't know whether it is true or not, but it works. Next day, if we can find a better theory which works better than the old, that becomes the truth. Science goes on changing every day.

Truth cannot change, but you can always find a better working hypothesis. If it is more workable, it is more true. Nobody knows what truth is. All that we can decide is, if something works it is true, and if something doesn't work it is not true. The criterion can only be the working.

Salih must be agreeing with Buddha. He is not bothered about the door, whether it is such or not such. He is bothered about those who are seeking, on the path, groping in the dark. He is talking to *them*. He says, 'Knock, knock continually.'

Whoever knocks at the door continually, it will be opened to him. And remember, it will be opened to *him*, not for all. If it is a question of the door being opened or closed, then one man can open it, and then it is open for all. Once opened it is opened, then all can enter . . . But it is not a question of the door at all. Everybody has to open it for himself, and nobody can open it for somebody else.

Buddhas only show the way. *You* have to travel, you

have to work it out. They can only give you indications. They can only give you indications of the maps of higher consciousness, workable hypotheses. You have to work them out, because deep down it is not a question of doing something, it is a question of being different from you as you are. A different quality of being is needed. That is the door! Salih is absolutely right.

This is the distinction between Patanjali and Tilopa. Salih is like Patanjali; Rabiya is like Tilopa.

> *Rabiya, hearing him one day, said: 'How long will you say, 'it will be opened'? The door has never been shut.'*

This is the statement of one who has attained. It is meaningful only to those who have attained. It is truer than Salih; that's why Salih did not contradict it, he simply listened. And nothing is said about what he said, how he reacted. He would not react because he knows Rabiya is right, but uselessly right.... Absolutely right, but of no use.

You cannot eat the absolute truth. You cannot drink the absolute truth. The absolute truth is like the water of the ocean—beautiful, but if you are there thirsty, of no use. For a thirsty man, sitting by the shore of the ocean, with tremendous waves coming, there is an infinity of ocean, but it is useless. Absolute truth is like the water of the ocean. When you are thirsty, you need a small spring, you need a small well, to drink. An ocean won't help, it is too salty. It will kill you.

Rabiya is absolutely true: the door has never been shut. Who will shut it? Nature is not against you, god is not your enemy. Who will shut the door? The door has always remained open.

Move back to the story of the prodigal son. The father's heart was never shut. Nothing was needed to open it, not even a knock was needed to open it. Just the message—or not even the message, just the rumour—that the son was coming back, and the father started preparing a feast for him. Just the rumour, not even a knock, not even a message from the son saying, 'I am coming', just the rumour that the son is coming back, and the father started creating a feast for him, a reception, a welcome.

This is the meaning of god as father. The heart of existence is always open for you. It is waiting, throbbing for you, just waiting for the rumour that you are coming back; you have been away long, long, far away.

Who will shut the door? Rabiya is absolutely right, but this is the standpoint of the *siddhas*, of those who have attained. Tilopa will talk in this way. Krishnamurti goes on talking in this way, but whatsoever he says is just like the water of the ocean—too salty to drink. It won't help anybody's thirst. A final statement of truth, of course, absolutely right, but absolutely useless.

Rabiya is saying something which can be understood only by the buddhas. But they don't need it! Salih, of course, understood it; that's why he remained silent, he wouldn't say anything. Of course Rabiya is right, but he won't say anything. And Salih continued to teach—even after this encounter with Rabiya he was heard again and again every day to say the same thing: *Whoever knocks at the door continually, it will be opened to him.* He didn't say a single word to Rabiya because there was nothing to be said; she was right. But that didn't change his own mind. He continued.

Once a messenger came to me saying that Krishnamurti would like to meet me. I said, 'That is beautiful. And whenever the possibility arises I will come and see him and meet him.' But it is going to be useless, because I am Salih and he is Rabiya. I am talking to the disciples, and he is talking to the sky. I am talking to actual people who are thirsty, and he is talking in a vacuum. Whatsoever he says is true but useless. And whatsoever I say may not be so true, but it is useful.

Salih continued. He didn't say even a single word to Rabiya because what to say?—she is right! The door has never been shut. But this truth is meaningful only when you have attained. When you have entered the door, then you come to know that the door has never been shut. But those who have not attained—if you say to them that the door has never been shut, you misguide them. You don't help them; rather, you hinder them, because if they hear that the door has never been shut, you don't know how they are going to interpret it. They are going to interpret it in this way: then there is no need to knock on it continuously, no need to knock when the door is not shut. And if they don't knock, the door is going to remain shut for them, because they will not open to it. You need a constant knocking.

It is just like Shankara used to say again and again; he used to use a metaphor: On a dark night a traveller is going along. Suddenly he sees a snake moving. He becomes afraid, he runs, backwards. But there is no snake—just a rope lying on the street, and the rope has moved because a wind came and moved it.

He saw the rope moving, just a slight tremor in the rope, and he thought: 'It is a snake!' He projects the snake, becomes afraid, as afraid as if the snake is real, and escapes from the place. But he has to go on, he has to pass that snake.

So he asks somebody. That man says, 'There is no snake, because snakes are not found in this part of the country. You need not be afraid. Maybe it is just a rope.'

But the traveller won't listen. He says, 'I have seen it myself, and not only have I seen it, it moved, and it seems to be a very long and dark, dangerous snake!'

Then another man who is listening to the whole dialogue comes with a lamp and he says, 'Come, follow me.' This man also knows that in this part of the country snakes are not found. He also knows that it is more possible that it is going to be a rope, because sometimes he has also encountered ropes on the street and thought that they were snakes, and always it was found later on that there was no snake—snakes are not found in those parts. But you can't tell this man, 'There is no snake, don't be afraid. You go ahead, don't bother about it.' That will not be of much help. He brings a lamp. Knowing well that there is no snake, still he brings a lamp. The man follows behind the lamp. They reach the place. There is no need to say anything: with the lamp the man can see it is just a rope. He laughs, thanks the man who has brought the lamp, and goes ahead.

Salih is the man who will bring a lamp, knowing well that there is no snake, just a rope. Rabiya will just make the statement, 'There is no snake to be found in this part of the country. Don't be foolish; go ahead.' She is absolutely true, but useless. This statement is not going to help this man. This statement can be understood only by those people who know that part of the country, who live there—but for them it is not needed.

If I were listening to Rabiya it would be useless to say to me that the door is not shut, because I know it. The question is not of me, the question is of those who don't know. If it is said to them it is going to become a hindrance.

This has been my observation: Krishnamurti has not helped people, he has created many hindrances. And he has been talking about truth and nothing else. He has hindered many people because he says, 'It is *you* who attain the truth.' It is absolutely true, nobody can help you—that too is true. But this assertion has not helped anybody, it has hindered. Many people listening to him have become very egoistic. They think: 'Nobody can help us. No master is needed. No reverence, no trust—we alone are enough.' And they have not reached anywhere. They have not become humble through it, they have become egoists.

Krishnamurti says no meditation is needed. Absolutely true, a hundred percent true. But people who have listened to him have not achieved that state which he means by 'no meditation.' And they are as miserable as anybody else. They come to me and they say, 'We understand that no meditation is needed, but still nothing has happened to us.' Then I tell them, 'Then do meditation. You have tried no meditation, now you try meditation.'

But they say, 'This is not right, because Krishnamurti says no meditation is needed.' Now he has created a barrier for meditations, and by his saying that no meditation is needed, these people have become addicted to the idea of no meditation.

I also know that no meditation is needed, but that state comes only after you have meditated for a long, long time. When you have been knocking continually, one day suddenly you become aware that the door is open: 'It is not shut, why am I knocking?' But this realization comes through knocking for years and years, and even for lives. The knocking doesn't open the door, the knocking breaks your sleep. The knocking itself creates a situation in which you become alert, jostled out of your sleep, shocked out of your sleep.

When I say meditate, I know that through meditation nobody reaches, but through meditation you reach the point where 'no meditation' becomes possible. Unless you meditate, how will 'no meditation' become possible? One has to go through meditations, and as strongly and as totally as possible. Nothing should be left out. You should bring your total energy to it. You should knock your head against the wall. Not that the wall will break and the door will open— the door is always open, but knocking your head against it, suddenly you will come out of your sleep. The dreams will break, not the door. The door has always been open.

I will tell you one anecdote. It happened: A man came to Nagarjuna, the great Buddhist mystic, and the greatest alchemist that India has produced. The man said, 'I would like to meditate, but I cannot. I try to concentrate on the name of god, but my mind goes on slipping here and there. I completely forget the name of god, and other things come into the mind. My mind is a crowd, and I cannot manage it in any way. Help me.'

Nagarjuna looked at the man and said, 'Forget about god. Tell me one thing: do you love somebody?'

The man felt a little awkward, embarrassed. He said, 'You have asked and I cannot be untrue to you. But don't laugh at me, I am a foolish man. I don't love anybody; I love only my buffalo. But I really love her, she is a beautiful being.'

Nagarjuna said, 'That will do, because it makes no difference whether you love god or the buffalo. Even a buffalo is a god—a goddess. So that will do. You just go into that cave, and sit inside the cave, and you just continuously think only one thing—that you have become your buffalo.'

The man said, 'This will do, I can do it. In fact, I am wondering how you came to know it, because sometimes I think...I love my buffalo so much that sometimes I think how it will be if I become a buffalo in my next life.'

Nagarjuna said, 'You go, and don't come out of it until I come and ask you to come out.'

One day passed. The second day passed. The third day passed. On the fourth day, in the morning, Nagarjuna reached the cave and he said to the man, 'Now please come out.' The man tried, tried but he would not come out. Nagarjuna said, 'What is the matter?'

The man said, 'You see? the door is so small...and don't you see my horns? I cannot get out of it!' Three days, continuously thinking that he is a buffalo, a buffalo, a buffalo.... He autohypnotized himself: he *was* a buffalo! Whatsoever you think, you become. Thinking creates your identity.

The man started weeping. He said, 'Now it seems that I will never in my life be able to get out of this cave. And for three days I have been hungry and thirsty, and now I cannot get out. You help me, please!' And tears started rolling down his face.

Nagarjuna said, 'It is difficult, I can see it is so difficult. Now you have to go back and again become a man. Now think that you are a man and not a buffalo. '

The man had to think for at least three hours that he was a man and not a buffalo—in three hours the buffalo disappeared, the delusion disappeared. He opened his eyes. He came out laughing, and he said to Nagarjuna, 'Whatsoever I needed, I have attained.'

Nagarjuna said, 'Now you know. You can meditate. But

through meditation one starts getting new identities. You are a worldly man; you meditate, then you become a spiritual man: a new identity. But to be spiritual is as wrong as to be worldly. The real thing only happens when there is *no* identity. Now this is a new illusion. But it helps. From the world you move to the spiritual. From being a householder you become a sannyasin. From being a materialist you become spiritual. You create a new illusion. To throw the old out, the new is needed.'

But, passing through the old to the new, there is a gap between the two in which you will be nobody, and once that nobodiness is realized, you can follow it. Then no meditation is needed. No methods are needed, no techniques are needed.

I am as much against techniques as Krishnamurti is, even more, but I am not talking to myself here. Krishnamurti is in a monologue; it is not a dialogue. He is talking to himself, he is not talking to you, you are just an excuse. He is in a monologue.

I am talking to *you*, otherwise what is the point of talking? And when I am talking to you, I look to your need. And the question is not: What is truth? The question is: If I say something to you, what are you going to do about it? If I say the door is not shut, you will stop knocking. That is the logical conclusion. If I say no methods are needed, you will drop methods, but then you will remain the same as you are.

A man who has compassion has to think how others are going to react to his statements. The statement is not the point—how you react to the statement is the point: what energy it creates in you, where it leads you. If that leads you towards truth, towards the door which is always open, then I will also say: Knock, and knock continually.

One day you will realize that Rabiya was right, Salih

was not right. But still, you will feel grateful to Salih and not to Rabiya, because without Salih you would never have been able to realize that Rabiya was right. This is the complexity. Rabiya cannot be a master, Salih can be a master; Krishnamurti cannot be a master, Patanjali can be a master— because being a master means that an enlightened person is relating himself to the ignorant ones. And when ignorance and enlightenment meet, there is bound to be a happening. In that happening the ignorant person will contribute something, and something will be contributed by the enlightened person. Something will be wrong, something will be right. And the whole art of the master is how to bring you out, by and by, slowly, step by step, layer by layer, towards himself.

He has to compromise with you. To help you to come towards him, he has to come towards you. In that coming, he will say things which are not absolutely true, cannot be. He will have to devise things which are in a way arbitrary. They are like boats. You use them, and when you have used them, when you have crossed the river, you leave them in the river and you go on. They are like ladders. You pass over them, and then they are useless. They are means, not ends.

Salih is saying something as a means. Rabiya is talking about the end. Both are true. Rabiya will be found, in the end, absolutely true. But Salih is true in the beginning, and the beginning *is* the end, because if there is no beginning there can be no end. Remember this: you have to take care of the beginning. The end will take care of itself. Rabiya, Krishnamurti, Tilopa—if you forget them, nothing is lost. They are the ends. But if you forget Patanjali, Buddha, Bodhidharma, Salih, then everything is lost, because they are the beginning.

You take care of the beginning and the end will take care of itself. The end follows the beginning. Go on knocking at the door. Continually knock at the door. And I know that the door has never been shut, it is open. But still you have to knock—only then will it open for you, because through knocking, you will be open to it.

Enough for today.

Four

Asking the Experts

A man who was believed to have died and was being prepared for burial, revived. He sat up, but was so shocked at the scene surrounding him that he fainted. He was put in the coffin and the funeral party set off for the cemetery.

Just as they arrived at the grave he regained consciousness, lifted the lid, and cried out for help.

'It is not possible that he has revived,' said the mourners, 'because he has been certified dead by competent experts.'

'But I am alive!' shouted the man. He appealed to a well known and impartial scientist and jurisprudent who was present.

'Just a moment,' said the expert. He then turned to the mourners, counting them. 'Now we have heard what the alleged deceased has had to say. You fifty witnesses tell me what you regard as the truth.'

'He is dead,' said the witnesses. 'Bury him,' said the expert.

And so he was buried.

Is EXISTENCE A problem? If it is a problem, then philosophers can help, then experts are useful. But philosophers have failed utterly. For centuries and centuries they have been thinking and thinking. Nothing comes out of their grinding, no conclusion is reached, no truth arrived at. Something is basically wrong with their attitude.

It is not that their competence is lacking, their competence is perfect. They are absolutely efficient. But somehow they have mistaken existence for a problem. It is not. It is not there to be solved, it is there to be lived! If it was a problem it could have been solved long ago. It is not a problem at all. It has to be lived. Life is not separate from you, to be tackled as a problem, it is *you*. Who is going to solve whom?

Existence is not there outside you. It is inside you, it is your very inside. And existence is not apart; you are part of it, organically one with it. How can a wave solve the ocean? The ocean is not a problem for the wave, it is something to be lived. And the ocean is not separate; in fact the ocean is waving in the wave. The wave and the ocean are not two things: they are one unity.

You are existence, existence is you. Who is going to solve it and how?

Philosophy starts from a wrong beginning. It takes it for granted that there *is* a problem. It never doubts the very ground—that maybe there is no problem. Once you start wrongly you go on and on, and if the first step has been wrong, the last is already missed. From a wrong beginning nobody can come to a right ending; that's why philosophy goes on theorizing, philosophizing. Its very attitude is such that it turns everything into a problem.

A great philosopher, a professor of philosophy, was ill, mentally ill. He was psychoanalyzed, treated. He started feeling a little better. And then the psychoanalyst said, 'Now it will be good if you go to the hills. It is hot in the plains and the climatic change will help you. So go to the Himalayas.'

The philosopher went. There he felt very good. The hills were covered with ice, and it was so silent that he felt a sort of euphoria bursting in him. Immediately he telegraphed his psychoanalyst: 'I am feeling happy. Why?'

The very attitude of philosophy is to make a problem out of any and every thing. If you are happy—why? That too becomes a problem. How to solve it? If you are sad, of course, why? If you are happy, again: why? It makes no difference to a philosopher what the case is—he creates problems out of it. A philosopher is a problem-creator. First he creates the problems, and then he starts solving them.

In the first place the problems are false, they are not there. Happiness is there. There is no question mark around it, the question mark has been added by the philosopher. Happiness simply exists, there is no 'why'. Existence *is*, there is no 'why'. Trees *are*, flowers *are*...birds singing, clouds floating in the sky—there is no why. The why is added by the philosopher, and once the why is added and the question mark is there, of course he has to solve it. And how can you solve a problem which doesn't exist? Whatsoever you do will create more problems. You will find one answer—you think it solves. Immediately that answer creates more questions.

So philosophy has been simply a search for more questions, more 'whys'. Not even a single answer has been given by it. For millennia philosophers have been grinding. Nothing comes out of it because in the first place nothing has been put in. The 'why' is empty. Philosophy is the most absurd effort of humanity.

Existence is not a problem to be solved, it is a mystery to be lived. And you should be perfectly aware what the difference is between a mystery and a problem. A problem is something created by the mind; a mystery is something which is there, not created by the mind. A problem has an ugliness in it, like disease. A mystery is beautiful. With a problem, immediately a fight arises. You have to solve it; something is wrong, you have to put it right; something is missing, you have to supply the missing link. With a mystery there is no question like that.

The moon rises in the night.... It is not a problem, it is a mystery. You have to live with it. You have to dance with it. You have to sing with it, or you can be just silent with it. Something mysterious surrounds you.

A philosopher has completely forgotten the language of mystery. Mystery is natural. Problems are man-created. If man is not on the earth, the mystery will be there, but there will be no problems. Crows will caw, and they will not ask why. Cuckoos will go on singing, and nobody will ask why. Trees will flower as they have been flowering always; nobody will sit underneath and philosophize. Life doesn't bother about philosophization. It is a foolish effort—but very ego-fulfilling, because you create the problem, then you try to find the solution, then more problems are created.... You start feeling that you are doing something great.

You are not doing anything. Nothing is there, just hot air, bubbles of hot air in the mind that you call thoughts. Ripples, confusion, chaos. A philosopher misses life completely. He bypasses life, completely unaware that there was something to be lived, loved; that there was something to be merged with; that there was something to float with; that there was something to dance with and become one with. A philosopher is a closed mind, completely life-proof. Life does not penetrate him.

And these philosophers become great experts about life

because they can talk, they are articulate people. They can create problems where none exist, and then they go on supplying answers for them. They are self-sufficient, they don't need anybody. They create the problems and then they create the solution. And then they create more questions and questions, and they go on and on. They create an illusion around them that they know.

We don't have a word like *philosophy* in Indian languages. This Greek word philosophy means love of knowledge. We don't have any word like that. And the word that we have is totally different: it is *darshan*. It means the capacity to *see*. Not love of knowledge, but love of realization. Not love towards more and more knowledge, no, but towards a greater, clearer vision. That's why we call those who have known, seers—those who have seen. Life has to be lived and seen, not thought about. Philosophy creates experts, and those experts go on giving answers to you which are false. The whole effort of philosophy is a false effort, and this is one of the greatest systems of human effort to know.

The second system is science. Science again takes it for granted that life is a challenge; not a problem in the sense of a philosopher, but a challenge. One has to fight. That's why scientists go on in terms of conquering nature: as if there is an enemy, not a problem, but an enemy who is challenging you and whom you have to conquer. Scientists become warriors, conquerors. They fight with nature. But how can you live if you start with hate? Science is based on hatred, enmity, fear, as if life is there surrounding you like an enemy: not like your mother, not something beloved, not caring about you, but ready to kill and destroy you. Science has taken the attitude of hatred, and through that, science goes on fighting. If you fight, you miss again.

Philosophy theorizes, and misses. Science fights, and misses. How can you live if from the very beginning your whole attitude is based on enmity?

A scientist lives a desert life. He may get the Nobel prize, but *life* never awards him. Life never comes any nearer to him. He does not allow that closeness with life. He is always in search of ways and means to conquer. The system of science is aggressive, it is violent. It is a rape against nature.

So scientists may get a few facts here and there. They may snatch something, just as a robber can. It is possible: you can steal, you can rob life of a few facts. Life will give those few facts to you very reluctantly. It is as if you gather a few crumbs from the table of an emperor, but you don't become the emperor...you remain a beggar, or a robber, and life was there ready to crown you as the emperor.

There was no need to fight because life is the mother—you come out of it! You are born out of existence, existence carried you in its womb; how can existence be inimical to you? It has given birth to you, it has protected you, it still protects you. You come out of it and you dissolve into it again. You are part of it: a hand raised by nature. Eyes, ears...through all your being nature is trying to reach a certain height of consciousness. You are not the enemy, you are the beloved son.

That is the meaning of Jesus' saying of himself, 'I am the son and God is my father. ' The Jews never understood him, what he was saying: he was saying that life is a family, existence is not inimical, it mothers you, it fathers you. You are the son, loved by it, nourished by it. Something is meant through you, some greater significance has to evolve in you. Don't fight, because if you start fighting the friend, you will create unnecessary barriers for yourself.

Science creates the attitude of fight; that's why science has been very very destructive. Philosophers have failed, but they have not done any harm to anybody. They have failed so utterly they cannot do any harm. Science has been a success, and science has completely crippled life. Now, in all the countries where science has become very developed, it has become a menace. The whole ecology is suffering. Rivers and lakes are becoming dead, trees are dying. The earth itself is dying, is on its deathbed. The whole atmosphere is poisoned. And there is panic in those who know, for there seems to be no possibility of stopping it—because who will stop it? Scientists themselves are impotent now. They have released the demon; now they don't know how to put it back in the bottle again. And the politicians won't allow them to put it back in the bottle.

Two types of mad people have joined together: the politicians and the scientists. The scientists go on supplying politicians with secrets and the politicians go on using those secrets in Hiroshima, in Nagasaki, and in everyday life. Technology is killing completely the whole of nature. Things are disappearing…because existence is a coherent whole: if you destroy one part of it, the whole is affected. Finally one day the whole system collapses. This is how it is happening.

Science has been a dagger driven into the back of nature. Philosophers have not done much harm—they cannot because they are absolute failures—but science has done much harm. The greatest enemy today is science. And why has it been so harmful?—because from the very beginning enmity has been at the base. Hatred, not love…enmity with life, not friendship. Science has created the idea in humanity that you are unaccepted guests here and you are not at home. You have to fight. From Darwin to Einstein, they have been teaching survival of the fittest—as if life is just a struggle! The fact is otherwise, just the contrary. Life is a vast cooperation.

Prince Kropotkin is nearer the truth than Charles Darwin. Prince Kropotkin says—and he is a religious man, a really religious man—he says that cooperation is the base of life, not struggle, and it is not a question of survival of the fittest, because if it is a question of the survival of the fittest, then might becomes right. It is not a question of survival of the fittest; most tender things also survive. Look at the flowers! They are not Adolf Hitlers, and they have survived. Look at the birds, the small birds, singing beautiful songs: they are not Genghis Khans and Alexanders, and they have survived. Life must be a deep cooperation—it is. Everything is cooperating; it is a cosmic whole, interdependent.

Look: the earth goes on feeding the tree, the sun goes on feeding the tree, the air goes on feeding the tree, and then a fruit is born. That fruit feeds you. It becomes your body, it circulates in your blood. It becomes your bones, it becomes your heart, it becomes your brain, it becomes the very marrow of your brain. Then one day you die. Insects start eating you. Then the insects die, they are reabsorbed in the earth. The trees start eating the earth. Again fruits will come. Your grandchildren will eat you in the fruits. Everything related, interrelated, connected. You have been eating your grandfathers, your grandmothers; they are again reabsorbed! You will be reabsorbed.

Waves come and go, the ocean remains—and each wave is connected with each other wave. Past and future—you are related to the whole past, you are a link; and you are related to the whole future that is going to be there. You are a link in the chain, and if one chain link is broken, the whole chain suffers. It is a cooperation. Nobody is independent and nobody is dependent. because even to be dependent you have to be separate. No, it is not a question of independence or dependence. Life is *interdependence*. Nobody is independent and nobody is dependent, everybody is interdependent.

So I call those messiahs pseudo who teach people independence, because it is a false attitude, untrue to life. Nobody can be independent. If you try it, you are being stupid. You can go to the Himalayas and you can try to be independent: you cannot be, because there also you will be part of the interdependence that is life.

Monks have been trying over all the centuries to become totally independent because they think if you are dependent then you are in bondage. So escape from the wife, escape from the children, escape from society; but where will you escape from oxygen? Where will you escape from water? Where will you escape from food? Where will you escape from the sun and the moon? Wherever you go you will remain part of the interconnected pattern of life.

You can never become independent, absolute independence is not possible, because that means you become an isolated unit, you become an island—and there exists no island. Islands that you see in the ocean, they also are not separate, they also are part of continents hidden under the sea. No island exists. Nobody can be independent. It is interdependence. It is a deep cooperation.

Don't start with enmity; otherwise you will destroy life and your whole energy will be engaged in destruction—and existence is creative. You can enjoy it, you can become one with it, only when you are creative. And science has been destructive. It is not needed. Or, a totally different type of science is needed, based more on Kropotkin and less on

Darwin. A totally different science is needed based on love, not on hate, based on Lao Tzu and not on Aristotle.

Science has to be Eastern if it is to be right. It need not be so logical. It has to be a little more loving, then it is not against nature, then it is not a rape, rather it is a courting. You court nature. Nature becomes the bride, you become the bridegroom. You court nature, you persuade her to reveal her secrets. A lover also persuades a woman, and the woman reveals everything that she can reveal, everything that she has. She reveals her very heart.

And then a man can rape a woman. The rape and the lovemaking may look similar from the outside, but they are not, because when you violate a woman she simply shrinks, she closes. You may violate the body, but you cannot violate the soul. The soul remains virgin. It simply shrinks back. A man who rapes a woman never touches her soul—he cannot. And that is what has happened with science. It has been a rape of nature. It could have been love.

And science has accumulated much expertise about everything. If you have to prove anything you have only to say that science says so: enough!—nobody questions it. It is proved already if science says so. Science is the model superstition. In the old days it was enough to say that the Vedas say so, or the Bible says so, or it is written in the Koran; and if you could show that it was written in the Koran—finished, then nobody asked whether it is right or wrong. If it was written in the Koran, in the Vedas, it had to be right; it was enough if you could prove that it was in the Vedas. Now it is enough if you can prove that scientists say so.

Who are these scientists? What have they been doing? They are experts. They have gathered a few facts. But they don't know what life is because life can never be known through analysis, through dissection.

You love a woman, a beautiful body, but you don't go to a surgeon to ask whether this body is beautiful or not. A surgeon of course knows many bodies, deeper than anybody else; he has been dissecting, he has cut thousands of bodies. But don't go to a surgeon because a dissected body is no longer alive, and beauty belongs to life. Analyzed, a thing becomes dead. Life exists as a whole. You cannot dissect it. If you want to know it, and the beauty and grace of it, you have to watch it while it is alive. You have to love it as it is— alive. If you try to cut it and find the innermost parts, and how they function and what is happening inside, you may come to know the mechanism of the body but you have missed the soul.

The soul lives in the unity—the unity *is* the soul. And the soul is greater than all the parts put together. The soul surrounds all the parts—in fact the soul keeps all the parts together. Once the soul has left a body, it starts deteriorating. Within hours it is dying, things are falling apart. You leave the body there a few days and it is already becoming one with the earth. Who was holding the whole as a whole? Who was keeping things together? What was the source of the togetherness?

A desire arises in me—I feel thirsty; my hand immediately reaches towards water. From where comes this unity? A desire arises—the desire is not in the hand, the hand never feels thirsty. My throat is feeling dry. I feel thirst. That thirst is recorded in the brain, is witnessed by the soul. The hand never feels thirst, but immediately, without any order, without any message given to the hand, if the throat feels thirsty the brain immediately starts functioning. Not a single moment is lost—the hand reaches towards water. The hand, the throat, the brain—they are functioning together.

There must exist an organic whole which keeps all parts together. That whole is the soul. You cannot dissect a body and come to know the soul, because the moment you dissect, it is gone. It is there only when the unity is functioning. It is the very unity.

If you go to the scientists to ask about life they have many answers, but all their answers belong more to death than to life, because they have been fighting, destroying, dissecting, analyzing. In the whole process they have missed life. They will never come to encounter it; that's why they always say that there is no soul—because they never encounter it in their lab. They have dissected many bodies and they have never seen any soul. Before they start dissecting, the soul has left. They will never come to know it, and science will go on denying that there is any soul, and science will go on denying that there is any god. But this is not the point, whether there is or is not a god, because the very method of science prohibits...the very method becomes the barrier.

Then there is a third system, which is art. These three systems produce experts: philosophy, science and art. These are the three dimensions in which the human mind functions. Art is not interested in theorizing, and art is not interested in dissecting; that's why art is closer to religion than anything else. Philosophers are the farthest. You may have thought otherwise, but philosophers are the farthest from religion. Even scientists are nearer, because if there exists a hate relationship it can be converted into a love relationship, because hate is nothing but love upside down.

So an Einstein can become religious more easily than a Bertrand Russell. At least he hates. At least he is fighting life—even fighting is a way to live; even fighting is an alive moment. A scientist is not just in theories, he is experimenting. A philosopher is sitting with closed eyes, thinking about 'woman': much fantasy. A scientist is raping a woman. At least that is better than the philosopher, at least a real woman is there. Maybe a right relationship doesn't exist between the man who rapes and the woman raped, but some type of relationship exists. Even the enemy is related to you.

The scientist can be converted—and it happens that many scientists by and by, as they grow older, with more understanding, start turning towards religion. But philosophers remain stubborn. To the very end they go on talking their nonsense and theories and this and that. A scientist by his whole life's effort of struggle, fight, murdering nature, may suddenly awake. His whole life may take a turn of one-hundred-eighty degrees. That's possible. An enemy can any day become a friend. You are related at least— wrongly, but related at least.

Farthest from religion is the philosopher, the system of philosophy. Closer than philosophy is science, and closer than science is art.

What is art? What is art doing in the world? Art is just like a child—enjoying the butterflies, running after them. Art is a childlike attitude. It tries to make life a little more beautiful. It is an interior decoration; it decorates life. It gives a quality of dream to life. Through painting, through poetry, through music, it enhances the beauty, the euphoria. It tries to give momentary pleasures, a quality, something resembling permanence. It is an effort to live, but it is still not religion. It does not accept life as it is, it tries to improve it; it tries to make it more beautiful. It feels as if raw life is not worth living. It tries to improve existence. It is nearer to religion because it tries to live, but still it is not religion.

Religion is the jump into raw existence as it is. Religion accepts totally. It says there is no need to decorate life; it is already such a beautiful poem that no Shakespeares can improve it, no Kalidases are needed. It is already such a tremendous poetry that all improvements are just futile. It is as if you are trying to put legs on a snake. Foolish! The snake is perfect, there is no need to put legs on the snake. And if you put legs on it then sooner or later somebody will come and try to fix shoes on the legs, and you will kill the snake!

Art is trying to put legs on the snake. There is no need—life in the raw is tremendously beautiful, it is utterly wonderful. To enjoy it nothing is lacking. The more you decorate it, the more false it becomes. It becomes like the painted face of a woman.

I have heard an anecdote. It happened that one saint was very much against women using any decorations for the face, powder, lipstick, this and that—he was very much against them. Another saint lived there also, just in the neighborhood, who was very much in favour of it. The first one used to say that as life is, it is beautiful, there is no need to improve upon it, and you cannot improve on it, it is the final word. The other used to say life is ugly, one has to hide it.

A woman used to go to listen to both the saints and she was very troubled and puzzled. She went to an expert, a logician, to ask what to do because one saint said this and another saint said that. The philosopher, the logician, pondered over it, meditated upon the matter, and he said, 'You do one thing: paint half your face...because when two saints are against each other this is the only logical answer. Be in the middle, follow the middle path. '

This has happened, this *is* happening every day to you. Somebody is saying something, somebody else is against it.

What do you do? You compromise. You paint half your face. You become uglier.

Life as it is, is perfect. That's why we say life is god. God means perfection; there is no beyond to it.

But art comes close, because it doesn't bother about theories, it does not bother about any fight. It simply tries to decorate. It simply tries to make it a little more beautiful so that you can enjoy it. But there it misses also, because life can be enjoyed as it is. In fact it can be enjoyed only as it is.

Art is childlike. Philosophy belongs to old age, to the cunning mind. That's why whenever you think of philosophers you always think them very ancient, old. Artists are always children, playing on the beach, trying to accumulate coloured stones.

It happens again and again that there come periods in art when the art simply becomes absolutely unsophisticated and childlike. That has happened with Picasso, and that is his appeal: he paints like a child. There is great art in it, but the painting looks like a child's, as if he has been playing with colours with no idea what to do...as if just by playing with colours it has happened. But a child has to grow because a child is only the beginning, not the end, and if the child grows rightly he becomes religious. If an artist grows rightly he becomes religious. If he does not grow, then he remains an artist.

For a philosopher to become religious is a long journey...very very difficult, almost impossible. Seems arduous. His whole being is at stake, he has to destroy himself completely; only then can he become religious. That's why philosophers have created a game. The name of the game is theology. It is not religion, it is just a trick of philosophers to feel as if they are religious. They have been thinking about truth, beauty, this and that, then they think about god. Theology means logic about *theos*, logic about god. They make god a problem also, and they start thinking about it. Theology is a false religion. It is part of philosophy, it has nothing to do with religion.

For a scientist it is difficult, but possible, to turn and take a hundred-and-eighty-degree conversion and become a religious man, because science and religion both belong to the age of youth. Just try to understand it: art belongs to the child, philosophy belongs to the old man, science and religion both belong to the young man. Both need energy. Science is hate, religion is love. Science fights with life, religion loves it.

A child is nearer to the young man because he will have to grow up sooner or later. Unless he is a retarded child he is bound to become religious. Every artist, if he moves, grows, will find one day he has entered the temple of the divine. Every poet, every musician, every dancer, if he goes on growing, if his growth is not stopped somewhere in the middle, then he will become religious. That is a natural consequence of being an artist.

A scientist will have to take a hundred-and-eighty-degree turn. He cannot grow into religion; he has to change himself, his direction. He can grow easily into a philosopher. So many scientists in their old age—Eddington, James Jeans—they all become philosophers. It is easy.

For a religious man it is impossible to grow into old age because a religious man never grows old; he grows and grows and grows, and becomes younger and younger. He never becomes old. Old age does not belong to the religious man because he lives moment to moment, so fresh. He remains young. He loves life so deeply that life nourishes his youth. An old man simply means somebody who has been rejected by life and is now getting ready for the garbage can, being thrown away. Used, now there is no need for him.

A religious man never grows old, that's why you never see a statue of Buddha as an old man. He became old, he lived for eighty years, but you never see a statue of Buddha, or Mahavira or Krishna or Rama as old, no. We have never painted a single picture of them as old because we know a religious man never grows old. The body grows old, but that is not the point; consciousness remains young and fresh.

A religious man never becomes a philosopher. It is impossible. It is not in the very nature of things. It is difficult for a philosopher to become religious, because he will have to go back. It is against nature to go back, but it is possible. Rarely it happens, very rarely, but it is possible; one can go back. Much is involved, investment is there—a whole life invested in philosophy; it is difficult to move back. Philosophers, to the very last, go on insisting on their theories, remain confined in them.

These are the four ways of living life. A religious man lives life without becoming an expert, he never becomes an expert because life is so vast—how can you claim expertise? Life is so infinite, beginningless, endless, how can you become knowledgeable about it? In fact the more you know, the less you feel that you know. The greater your knowing becomes, the more intensely ignorance is felt. When knowledge becomes absolute, the man of religion simply feels that he doesn't know anything. He is not an expert.

So if you find anybody expert in religion, know well he is not a religious man. He may belong to the false discipline of theology. Theology is the false coin which tries to deceive people that it is a religion. Christianity died because of theology; too much theology suffocated it.

The Jews could not kill Jesus. They crucified him, but he survived. Then the theologians—and Christianity has produced great theologians; in fact Christianity has not produced anything else, just rotten theology that has suffocated Jesus completely—they murdered him. Jesus was not murdered on the hill of Golgotha, he was murdered in the Vatican.

Religion is always killed by theology; it is a dangerous, cancerous growth. Religion never makes you an expert, it never makes you a pundit. A man with eyes can never become a pundit because life is not a theory, it is not a scripture; it is not a hypothesis to be learned, it is a mystery to be lived. And the more you move into this mystery the more you are lost.

A day comes when life is and you are not. A day comes when you are dissolved completely. The wave has disappeared into the ocean. This is the final, the ultimate—what in India we have been calling *samadhi*, the enlightenment, *sambodhi*. When you are no more you have become a buddha.

Now, this small parable.

> *A man who was believed to have died and was being prepared for burial, revived. He sat up, but he was so shocked at the scene surrounding him that he fainted. He was put in the coffin and the funeral party set off for the cemetery.*
> *Just as they arrived at the grave he regained consciousness, lifted the lid, and cried out for help.*
> *'It is not possible that he has revived,' said the mourners, 'because he has been certified dead by competent experts.'*

When competent experts have said that he is dead, how

is it possible that he has revived? People believe in theories, not in life. The man is there alive and crying for help, but no, their eyes are closed by theories, knowledge, and competent experts have given the certificate that he is dead. How can they be wrong? It must be an illusion: 'Maybe we are hallucinating, or maybe this man is hallucinating: he is dead and he thinks he is not. Something has gone wrong, because how can the experts be wrong?'

And don't laugh, because this is your attitude also. If something is said in the Vedas and life denies it, you will forget life and you will believe in the Vedas. You will say, 'How is it possible? The *rishis* of the Vedas, the great experts, they say this is not so. Something must be wrong in life. Life can go wrong, experts never go wrong.'

It has happened so many times, it is happening every day, with you, with others.

When for the first time astrologers and astronomers proved that the earth is round-shaped, not flat, the pope of the Vatican denied it. He said, 'How is it possible? Because in the Bible it is said that the earth is flat.'

They had all the proofs that the earth is round but the Christian theologians wouldn't listen. They said, 'How is it possible? The earth *has* to be flat. How can the Bible be wrong? The Devil must be playing tricks with your minds; that's why you are finding these arguments. But you cannot deceive us, we know the word of God.'

Then it was proved that the sun is not moving around the earth as it was believed. Just the contrary, the earth is moving around the sun. Every proof was there, and not a single proof existed against it. But again Galileo was called to the court of the pope, and he was forced to take his statement back.

Galileo, on his knees in the court, said, 'I also believe that the sun must be moving around the earth, because it says so in the scriptures, and I must apologize for making a statement that the earth moves around the sun.' And he said to the pope, 'My Lord, if you wish I can write another book to prove that the scripture is true. But one thing I must say: Even if I prove it, it makes no difference, the earth is moving around the sun. Nothing can be done about it. I can write a book to disprove my argument—that is nothing, that is not the point.'

Galileo must have been a rare man. People think that he was a coward; I don't think so. People think that he was a coward because why should he apologize? He should have become a martyr. But as my feeling goes martyrs are almost always foolish, stupid people. Ninety-nine percent are stupid. Galileo must have been a very very understanding man.

If you live with fools you have to accept their foolishness. Why unnecessarily become a martyr for just this ordinary thing? And whether the earth moves around the sun or the sun moves around the earth, what difference does it make? Why waste your life for it? He must have been a very rare, understanding man. He was not a coward at all. He was not foolhardy, that's right, but his statement is beautiful in the end. He says, 'But I cannot do anything. I can prove it, but that sun won't listen, and neither will the earth follow.'

It happened that Galileo made the first telescope, and he asked his friends—university professors, priests—to come and see through it, because many stars were there which could not be seen by the naked eye but they could be seen through this telescope. Nobody was ready to look through it, because everything is counted in the Bible, and it is said how many stars are there, and God created only that amount, that number, and how can you suddenly find more with an instrument? That instrument must have been supplied by the Devil!

Nobody was ready to look through it—so afraid... because maybe you can see some stars there which are not written about in the scriptures. Then there will be trouble. When a few courageous people tried to look, they looked and they laughed and they said, 'You must have been playing tricks!' The stars were there; this Galileo must be playing tricks.

This has been the attitude, that life has to follow the scriptures, life has to follow the theory. So don't laugh about these people—they are following a well-established law of foolishness.

'It is not possible,' they said, 'that he has revived, because he has been certified dead by competent experts.'

I have heard: It happened that somehow Mulla Nasruddin's wife's name was missed in the voters' list. Then there was an election, and his wife was very anxious to vote, but her name was not there. So Nasruddin took his wife to the election commissioner—and not only was the name not there on the list, it was said that his wife was dead. Of course his wife was very furious, and she was more furious because Nasruddin was taking the thing with much ease. He was not disturbed and he was not angry, and he should have been because how dare these people count her as dead when she was alive? She was very angry. They went to the commissioner and she told him, 'This is not right. I am alive! And in your list it is said that I am dead. What is this?'

She was so angry that Nasruddin said, 'Wait. You cannot fight with the officers. They must be right; how can they be wrong? Of course they know better than we do, and you, a foolish woman, not educated at all, trying to argue with a great officer? If they write that you are dead, you must be dead. Experts cannot be wrong.'

'But I am alive!' shouted the man.

And life is shouting all around you, but you have never listened to it. You are too engaged with experts. You go on reading your Ramayana, your Bible, and life is all around shouting, 'I am here! Look at me!' It shouts through the birds, through the trees, through the rocks, through the clouds—but you are deaf. Your ears are filled with the scriptures and the experts and the theoreticians. You are reading your book, you are looking in the book, you are searching for life in the book.

Ramakrishna used to say that this happened: The wife of a disciple of Ramakrishna told her husband that in the neighbourhood, just two or three houses away, a house had burned down in the night. He was an educated man. Immediately he took his newspaper and went through it. The wife said, 'What are you doing?' He said, 'If the house has really burned down then there must be news of it in the newspaper, and it is not there. I don't think that house could have burned down, it must be a rumour.' Just three houses away—but you have to look in the newspaper, you have to check in the newspaper. The newspaper has become more alive than life. Words have become more meaningful than facts.

Existence has gone far away from you. Between you and existence there is a vast wall of China, made of words, theories, scriptures, religions, philosophies. It is difficult to penetrate the wall and reach existence; that's why you are so miserable, so thirsty, so starved. You have not lived at all. You have been just dragging yourself along.

> *'But I am alive!' shouted the man. He appealed to a well-known and impartial scientist and jurisprudent who was present.*

There he also committed the same mistake as the mourners were committing, because he also belonged to the same crowd. Sometimes I think, reading this story, that he may also be thinking inside: Maybe they are right, because how can the experts be wrong? Maybe I am deceived!...because he was part of these mourners, of the same crowd. He was not a different man but a member of the same group. He must also be thinking inside: I feel that I am alive, but who relies on his own feelings? You also don't rely on your own feelings. You feel suspicious. Who knows?—you may be wrong. The man was alive, he was feeling alive, he was shouting, 'I am alive!' but still he appealed to the wrong man—a well-known and impartial scientist.

First, he was a scientist, which means he was an expert about dead things. No scientist ever encounters life, he cannot. His methodology debars it. A man who knows about dead things—appealing to him about life was a wrong step, and the step was even more wrong because the man was well-known. When an expert is not well-known sometimes he can put his expertise aside; nothing much is at stake. But when a well-known expert is there he has to save his expertise. The question is not whether this man is alive or not; the question is, he has to save his prestige of being a well-known scientist. A small man can commit suicide but not a well-known scientist. An immature scientist may have looked at the man and thought: Maybe he is alive. But that would mean that he was immature, not really well-established.

The more a man is established the more he has invested in it and the less is the possibility for him to allow any new fact to arise. He will have to push away the new fact because the new fact, if accepted, will destroy the whole old pattern. More established people are less rebellious, they have to be. They cannot afford rebellion. This is one of the basic tricks that societies play against revolution.

In India, for five thousand years there has been no revolution because we gave the brahmins so much prestige. The man of knowledge was made the highest, the topmost; the man of knowledge was the base of the whole establishment. Who will rebel? Because to rebel you first have to be a brahmin, an intellectual. Only the intelligentsia rebels. But if the intelligentsia is made the very base of the establishment, then nobody can rebel, there is no possibility. All the brahmins in India were the topmost people. They could not afford to be rebellious because in rebellion their prestige would be lost. If the establishment is lost, they are lost. They exist with the establishment. They cannot afford rebellion.

And the same trick is being played in Soviet Russia. That's why in Soviet Russia there is no possibility of any revolution, no possibility at all. The same trick. They must have learned it from the Hindus, because India is the only country which has been on earth for thousands of years without revolution, the only social structure with no rebellion, no possibility of any rebellion—they must know some secret. The man who gave Hindu society its foundation, Manu, must have known the secret.

And now, Marx plus Manu is the structure of Soviet Russia. They pay much respect to authors, professors, writers, novelists, scientists—the brahmins, the intelligentsia. Again, in Russia the brahmin is the highest, the top class. Now there is no possibility of any revolution there, because who will revolt? Labourers, *sudras*, never revolt; on their own they will never revolt. The intelligentsia is needed to provoke them, but who will provoke them?—because a revolution will go against the intelligentsia itself. Warriors, soldiers, they never revolt, they are the most obedient people in the world, soldiers—the *most* obedient, even foolishly obedient. Their whole training is for obedience. They never revolt. And business people of course cannot revolt, because they will be robbed in a revolution. They have much to lose. Business people never revolt, *vaishyas* never revolt—they cannot. They are always against revolution. That's why in America revolution is not possible, because the whole country consists of the middle class, the whole country is the business class, vaishyas. In America revolution is not possible—who will revolt? The major part of the country is middle class. A middle-class mind is always trying to reach the top. He has no time for revolution, and any revolution will disturb his own ambition. Vaishyas are never revolutionaries.

Warriors, soldiers, *kshatriyas*, are the most obedient part of a country. They never revolt. Whosoever rules, they follow him. Sudras have no mind—labourers, the proletariat, they have no mind to revolt. They are contented with whatsoever they have. They drag on with it. They don't hope much. They are not frustrated. To create the frustrations, brahmins are needed. The brahmin is the only revolutionary class, and if you make the brahmins the top, then revolution is killed from the very seed, burned. Experts can never be revolutionaries. They are the brahmins. They are already so established that they would not like any change.

The man appealed to the wrong person. He appealed to a well-known and 'impartial' scientist—and there is one more condition: impartial.

This is something to be understood, it is a very delicate point. Science thinks that it is impartial, science thinks that it is impersonal knowledge. This is wrong. No knowledge is ever impersonal, all knowledge is personal. No knowledge is impartial, all knowledge is partial, because the knower enters into the knowledge, he cannot remain outside of it. Whenever you know something, *you* know. You have entered into it, you have become part of it. That's why in Soviet Russia a different type of science exists than in America—because they have different investments, different commitments.

In Stalin's Russia, many scientific theories were denied. They were not accepted because they were against Marxism, so nobody would talk about them, nobody would discover them. They were discovering something else. In Soviet Russia, Freud's psychoanalysis is not accepted. Not a single psychologist there says that Freudian analysis is right, no. The whole world has said so, but not Russia.

They have their own psychology—Pavlovian. Pavlov is their Freud because he supports communism, because he says there is no soul, no mind: man is nothing but behavior, a mechanism; biological, but still a mechanism. And the whole point is how to condition it. Wrong conditioning leads to psychic illnesses, right conditioning will change the man. There is no need for psychoanalysis. Psychoanalysis is bourgeois, it is capitalistic. Freud has not entered into the Soviet bloc.

They have their own psychology, and they also think they are impartial, and Freud also thought he was impartial. In fact, impartial knowledge is not possible, because the man who finds it, he has his own bias, his own prejudice. He has his own knowledge, he has his own mind; it colours the whole thing. Nothing is impartial.

Only one possibility exists of impartial knowledge, and that is when you have lost your mind completely. We in the east say: Only a buddha can be impartial, a buddha, who has no mind, who has no self, who has no prejudice, no ideology, who lives in emptiness—he can be impartial. But a man who lives in mind—how can he be impartial? His mind is going to colour, his mind is going to interpret.

This man must have been a very well-known scientist, 'impartial'—because what he did proves that he must have been well-known, and he must have been thinking that he was impartial. That impartiality killed the man. He appealed to the wrong man.

> *'Just a moment,' said the expert. He then turned to the mourners, counting them. 'Now, we have heard what the alleged deceased has had to say. You fifty witnesses tell me what you regard as the truth.'*

Of course, this is the only way to be impartial: Take votes. And of course the majority is always right, truth is to be proved by majority. This is how the whole world is run by experts—truth is to be proved by majority. And in fact just the reverse is the case: the majority always believes in lies, because the majority consists of fools.

Democracy basically is mobocracy. It cannot be otherwise. You have to ask the fools who is right, what is right, and there is a tendency in the mob to follow others. The mob has no standpoint of its own. It is a chaos. Somebody raises his hand, the others follow. The mob are like sheep.

One teacher was asking a small boy—because the boy was the son of a shepherd—he asked, 'You have ten sheep. Five jump out of the fence, how many are left behind?'

The boy said, 'None.'

The teacher said, 'What! You can't even figure it out? Five have jumped out, and there were ten in the beginning, so how many are left?'

The boy said again, 'None.'

The teacher was at a loss. He said, 'Then you can't figure it out?'

The child said, 'You may know figures, but I know sheep. None is left. Even if one jumps out, that will be enough; the other nine will follow.'

And he is right. What did this impartial, well-known scientist do? He did a democratic thing.

> *'Just a moment,' said the expert. He then turned to the mourners, counting them. 'Now we have heard what the alleged deceased has had to say. You fifty witnesses tell me what you regard as the truth.'*
>
> *'He is dead,' said the witnesses. 'Bury him,' said the expert. And so he was buried.*

And so you have been buried. Your experts have buried you. Your scriptures have buried you. Your theologies have buried you. You were alive but you went to ask the experts.

Don't go to the experts, go to life itself. Don't go to the scriptures, go to existence itself. Don't ask the theoreticians, ask life itself.

The man was just foolish. He should have run from the expert. The moment he had seen that a well-known scientist, an impartial man, was there, he should have jumped out of the coffin and run as fast as possible—that was the only way to save himself.

And you also should do the same: jump out of your coffin and run as fast as you can from all your experts; otherwise they will kill you. They have already killed you. They will bury you. If you want to be alive, listen to life, not to knowledge. If you want to be alive, listen to your own heart. What a foolish man that man must have been who asked the expert to decide!

Remember, your own *heart* is the only judge. No other judge exists. Listen to it. Listen to the inner voice, and follow it, wheresoever it leads. If you listen to the inner voice, if you don't bother about theories, if you make contact with life itself, direct and immediate, you will attain to the ultimate.

God is waiting there, alive and kicking. And there is nobody who is hindering you except yourself. Just don't come in your own way.

Enough for today.

Five

Mind Games

There was a man who lost his axe, and he suspected the boy next door.

He watched the boy walking—he had stolen his axe. His expression, his talk, his behavior, his manner, everything about him betrayed that he had stolen the axe.

Soon afterwards the man was digging in his garden and he found the axe.

On another day he saw the boy next door again. Nothing in his behavior and manner suggested that he would steal an axe.

EVERY MAN, AND you are included in it, lives a closed life, lives in his own world. There is not one world around you, there are as many worlds as there are minds. Each mind has its own world and is closed. Sometimes you come in close contact with other worlds, but that is only on the periphery. Your centres remain separate, and they go on living in their own capsule.

The mind is a wall around you. You are enclosed in it as a prisoner. But the wall is transparent. It is a glass wall made of only thoughts, prejudices, theories, scriptures; that's why you cannot touch it, that's why you are not even aware of it. But you live behind it, and whatsoever you see and feel is not the fact. It is an interpretation.

You look at a woman and you feel: How beautiful! This is an interpretation. Somebody else may not agree with you. And somebody else may absolutely disagree with you. You think she is the paradigm of beauty, and somebody else thinks that she is just homely, can be tolerated, that's all. And somebody else thinks that she is positively ugly, the worst that he has ever seen; she is a nightmare, not a beautiful dream.

What are they talking about? Are they talking about the same woman? How can it be that they are talking about the same woman and they differ so much? They are not talking about the same woman. The same woman is an illusion. They are talking about different interpretations. The woman is being used just like a screen, and they are projecting their own minds on her. They are seeing whatsoever they want to see. They are seeing whatsoever they are capable of seeing. They are seeing whatsoever they are conditioned to see from the very beginning. It is an interpretation, it is not a fact.

That's why aesthetes for centuries have been trying to define what beauty is. They have not yet been able; they will never be able to define it because beauty is not a fact. It doesn't belong to the world of reality, it is an interpretation—and so is ugliness.

And the same is true about all dualities, because the reality is one. The reality is not two. It is neither ugly nor beautiful; it is simply there without any beauty and without any ugliness. There is no question of any comparison because nothing else exists besides it. It is the only reality. There is no other reality, so how can you compare what is beautiful and what is ugly, and what is good and what is bad, and what is divine and what is evil? No, only one exists. All divisions are of the mind.

You say someone is good, some other man is bad. You think someone is a saint and you think someone else is a sinner. All projections, all interpretations. That's why Jews thought Jesus to be a criminal. And Christians think him to be the only begotten son of God, the greatest who ever walked on earth. And Jews—they thought him to be the worst, sin incarnate.

When they crucified Jesus, they didn't crucify him alone. On both his sides were criminals; three persons were crucified together. He was crucified like a criminal. Not only that, every year the viceroy of the country, the Roman viceroy, had the power to forgive one person, to release him from the death penalty. Four persons were to be crucified—Jesus and three others. The other three were murderers, and when the viceroy asked the Jews, 'I can free one man'—and he was thinking of Jesus because to him it looked as if he was just innocent, childlike. It was simply unjust to kill this man.

The viceroy was not a Jew, his standpoint was different; he could not project the same idea as Jews were projecting on Jesus. He could not see the badness, the evil. He talked to Jesus and found he was a simple man. Maybe too bold, maybe too bold because of his innocence; he may have been saying things in a metaphorical way, but he never meant it. He wanted—deep down in his heart was the idea that the Jews would ask for Jesus to be forgiven.

But no, the Jews wouldn't ask for Jesus. They decided for a criminal, a murderer. Barabbas was his name. They decided that he should be freed but Jesus had to be killed. Jesus died like a criminal. What happened? Why are the standpoints about Jesus so contrary, so diametrically opposite?

Not that Jesus is the problem, the problem is of the interpreting mind. You call somebody good and you call somebody bad, but have you ever thought—what is goodness? Can you define it? Has anybody ever been able to define it?

One of the greatest logicians of this century, G.E. Moore, has written a book. The name of the book is *Principia Ethica*— one of the rare books, so penetrating, so logical—and he starts by asking 'What is good?' And a man of the calibre of G.E. Moore is rarely born. You cannot find anybody else in this century who has such an acute penetrating quality of the mind.

He starts by asking: What is good? and he ends the book by saying that good is indefinable. He works hard through the book, round and round he goes, tries many ways to penetrate the mystery of good, and fails. And this is the conclusion: you dig the whole mountain and not even a mouse is found; good is indefinable.

But that has been known forever—that good is indefinable. The question is, Why is good indefinable? Why is beauty indefinable? It is indefinable because it doesn't exist as a fact in the world, it is an interpretation. It depends on the mind. It is just like, like and dislike.

Somebody says, 'I like this flower,' and you can say you don't like it. There is no quarrel about it; we know that likings differ. Beauty is also like, like and dislike and good is also like, like and dislike. They are not facticities in the world. You bring your own idea to the fact, and between your idea and the fact a notion is born: you say it is beautiful. It fits *your* idea of beauty.

But your idea is not universal, it is personal to you. That's why Sufis insist that all knowledge is personal. No knowledge is impersonal. They insist that all knowledge is partial, no knowledge is impartial, cannot be. Only a man like Buddha,

Jesus, Mohammed, is impartial—but then he has no knowledge. He has no mind to interpret. He looks at reality, he simply looks! He does not bring any idea to reality. He is passive. His mind is not an activity. He is alert, but just receptive; he does not project.

That is the difference between a buddha mind and an ordinary mind. An ordinary mind is an active agent. It is not like a mirror. It is not just showing whatsoever is the case; no, it penetrates *actively*. It brings its own ideas to reality. It colours reality, it gives a shape. It gives a form to reality which is not there, which has been brought by the mind itself.

The flower is there; the mind says, 'Beautiful.' Only the flower is there—nothing of beauty, nothing of ugliness. The mountains are there. Nothing beautiful, nothing ugly; they simply are there. Existence simply is. It is not divided. Mind brings its knowledge, divides it, and then you go on and on, and you never become aware that a subtle wall surrounds you. Because of that wall you are unable to penetrate reality. One has to become passive. Remember: alert, but passive—that is my definition of meditation. Alert but passive.

Just the other day somebody sent me a small cartoon. I loved it. Two men are standing—maybe neighbours, friends—and one says to the other, 'I hear that your son has started meditating.'

The other says, 'Yes, he has started meditating. And I think it is far better than just sitting and doing nothing.'

But that is the meaning of meditation!—just sitting and doing nothing. If you *do*, it is not meditation.

Alert, and passive. Says Zenerin: Sitting quietly, doing nothing, spring comes, and the grass grows by itself. Nothing has to be done, because once you do, *you* are there. Once you do something you have changed reality; already it is no more the same. Don't do anything. Just watch. Be passive but alert. Aware, nondoing, sitting quietly...suddenly the reality is there. The mind is dropped. When the mind is not, then you know what is real. The mind won't allow you to know the reality, because the mind goes on creating its own hallucinations.

Once I was working as a teacher in a university, in a far corner of India. I lived in the bachelor quarters and shared my room with a colleague, a very gentle, good-hearted man, simple. But then came the festival of Holi, and he took some *bhang*, a psychedelic—and he had never taken it before. So he went completely crazy. He was found in the street naked. He was caught, and the whole night he had to stay in the police station. That disturbed that poor soul, and that disturbed him so much, he became paranoid.

He came back—I had to go and find him, where he was. I found him in the police station; I persuaded the police officer that he was a simple man, just a victim of some friends, and he had never taken bhang before, so it affected him too much. I brought him back. But from that day he became afraid, so afraid that a car would pass and he would jump on my bed and he would say, 'The police are coming!' In the night, somebody would be knocking at somebody else's door, and he would immediately hide under my bed: 'The police are coming!' He became so afraid that it became impossible for him to go and teach, because anywhere you can come across a policeman.

Twenty-four hours a day I watched him, because he was just an exaggerated case of ordinary humanity. And when a case is exaggerated you can watch more easily. He started creating fantasies of his own, nightmares, that the government was conspiring against him. An ordinary teacher in a university, why should the government bother? There are many other things to bother about.

A simple-hearted man, but now he created in his own imagination—he worked it up, and the more he worked it up the more he got into it—that the whole world was against him, and everybody was watching him, and they were just trying to find an opportunity to catch him and throw him into jail. He stopped going outside the room. Even if I came back he would look first from the window, make certain that it was me and not somebody else trying to deceive: maybe the police have come, or somebody else—the enemy. When I came, minutes would pass, even sometimes half an hour, then he would open the door, when he was absolutely convinced that it was me and nobody else.

Then it became too much because I also could not sleep or rest—the whole night, the whole day! Even if just a breeze came on the door and knocked he would jump up and hide in the cupboard. So I had to do something.

I went to the police station, I persuaded those men: 'You have done this. Now help me—because he says that the police have some documents against him. So you please come tonight, bring a file, just a false file, because there is no document against him or anything, he has never done anything else other than this taking bhang once. So you bring a false file, his name written on it, with many papers inside—any papers will do, and you beat him hard. A shock is needed, otherwise he will not come out of his enclosure, and he is shrinking and shrinking inwards. So you beat him hard, don't be worried. Hit him hard. And bring the chains, put him in chains, then I will try to persuade you, and I will bribe you in front of him, so he is satisfied that now the case is closed, and you burn those files in front of him.'

That was arranged—a mock show. And it worked. He was beaten hard, really beaten. But when they were beating him he was looking at me and saying, 'Look. It is happening as I said, and nobody listened to me!' He was feeling a deep satisfaction also in it, that finally he was proved right. When they were putting chains on him, he winked at me, and he said, 'Look at the file: my name.' But he was shocked. Then I bribed the police, the file was burned and the matter closed.

While watching him for one month continuously I became aware that he is not in any way different from ordinary human beings. No qualitative difference, just the difference of quantity, degrees. He may be at the topmost rung of the ladder, you may be just in the middle, and somebody may be just in the beginning; but the difference is of degrees, not of quality. Whosoever has a mind is mad in some way or other. Mind IS madness. But you may be mad, and you may not know it, because all others are mad to the same degree. You fit together; there is no problem.

There is an old Sufi story: It happened that a witch came to a capital town. She threw something into the well, chanted a mantra, and said, 'Whosoever will drink the water from this well will go mad.' The capital had only two wells: one for the ordinary humanity, another was in the palace for the king and the prime minister.

Of course, people had to drink, knowing well that they will go mad. But there was no other way—that was the only well. They were not allowed to go to the palace to get water from there.

So the whole town by the evening, when the sun was setting, became mad. But nobody was aware, because when everybody goes mad, how can you be aware of it? As hippies say, everybody was doing his own thing. People were dancing naked, crying, screaming; women were running naked on the streets. People were doing all sorts of yogas...somebody standing on his head, somebody doing other asanas—the whole town was in a nightmare. Much rejoicing was going on. People were celebrating and jumping and screaming—the whole town was awake!

Only the king and the prime minister were sad, very sad: 'What to do? The whole town has gone mad, and poor souls, they are not even aware of it because when everybody goes mad, how to judge?' In fact, the prime minister and the king became suspicious of their own sanity. Maybe the madness had happened to them, because the whole town seemed blissfully unaware. Thousands of people, and they had all gone mad, and nobody thought that anybody was mad.

In that town of course the king and the prime minister became suspicious of themselves: maybe the madness had happened to them! And by midnight there was great trouble, because the whole town gathered and the town also became aware that something had gone wrong with the king and the prime minister. A rumour spread that the king and prime minister had gone mad. And of course everybody agreed.

They surrounded the palace. The guards were mad, the police were mad, the army was mad, so there was no protection, and they started demanding, 'Either you come back to your senses, otherwise we will dethrone you.'

The king said, 'What to do?'

The prime minister said, 'You talk to them, and I will run and fetch some water from the well, because there is no other way now. In this mad capital, if we want to survive even for a single minute we have to be mad.'

He fetched some water from the well of the town. They both drank, they both started dancing, they threw off their clothes—and the whole town was happy that the king and the prime minister were back to their senses, they had regained their sanity.

The whole of ordinary humanity is mad because mind IS mad, and whatsoever you see through the mad mind is just your own interpretation of reality. It doesn't exist anywhere else than within your mind. It is an idea.

A madman lives closed in his mind. You are also closed. Maybe not so closed, but closed. Maybe here and there, there are a few apertures and sometimes a little light breaks in. But you are just like the whole crowd, so you don't have any comparison.

Scientists say that if suddenly god decides to reduce everything to one-tenth of its size nobody will become aware of it. If you are reduced—you may be six feet, and you are reduced to point six feet, but everything is reduced in the same proportion. The tree that was sixty feet is reduced to six feet, and the mountain that was six thousand feet is reduced to six hundred feet. If everything is reduced in the same proportion—you become point six feet and everything comes down in the same proportion—nobody will ever become aware that anything has happened. How can you become aware? Even your yards will be reduced. Nobody will ever become aware.

You become aware only when you don't fit; otherwise you are not aware. And the reverse is also true: when you become aware, you don't fit. The more you become aware, the less and less will you fit with ordinary humanity. A Jesus is an outsider; he becomes a stranger to you. He fits with existence perfectly, but with this mad world he does not fit at all. On the contrary, you think that he is mad. A Socrates, a Jesus, a Buddha are thought to be mad; something abnormal has happened to them. You live in such abnormality that a normal, healthy man will look abnormal to you.

Sufis say the mind is the disease. And all those who have known agree with them. And the trick is such that whatsoever the mind thinks, it always finds there...because first you put something in reality and then you read it. With the right hand you put it, with the left hand you read it and you think you are reading reality.

I am talking to you. But you are not listening to me, to what I am saying. You cannot; there is no possibility. You may be listening to a thousand and one things. You will be listening differently from one another. Your interpretation will be yours, your friend's will be his. And if after this talk you gather together and decide what you have heard, you will be surprised: everybody has heard a different thing, a different story, because the mind is there continuously adding, deleting, interpreting, philosophizing....

You are not simply hearing me. You are active. And if you are active, you will miss me. An active mind is the barrier to understanding anything. A passive mind is needed. A vacant mind is needed, empty of all thoughts. You become like a mirror. You simply *listen*. You don't try to think about it because if you think about it, you miss. You have gone astray, you have already gone far away.

Simply listen! Listen to me as if you are listening to music. Listen to me as if you are listening to a bird, or to a river. Simply listen passively. To listen passively is to become a learner. To listen passively is to learn. There is no other way to learn.

This is one of the most fundamental things to be understood. Otherwise you can read the Gita and the Koran, and you will not be reading the Gita and the Koran at all, you will be reading yourself. Through the Koran you will be reading your own mind. You move in a vicious circle, and the wall surrounds you—but it is very subtle and you cannot see it and you cannot feel it. Once you understand that the mind is the wall, you start dropping it.

Be with the trees sometimes and don't say anything, don't verbalize, just be. Sit under a tree. Many flowers have come to it. But don't verbalize. Just look at the flowers, look at the tree, touch the tree, embrace the tree, kiss the tree; but don't verbalize! Do whatsoever you want, simply don't verbalize. Don't bring the mind in. Allow the tree and your reality to be together. Don't have the mind in between. Drop the mind. Be related directly and immediately with the tree. Be related directly and immediately with the sky. Be related immediately and directly to me...or to your beloved or friend.

Remember only one thing: the moment you bring in the mind, you bring madness. The moment you bring the mind in, you bring the distorting factor, the frustrating factor.

Can you be a no-mind? That is the only possibility to know reality.

Now this small parable.

There was a man who lost his axe, and he suspected the boy next door.

Once you suspect, the mind has become active. Now the suspicion is there, and the suspicion will start projecting things. The man suspected the boy next door.

He watched the boy walking—and of course, he was absolutely certain that in the very walk he could see the thief. The way he was walking was the way thieves walk—*he had stolen his axe. His expression....* The eyes of the boy were trying to hide something. He was not looking directly, he was avoiding: he was the thief. His talk was roundabout. He was trying to deceive: he was the thief. His behavior was not normal...something abnormal, something on his heart, heavy. He was no more the same as he used to be. The axe was heavy on his head. His manner...all gave the man proofs, everything about him betrayed the fact that he had stolen the axe.

You also know that this happens to you. Once you suspect a thing you start projecting it. Once the suspicion enters, the seed is there. Then everything changes.

If you are in love with a woman—and she may not even have dreamed that she is in love with you, but if you are in love, then everything—the way she walks, the way she says hello, the way she stands near you, everything helps: she is in love. You become more and more certain that she is in love. She may not even have suspected, the very idea may not have occurred to her, but you are certain. She may be just the same, but you are no more the same—your mind is carrying something in it, a seed, a projection. Your mind is loaded with an idea. Or, you suspect your wife or your husband of being unfaithful. Once the idea enters then you will find proofs.

Remember this, this is what madness is: first you decide and then you find proofs. And you will always find them. Life is vast. Once you decide—and this is the path of madness, that first you decide then you start finding proofs. Those proofs are not real proofs, those are pseudo-proofs. They are more or less rationalizations. But you have already decided the case.

Proofs should be first, and then the decision. But people decide first, then they always find. Remember, whatsoever you decide, you will find. Nobody can prevent you from finding it. If you decide there is a god you will find one. If you decide there is no god you will find that there is no god. If you decide that the number thirteen is a bad omen, it is evil, you will find proofs every day that number thirteen has something evil in it. On the thirteenth day of the month something will go wrong. It goes wrong every day, but then you don't take notice of it. But on the thirteenth, you take notice. In America, in many hotels they don't have a thirteenth floor because nobody wants to stay on the thirteenth floor. So after the twelfth floor comes the fourteenth. The thirteenth never comes.

I was reading one article: A man has found thousands of things to prove that the number thirteen belongs to the devil. He has accumulated thousands of facts: on the thirteenth of each month—how many murders are committed in the world, how many robberies, how many people commit suicide, how many auto accidents, how many people become mad on that date, the thirteenth. He has accumulated thousands of facts. Somebody sent me the article—he was also impressed. One has to be impressed; the man has forced so many facts to support the idea.

I wrote to the man who had sent me the article, 'You try to find the same about the number twelve, and you will find the same number of murders, robberies, heart attacks, suicides, people going mad. Any number will do. You just decide first on the number, and then you go on looking in life and you will find.... If you decide that number thirteen is a good number, then you will find some other facts: how many people get married, how many children are born, how many people fall in love.'

On the date of the thirteenth, people get married, people

get divorced also. It depends on you, which you choose. People are born and people die also. In reality every day is the same. Reality does not favour. But your mind...if it starts working, you will find....

People come to me—if they have decided that I am a bad man, almost always they find proofs. Nobody can prevent them; they will always find proofs. Life is vast. It is both summer and winter. It is both good and bad. It is both right and wrong. It is just like two wings of a bird—you cannot be without both. A man comes who has decided that this man is bad—he will find all proofs. Another comes who has decided that this man is good—he will also find all proofs. Life gives you ample opportunity. All alternatives are open.

Once that man suspected that this boy had stolen his axe, he watched him walking, and in the very walk he could see the thief. Everything about him betrayed that he had stolen the axe.

Soon afterwards the man was digging in his garden and he found the axe.

Suddenly everything changed.

On another day he saw the boy next door again. Nothing in his behavior and manner suggested that he would steal an axe.

Everything changed. The boy remains the same. The boy is not even aware of what is happening. He had become a thief, now he is no more a thief—a beautiful, nice boy, very good! Look at his walk—so innocent. The boy remains the same but the mind of the man has changed.

If you bring your mind to reality you will see something which is not there. You may miss something which is there. Hindus call this bringing of the mind to reality, maya. This is the root cause of all illusion.

If you want to understand the Hindu concept of maya, this is the base. If you live through the mind you live in maya, you live in illusion, you live in your own projections and ideas. Layers of your thoughts hide you from reality and hide reality from you. Dropping the mind is dropping the maya, the very base of all hallucination. Once the mind is not there, suddenly that which is, is revealed. And that is god, not your ideas about god.

A Hindu will always find Krishna playing on the flute; no Christian ever finds Krishna playing on the flute. In fact, to a Christian mind all this playing on the flute and girls dancing around looks a little bit profane. It doesn't look right. Krishna looks like a hippie. Christians cannot think of him as a god. Impossible. A god should be serious. In fact a god should be always on the cross, a martyr, carrying the whole burden of humanity, trying to rid humanity of all sins. How can he be playing on the flute? Impossible. He is the saviour of sins; he is carrying a mountain load—of all humanity. The fate of humanity depends on him—and he is playing with girls? Krishna looks like a playboy. No, not like a god at all.

To Christians, Jesus comes sad, the saddest you can imagine—the very face more like death than like life. Crucified. Death worshipped, not life; very serious. Christians say that Jesus never laughed. It may not be true but Christians have that idea. How can god laugh when there is so much misery, when there is so much sin? How can god laugh when there is Vietnam and when there is Cambodia and when there is Israel and all types of wars and killing and murder? How can god play on a flute? Impossible. He should be serious, on the cross.

To a Christian mind the cross is the symbol, not the flute. But to a Hindu, to think of god on the cross will look simply absurd, because god should be a laughter, a singing, a rejoicing, a celebration! A god should be blissful, playing on the flute, because the whole existence is a celebration.

You never see any flower on the cross, you never see any bird on the cross, you never see any river sad, any mountain sad. The whole existence is playing on the flute. That is the meaning of Krishna playing on the flute: the celebration that goes on all around, continuously. And the feminine energy dancing.

That's how a god should be: both polarities meeting in him, in a deep embrace with his own energy, with his own creation. The creator and the creation, the male and the female, the yin and the yang, the positive and the negative must be dancing together—otherwise there can be no dance. How can a man dance alone? It will look foolish. For what?…Because man is half, and how can a half dance? Only a whole can dance.

When the circle becomes whole the dance happens by itself, on its own accord. There is no need—celebration comes on its own accord. It simply happens—just like that. It happens!—Krishna is not trying to dance, he is not an actor. He is not manipulating. The female energy is there, and the male energy is satisfied, a deep content. A meeting, a marriage. The dance is spontaneous.

Hindus cannot think that Jesus never laughed. If he never laughed, then he does not know anything. He must be laughter itself—the deepest that is possible. Jesus must be a belly-laugh;

anything else is not possible.

But these are conceptions. A Hindu will think in his own terms, then a Hindu god appears; a Christian thinks in his own words, in his own phraseology, ideology, and a Christian god comes. But both are mind creations. Neither is true, both are projections.

Unless all krishnas and all christs drop, you will not be able to know reality. They are all dreams, created by you. Beautiful dreams, but dreams still.

When you alone are left, a passive alertness, doing nothing, just being, suddenly the reality bursts into an explosion. And it is not going to be according to any ideology, not Hindu nor Christian nor Mohammedan. All ideologies are transcended. Ideologies are very narrow. Reality is infinitely vast. It cannot be contained by any idea. It cannot be contained by any concept. It cannot be present.

Mind is too narrow a thing: it cannot surround reality, it has to dissolve into reality.

When you are not a mind, reality is. And reality is god. And that god—you will not find that it fits with Hindus or it fits with Christians. It fits with nobody. It cannot. Hence I go on insisting that religion is not Christian, not Hindu, not Buddhist. Religion knows no adjectives, religion knows no labels. It is life itself, in its tremendous vitality, in its unlimited expanse, in its endless, beginningless flow.

God is life. And all concepts are poor, and if you become too much attached to the concepts, you will *find*—this is the trouble. A Christian will find that his god is true, because he realizes it. A Mohammedan will find that his concept of god is true, because he finds it. And they all say, 'We have experienced!' And how can you deny the experience? A Hindu finds his own god. Mind is self-fulfilling. Whatsoever you have as an idea, you will find as a fulfilment. You will find whatsoever you seek. But whatsoever you find will be only a projection of the mind.

Then what to do? Truth cannot be sought through the mind. The mind has to be dropped if you want to seek truth. To truth, to reality, to life, to existence, you have to come completely stripped of your mind, completely nude, completely innocent of all ideologies, completely empty, totally empty. Only then you come to truth. Otherwise, whatsoever you come to is your own mind playing tricks with you. And you can go on deceiving, for many lives you have done that.

It is time, the time is absolutely ripe to drop out of this game. You have played it long enough, more than it was necessary. Drop out of the game! And the game is this: if you have an idea, the mind will create the dream, and the dream will be thought of as reality.

Reality is never known through the mind because mind is the known, the past, the dead. The past has to cease for the present to be. The known has to cease for the unknown to be. The mind has to cease for god to be. You have to drop all that you have. If you can drop it, if you don't cling, the greatest revolution, the greatest mutation becomes possible within you.

Meditation means a state of no-mind.

Every day, *every* day, I come across the same trouble: you have read in a book that the *kundalini* rises in a certain way. If you have read it in the book it *will* rise! And then it will be difficult for anybody to prove that you are wrong, because you have the experience, and you say, 'I have felt the experience, how can you say that I am wrong? I have felt the snake of kundalini rising in the spine. It goes with tremendous energy, upwards.' And you *feel* it—and the feeling is so solid that no doubt arises. But I tell you it is your mind. Because there are people who have never heard of kundalini; then it never arises, then it is never felt. They have also attained. Jainas never talk about kundalini, but a Mahavira attains to the ultimate unfoldment of being without any kundalini. Buddhists never talk about kundalini. Hindus talk about it—then it arises.

Buddhists talk of four chakras; then a follower of Buddhism feels only four chakras. Hindus talk of seven chakras; a follower of Hinduism feels seven chakras. Once I told a man who was feeling seven chakras, 'You don't know there are thirteen chakras?'

He said, 'What! Thirteen? But I have felt only seven up to now.'

'Six more are left,' I told him. 'You go and try, and when you have felt the thirteen all together, then come to me.'

After six months he was there. He had felt thirteen—and the man was not deceiving, he was deceived. He was not a liar, he was not lying to me; he is a sincere man.

Mind can create experiences. So remember, I repeat again and again, that spirituality is *not* an experience. It is the experiencer, not the experience; the witness of all experiences, not any experience in particular. When all experiences have been transcended, then you come to the spiritual experience. Spiritual experience is not an experience of this or that. Simply *you* are left with a consciousness, not experiencing anything.

The greed to experience is of the mind, and when it is fulfilled the mind feels very gratified, even with foolish things. What can you gain out of the feeling that energy is rising in the spine? It is just a sensation—and created by the mind. The mind is powerful.

Have you seen somebody walking on fire? red-hot coals? Now it is a proven fact that people can walk on them. Just a few years back in Oxford University, a yogi from Sri Lanka walked on fire—with all scientific arrangements so that he could not deceive. He was not deceiving!—he walked on fire. What happens when a yogi walks on red-hot burning coal? He is not burned—what happens?

The mind has tremendous capacities. If the mind feels that the fire is not going to burn, if the feeling is absolute, total, the very feeling becomes a protecting energy all around you. Then your feet are not touching the coal. In fact between the coal and the feet there is a pad of unknown energy. And the fire is not passing through; an invisible pad of energy protects you. It is your body aura, concentrated there under your feet. You are not walking on the fire really, you are walking on your own energy. It protects your feet like a shoe, a shoe of energy. The mind has forced it.

It happened that a professor of the university became so captivated seeing this man walking on fire, he became so certain, that he came near. When he came near, the yogi who was walking on the coals pulled him on to the course and he also walked. He had never tried it before and he was not a trained man. What happened? Even in a certain moment if you have total belief, immediately the body is protected.

Now medical science has become aware of certain phenomena. One of them is really very peculiar, and the phenomenon is this: every country has different types of prevalent diseases, and every community, every religion, sect, has different diseases occurring more.

For example, Eastern people are more prone towards epidemics: plague, cholera, more prone towards communal diseases, infections and diseases which spread by infection, because in the east the individual doesn't exist much. Only the community exists. In an Indian village, the village exists. Nobody exists as an individual; the community exists. When the community is too large, infectious diseases will be prevalent, because nobody has a protective aura around himself. If one becomes ill, then the whole community by and by will become a victim to the illness. And in the same community there can be a few westerners—they will not be affected by the infection.

In fact, just the reverse should be the case, because a western man in India should be more prone to diseases because he is not immune. He is not immune to this climate, to such diseases; he should become a victim sooner. But no. For the last hundred years it has been observed that whenever there is an infectious disease, Europeans are protected by some unknown force. Indians become victims.

The Indian mind is more a communal mind. The European mind is more egoistic and personal. So in the West certain other diseases are prevalent. For example, heart attack; it is an individual disease, noninfectious. In the East heart attack is not so common unless you are Western, you are educated in a Western way and you have become almost Western. In the East, heart attack is not a big problem, diabetes is not a big problem, blood pressure is not a big problem—these are noninfectious diseases. Christians are more prone to them. The Western mind lives as an individual unit. Of course, when you live as an individual unit, the community cannot impress you too much. You will be protected from infections.

In the West, infections have disappeared by and by, but people are becoming more and more personally ill. Heart attacks, suicide, blood pressure, madness—these are individual diseases. They don't carry any infection. Tenseness, anguish, anxiety.... In the East people are more at ease. You don't find them too tense. They don't suffer from insomnia. They don't suffer from heart illnesses. From that they are protected by the community. Because the community has no heart. If you live a communal life you cannot suffer from a heart disease.

This is a rare phenomenon. It means your mind makes you available to certain diseases, and keeps you protected against certain diseases. Your mind is your world. Your mind is your health, your mind is your illness. And if you live with the mind, you continue to live in a capsule and you cannot know what reality is. That reality is known only when you drop all types of minds—communal, individual, social, cultural, personal ... Then your mind becomes universal. Then your mind becomes one with the mind of the universe.

When you don't have your own mind, your consciousness becomes universal. God is known not as an object. Truth is known not as an object. You become the truth. You become god himself. That is the meaning of al-Hillaj Mansoor's famous assertion: *Ana'l haq*. He says, 'I am god; *Aham brahmasmi*, I am the brahman.'

Sufis believe in the universal mind. And they want you to drop the individual mind, the communal mind, the social mind. They want you to drop all the barriers that divide you from the universal mind. You become a drop in the ocean. You become the ocean, only then you know what it is. Only then you know what existence is, never before it. The mind has to die.

Until you die, god will not be possible for you. God is not an experience. He is never separate from you. You cannot look at him because he is hidden in the looker. You cannot confront him. Where will you confront him? He is hidden in you.

I would like to tell you a story, a very old Hindu story. It is said, god created the world. Everything was going well. Then he created man, and something went astray. With man trouble started. And in those days god used to live on the earth. He had created this earth to live on, and to be here and in it. These trees and these flowers, and these rivers and mountains—for what should he create them? The story says he created the earth to live on, to be here. And he was here, and everything was going well with the birds, trees, rivers and animals; everything was perfect.

Then he committed a mistake: he created man, and trouble started, because man started complaining. He would not see if it is night, midnight, and whether god is asleep, he would come and knock at the door with his complaints. He was always there. Man started driving god crazy—his complaints were infinite. And the problem was this: if you solve one man's complaint, then the very solution creates another man's complaint.

Somebody says, 'I need rains today.' And if god gives rains, somebody else comes and he says, 'You have destroyed my house—I had just painted it!' But somebody was needing it for his garden. It was impossible to satisfy all, so god asked his advisers what to do. Somebody said, 'You had better go to the Himalayas and hide there.'

God said, 'You are right, but you don't know the future. Sooner or later a man named Edmund Hillary will come even to Everest. They will not leave me alone there. And once they know I am in the Himalayas, the whole world will go there. No, that won't help much. For a time, okay, a temporary arrangement, but you don't know this man Edmund Hillary. I can see him already approaching, because I can see the future.'

So they said, 'Then it will be good if you go to the moon.'

God said, 'No. For just a little while it will help. But man is going there. Man is going everywhere.'

Then one old adviser whispered something in god's ear, and god nodded and said, 'Yes, you are right.'

That old man said, 'Better hide yourself in man himself. Go deep into his heart and hide yourself there.'

God said, 'You are right, because he will never suspect....' This is the one place rarely possible for any man to suspect that god can be—within you.

God is not an experience. He is hiding in you. You are just a hiding place. God is not an experience, he is the experiencer of all experiences.

Become passive, alert, and suddenly you will find him within yourself. The story is true, absolutely true...because I followed the story and found him. You also follow the story. It is not a fiction; it is absolutely, literally true. He is hiding in you.

Enough for today.

Six

Blind Man's Buff

Saadi said:
'A man had an ugly daughter. He married her to
a blind man because nobody else would have her.'
'A doctor offered to restore the blind man's sight.
But the father would not allow him for fear that
he would then divorce his daughter.'
Saadi concluded:
'The husband of an ugly woman is best blind.'

MAN IS IGNORANT, blind, as if living in sleep, drunk, not aware. This is the situation. This has always been so. Many cures have been invented, many methods to awaken him. But he resists. So the real problem is not ignorance but the resistance. Ignorance can be cured, but man insists on remaining ignorant. His eyes can be opened—the medicine exists, the doctors are there but man is not ready to open his eyes. He is against it.

This is the real problem. Ignorance is not the real problem; it can be cured. It is a simple disease, there is no complexity in it. But something in man is against curing it. There seems to be a great investment in it, as if with ignorance many other things will disappear; as if man clings to ignorance in the hope that something valuable is hidden there, a treasure.

Once it happened: A man was brought to me; his wife

brought him. He was seriously ill but he wouldn't go to the doctor, and he would deny absolutely that he was ill. He would say, 'What is the need to go to the doctor's? I am not ill. I am perfectly healthy. Something has gone wrong with my wife—she has become neurotic, she is obsessed with the idea of bringing me to the doctor's...not only that, she wants to hospitalize me. For what?'

The man was really ill, and he was saying these things to me: 'I am not ill. What is the purpose? Why are people forcing me? What do they want? There must be something they want out of it. All my relatives, my wife, my children—they are all conspiring against me, and I am perfectly healthy!'

I could see that the man was trembling, his face was ill and pale, his body weak, his eyes murky, with no health around his body, no well-being. What to do with this man? Why is he insisting...? I asked the wife the details.

She said, 'He has always been afraid of death, always afraid of illness. When he was healthy, then too it was difficult for him to go to the hospital, even if some relative was there, or friend; even to see and visit the patient was difficult for him. The moment he goes near a hospital something in him catches fear—death, the idea of death. And now it is creating trouble because he is ill and he won't go—and he insists that he is not ill so what is the use of going to any doctor? Why should he go?'

I looked at the whole situation. The man was really afraid. I told him, 'Your wife has gone really mad. You are perfectly healthy'—he smiled, his face changed—'nothing is wrong with you.'

As if a new lease of energy, something came up. He started laughing and he said, 'I always suspected it. You are the only man who has understood me. Nobody understands! I am perfectly healthy.' And he told his wife, 'Look! Look at what Osho says: I am perfectly healthy. Do you need any other certificate?' He asked me, 'Now there is no need to go to the hospital?'

I said, 'Absolutely no need to go to any doctor, to any physician. Don't think of it, you are perfectly healthy. Rarely have I seen such a healthy man.'

He smiled, but a suspicion was there in his eyes. He could not believe me completely—how could an ill man believe me? He knows deep down that he is ill, but he is afraid to accept the fact. Then he said, 'Then there is no need?'

I said, 'There is no need, but just for your neurotic wife, it will be good if you go to the doctor. You are perfectly healthy—but this poor woman is suffering so much.'

He laughed. He said, 'Then I can go. But are you certain that I am not ill?'

I said, 'Absolutely certain. Nothing is wrong with you. But just to console this poor woman, go to the doctor and let your body be examined. There is nothing wrong.'

He said, 'Then I can go.' And that's how he was caught in the hospital.

And the same is the trouble with you. The same is the trouble with every man. You are afraid of something. From Socrates up to now, or from the Vedas up to now, all those who have had any glimpse of themselves have been insisting on self knowledge: Know thyself. Nobody listens to them, nobody really listens to them. Everybody creates a protective armour around himself *against* self-knowledge. Something seems to be at risk. And the problem seems to be very complex. Why are you afraid of self-knowledge?

In your ignorance you have a certain feeling of blissfulness. Ignorance gives a false feeling of blissfulness because one lives on the surface. In fact one doesn't live, one simply drifts. Irresponsibly one drifts. With self-knowledge enters responsibility. You cannot be as you are if you know yourself. You cannot indulge in whatsoever you are indulging if you know yourself. You cannot remain the same if you know yourself. There is going to be a radical change through self-knowledge, and that change seems to be too much. You feel almost established. You feel almost in comfort.

You have made a house; you think this is the home. But you have made the house on the road. The journey has not yet ended, but you have convinced yourself that the end has come. Now, to know yourself will mean again a beginning, again a birth, again moving. Now, to know yourself will mean this is not a house where you are staying. This may be a serai, a *dharmshala*, but it is not a home. For an overnight stay it is good, but in the morning—the journey.

You feel comfortable. Even in your misery, anguish and anxiety, you feel comfortable because everything looks familiar. If you start trying to know yourself you are moving into the world of the unknown, the unfamiliar. That gives fear, a trembling comes. Why bother? Things are going well— not so well that you *know*, but still, somehow well. Things are drifting, time is passing. Half your life you have lived, only half is left; you can drift the same way. And then comes death, and oblivion. And nobody knows where one goes. Why bother about self-knowledge?

In your ignorance you have created a comfortable, established life, a secure life with a bank balance, insurance, the government, the society, membership of a religion, the church—you have created a false world around you. Nothing is protective, it just gives the notion that you are protected. Nothing is secure—just an illusion of security.

You have a wife—what is secure in it? Tomorrow she can fall in love with someone. She fell in love with you, one day you were also a stranger to her; she can fall in love again with another stranger. She could fall in love with you, so what is wrong in falling for another stranger? You were a stranger one day. You could fall in love with this woman, you can fall in love with another woman. What is secure?

But man tries to create a notion of security. You have a marriage certificate, that is your security; you can go to the court. But what type of security is it if the court is needed to protect love, if the policeman is needed to protect marriage, if the vast machinery of government, of violence, is needed to protect your love? What type of security is this? You are not together, you are forced to be together: the government is forcing, the police are there with the bayonet.

And the government is nothing but the agency of absolute violence. No government can be nonviolent; a government has to be violent. It is violence, pure violence. Are you in love really? Or just protected, forced, by bayonets and the courts and the laws...? But it gives a feeling that things are secure.

With self-knowledge again a chaos is born, a chaos which unsettles everything, which unsettles all values. It is a transvaluation of all values. You again have a new vision. You look at the world—not with the old eyes, nothing will seem to be the same—as if you have been suddenly thrown into a strange world.

You were fast asleep, comfortably tucked in your blanket, sleeping, having a beautiful dream, and suddenly self-knowledge awakens you. The dream is not there. You may have been an emperor in the dream—and all beggars always dream that they are emperors. They have to substitute. A dream is a substitute; whatsoever you don't have in life, you substitute in your dreams.

Suddenly you are no more an emperor. The dream disappears, the cozy comfort of sleep disappears. The day breaks, the sun has risen, and the world of worries, responsibilities, anxiety—this is nothing. When one awakens, then for the first time one feels responsible. And not responsible as an obligation—no, one simply feels responsible, without any obligation in it. It becomes part of one's being.

You also feel responsible, because this woman is your wife, so you are responsible to feed her and look after her. You have to go to work and to the job. You have children, you feel responsible.... But this responsibility is just a duty. You have to do it, so you do it. But you are not really responsible, it is not coming from the heart.

When somebody awakens he becomes responsible for whatsoever he is; even for his breathing he becomes responsible. And he becomes responsible for the whole existence; whatsoever happens anywhere he feels that he is part of it. If there is violence in Vietnam, he feels: 'I am part of it, I am responsible for it—not related at all, but still responsible.'...Because a man of self-knowledge comes to know, 'No man is an island, and the whole existence is interlinked. The whole existence is one, one organ. We are waves in it, and whatsoever happens in the world, I am responsible. Not only for whatsoever is happening today: for whatsoever has happened in the past I am responsible, and for whatsoever is going to happen in the future I am responsible, because now I have become a conscious part of the whole. Up to now I was an unconscious part. Somebody was killing somebody else—I was not responsible. I had a small responsibility around my family, my wife, my children, and that was all. Somebody is killing somebody else—how am I responsible? No, that doesn't bother me.'

But a man of knowledge, a man of awakening, a buddha, knows now consciously that he is part of every leaf and every tree, and every tree and every leaf is part of him. The individuality is no more there, he has become universal. The self is a universal entity, it has nothing to do with you. The self is *Brahman*.

Your hidden being has nothing to do with you. Your innermost centre is the very centre of existence itself. One suspects it somehow. One feels the tremors on the surface of this phenomenon. One doesn't want to awake—it will be too much responsibility.

Right now you may be moral or immoral, but your morality and immorality are just on the surface, a conditioning. A society thinks something is moral—it conditions you. But you are not moral yet. Only a man who has awakened becomes moral, moral in the sense that now nothing wrong can happen through him. Not that he avoids wrong, not that he tries to do good; now there is no effort to do the good and no effort to avoid the wrong.

With awakening, with awareness, only that which is true, that which is good, that which is right, happens. That which is untrue, evil, bad, does not happen. It is just as if you have lit a candle in the room and the darkness disappears. When one is awake the immorality, the sin, the evil, disappears. One has, for the first time, virtue.

This has to be understood, because it is one of the most delicate things. A perfect man has no character; he can't have. He has consciousness, not character. You have character, no consciousness. Character is a poor substitute for consciousness, a very very poor substitute. That's why your life is a life of poverty—impoverished.

What is the difference between character and consciousness? When I say Buddha has no character, try to understand it. A buddha can't have any character, there is no need. Character means you are not so alert, you cannot be allowed total freedom to be. A character hangs around you to force you to do the right thing.

We teach every child not to be untrue, not to steal, be true. Why?—because we can't rely on the child himself, his consciousness. We have to force a pattern over his being. We have to give him a character. Character means a conditioning. If you go on enforcing, a character means just a dead pattern given from the past. And then the being of the man starts flowing through the lines that the character allows. He is not free.

A man of character is in bondage. He is a slave, a slave of a particular society he happened to be born in. He may have a Hindu character or a Mohammedan character; both are slaves. He may have a Christian character or a non-Christian character; both are slaves. He is a slave of the society; the society has forced his mind to learn certain things. Now they hang around him. He cannot go in any way different from his character. If he goes, then he feels guilt. That guilt brings him back, because it is too much.

A man of character has a conscience. The perfect man has no conscience, no character. He is simply conscious, but being conscious is enough. He does not live his life through the past, he lives his life here and now. And he is aware, so he need not have concepts from the past, routine morality from the past; he need not have any notion of what is good and what is wrong. It is not needed.

Look: if a blind man is sitting here and he wants to go out, he will start inquiring where the door is. He has to inquire, he has no eyes. And even if he has inquired from you he would like to inquire from a few other people because, who knows, you may be deceiving him. How can he trust you? He will inquire from a few others, 'Where is the door?'—because many times people have played tricks on him. People are cruel. They even play tricks on blind men. They will say: 'This is the door'—and the wall is there, and the blind man has stumbled many times, and then people laugh.

People are ugly. He cannot trust them. He will have to ask a few more, and if everybody says, 'This is the door,' only then can he believe, at least ninety-nine percent. Then too he will grope for the door with his stick. He cannot just go, he has to check.

This is what a character is. A man who is not conscious—he has a character. Character means notions, values, given by others. He has a conscience. Conscience is a trick played by society on the blind man. Conscience works if you go 'wrong'; wrong means, if you go against the society. The society may itself be wrong altogether—that is not the point. If you go against the society, the society has put the idea inside you that you are doing something wrong and you will suffer through it. You yourself will feel condemned. You will feel rejected by yourself—not worthy, not valuable. You will feel a deep rejection, a repulsion against yourself. This is the trick of the society. You are punished by your own being.

The society has placed the court and the constable on the road, and a conscience inside you. Conscience is the constable standing inside and the constable is the conscience standing outside. The society tries to control you from the outside and the inside, both. It appreciates if you follow. It awards you, rewards you, if you follow. It punishes you, condemns you, if you go astray.

A man of perfect awareness has nothing to do with character. He comes out of it. He has no conscience because he has consciousness. He is like a man who has eyes. He doesn't ask, 'Where is the door?' He himself can see. And he doesn't grope with his stick—where is the door? There is no need, he has eyes. In fact, a man who can see does not think at all: Where is the door? Even thinking is not needed. When he wants to go out he simply goes out, without even thinking: Where is the door, what is the door, and how to go through it? He may not even for a single moment think about the door, he simply passes through it. A man of awareness simply passes through the door, he doesn't stumble against the walls. Whatsoever he does is good. He never repents. He has no conscience, he never feels guilty.

He lives moment to moment. He does not live out of the past, he lives in the present. He does not live out of the future, he lives just here, just now. This is all. His existence culminates, converges, on the only existential moment that is—here and now.

You live through the past. Your parents are still guiding you. Your society is still following you like a ghost. You live through the past—the Bible, the Vedas, the Koran still guiding you—the dead leading the alive. Mohammed, Manu and Marx, they still go on forcing you to move in certain directions. You are not an alive man yet, because the dead are still your leaders. Or you live through the future. Either through the past which is no more, or through the future which is not yet. Rewards in heaven, or rewards on this earth; some future rewards—respectability, honour, hope of gaining something in the future—these are the forces that lead you.

A man of awareness is not controlled either by the past or by the future. He has nobody to force him. The Vedas are no more on his head, Mahavira and Mohammed and Christ no more force him to move anywhere. He is free. That's why in India we call him a *mukta*. A mukta means he who is totally free. He *is* freedom.

In this moment, whatsoever the situation he responds with full awareness. That is his responsibility. He is capable of response. His responsibility is not an obligation, it is a sensitivity to the present moment. The meaning of responsibility changes. It is not responsibility as an obligation, as a duty, as a burden, as something which has to be done. No, responsibility is just a sensitivity, a mirror-like phenomenon. You come before the mirror, and the mirror reflects, responds. Whatsoever happens, a man of awareness responds with his totality. He does not hold anything back; that's why he never regrets, that's why he never feels guilty— whatsoever could be done, he has done, he is finished with it. He lives each moment totally and completely.

In your ignorance everything is incomplete. You have not completed anything. Millions of experiences are inside you, waiting for their completion. You wanted to laugh, but the society wouldn't allow it. You suppressed it. That laughter is waiting there as a wound. What a miserable state—even laughter becomes a wound! When you don't allow laughter it becomes a wound, an incomplete thing inside you waiting and waiting and waiting someday to be completed.

You loved somebody, but you could not love totally, the character prohibited it, the conscience wouldn't allow it. Even when you are with your beloved in the dark night, alone in your room, the society is present. The constable is standing there and watching. You are not alone. You have a conscience, your beloved has a conscience: how can you be alone? The whole society is there, the whole marketplace is standing all around. And god, looking from the top, watching you, what you are doing, god seems to be the universal peeping Tom—he goes on looking.

The society has used god's eyes to control you, to make you a slave. You cannot even love totally, you cannot hate totally, you cannot be angry totally. You cannot be total in anything. You eat halfheartedly, you walk halfheartedly, you laugh halfheartedly. You cannot cry—you are holding thousands of tears in your eyes. Everything is a burdened thing, loaded; the whole past you are carrying unnecessarily. And this is your character.

Yes, I say to you, a buddha has no character because he is fluid, because he is flexible. A character means inflexibility. It is armour-like. It protects you from certain things, but then it kills you also.

Just now India has absorbed a small Himalayan country, Sikkim. It is the same game of politics. China absorbed Tibet; then India was against—now they have absorbed Sikkim in the same way; China is against.

The king of Sikkim, the *chogyal*, is under house arrest. But the Indian government says that he is not under house arrest, the military is surrounding his palace so that nobody enters and harms him, because people are against him. So the Indian government is protecting him; he is not under house arrest but under protection, because his own people are against him and they may kill him, or they may enter the palace, they may burn the palace. So the Indian government says, 'The military is there to protect him from his people.' And he goes on saying that he is under house arrest and he is not allowed to go out.

This is what is happening to everybody. You are under house arrest by the society. The character is the army around you. But the society says, 'You are not under house arrest. We are protecting you; otherwise you may do something wrong or something wrong will be done to you. It is a protection.'

But as I see it, everybody is under house arrest. And this is a subtle house arrest; even if you escape to the Himalayas you cannot escape it, because character is now something inbuilt in you. It is not around you, it has penetrated you. It is not like a dress that you can take off; it is now like the skin. You cannot peel it off easily. It is going to be hard. It is going to be a *tapascharya*, an austerity.

That's why you are afraid to leave your ignorance, you go on protecting it because you feel it protects you. Ignorance is not a simple thing; otherwise the cure exists. There are a thousand and one complexities in it. You want to remain ignorant, you insist. You like to remain ignorant because in your ignorance in the past you have created a volcano within you, a volcano of incomplete desires, incomplete experiences. That volcano is there, suppressed but alive, waiting for the moment when it can explode and throw you to thousands and millions of bits.

You are afraid. You don't want to go in, you want to go out. Everybody is interested in going out, nobody is interested in going in, because the moment you think of going in you think of many things that are there, hidden. *You* have suppressed them, nobody else, so you know well that anger is there, hatred is there, sex is there, greed is there, jealousy is there.... Thousands of things are bubbling and boiling and any moment they can explode. It is better to go out, not to go in. It is better to escape somewhere and you have tried many ways to escape.

People want to remain occupied. If they have nothing to

do they will find something to do, something or other. They may start reading the same newspaper again. In the first place it was rubbish, so why are you reading it again? Nothing to do—and you would like to do something, because whenever you are not doing anything, suddenly the energy starts moving inwards. If it has something to cling to, only then can it remain out.

Sitting alone you feel restless. You want to go to the club, to the theatre, or just to go and move in the market so that you are occupied. At least walking, looking at the shops, at the shop windows, or talking to people about absolutely nonsense things—neither you need to talk, nor do they want to listen, but people are talking and talking—somehow, something to cling to....

People are busy without business. And they may say that they would like to rest, but nobody wants to rest because if you really rest it automatically becomes a meditation and you start falling inwards. You start moving towards your inner centre and fear grips you. You become afraid. So go to the market, go to the club, become a member of the Rotary Club, the Lions Club—thousands of stupidities exist all around for you to waste your time in.

Do something. And if you cannot find anything, or if to be a Rotarian is difficult, or you are not rich enough and you cannot go to the restaurant, you can go to the church, you can go to the mosque, you can go to the temple. They are at least free; there you can chant, 'Hare Krishna, Hare Rama,' and get occupied. Or you can listen to a stupid priest who is repeating the same thing again and again. But at least you are occupied. Remain occupied. Go on moving outwards and cling to something exterior, because if you don't cling, suddenly the energy starts moving inwards.

When people come to me and they ask, 'How to meditate?' I tell them, 'There is no need to ask how to meditate, just ask how to remain unoccupied. Meditation happens spontaneously. Just ask how to remain unoccupied, that's all. That's the whole trick of meditation—how to remain unoccupied. Then you cannot do anything. The meditation will flower.'

When you are not doing anything the energy moves towards the centre, it settles down towards the centre. When you are doing something the energy moves out. Doing is a way of moving out. Nondoing is a way of moving in. Occupation is an escape. You can read the Bible, you can make it an occupation. There is no difference between religious occupation and secular occupation: all occupations are occupations, and they help you to cling outside your being. They are excuses to remain outside.

Man is ignorant and blind, and he wants to remain ignorant and blind, because to come inward looks like entering into a chaos. And it is so; inside, you have created a chaos. You have to encounter it and go through it. Courage is needed—courage to be oneself, and courage to move inwards. I have not come across a greater courage than that— the courage to be meditative.

But people who are engaged outside with worldly things— or non-worldly things, but occupied all the same, they think— and they have created a rumour around it, they have their own philosophers—they say that if you are an introvert you are somehow morbid, something is wrong with you. And they are in the majority. If you meditate, if you sit silently, they will joke about you: 'What are you doing?—gazing at your navel? What are you doing?—opening the third eye? Where are you going? Are you morbid?...because what is there to do inside? There is nothing inside.'

Inside doesn't exist for the majority of the people, only the outside exists. And just the opposite is the case. Only inside is real; outside is nothing but a dream. But they call introverts morbid, they call meditators morbid. In the West they think that the East is a little morbid. What is the point of sitting alone and looking inwards? What are you going to get there? There is nothing.

David Hume, one of the great British philosophers, tried once...because he was studying the Upanishads and they go on saying: Go in, go in, go in—that is their only message. So he tried it. He closed his eyes one day—a totally secular man, very logical, empirical, but not meditative at all—he closed his eyes and he said, 'It is so boring! It is a boredom to look in. Thoughts move, sometimes a few emotions, and they go on racing in the mind, and you go on looking at them— what is the point of it? It is useless. It has no utility.'

And this is the understanding of many people. Hume's standpoint is that of the majority: What are you going to get inside? There is darkness, thoughts floating here and there. What will you do? What will come out of it? Had Hume waited a little longer—and that is difficult for such people— if he had been a little more patient, by and by thoughts disappear, emotions subside. But if it had happened to him he would have said, 'That is even worse, because emptiness comes. At least first there were thoughts, something to be occupied with, to look at, to think about. Now even thoughts have disappeared; only emptiness.... What to do with emptiness? It is absolutely useless.'

But had he waited a little more, then darkness also disappears. It is just like when you come from the hot sun and you enter your house: everything looks dark because your eyes need a little attunement. They are used to the bright sun outside. Comparatively, your house looks dark. You cannot see, you feel as if it is night. But you wait, you sit, you rest in a chair, and after a few seconds the eyes get attuned. Now it is not dark, a little more light.... You rest for an hour, and everything is light, there is no darkness at all.

If Hume had waited a little longer, then darkness also disappears. Because you have lived in the hot sun outside for many lives your eyes have become fixed, they have lost the flexibility. They need tuning. When one comes inside the house it takes a little while, a little time, a patience. Don't be in a hurry.

In haste nobody can come to know himself. It is a very very deep awaiting. Infinite patience is needed. By and by darkness disappears. There comes a light with no source. There is no flame in it, no lamp is burning, no sun is there. A light, just like it is in the morning: the night has disappeared, and the sun has not risen.... Or in the evening—the twilight, when the sun has set and the night has not yet descended. That's why Hindus call their prayer time *sandhya*. Sandhya means twilight, light without any source.

When you move inwards you will come to the light without any source. In that light, for the first time you start understanding yourself, who you are, because you *are* that light. You are that twilight, that sandhya, that pure clarity, that perception, where the observer and the observed disappear, and only the light remains.

But it takes time. In the beginning you will feel chaos. One has to pass through it. And nobody else can do it for you, remember, you have to pass through it. The master can only do this much—he can help you to pass, he can give you courage. He can say, 'Don't be afraid, just a few steps more.'

It happened: Buddha was moving from one town to another. They had lost their way. They asked a few villagers on the way, 'How far until the next town?'

They said, 'Just two miles,' as is always said in India. Whether it is fifty miles or twenty miles, it makes no difference; villagers always say, 'Just two miles.'

Buddha and his disciple Ananda, they walked two miles but there was no sign of any village coming nearer. They couldn't see any possibility that the village was any nearer. They asked again a few villagers, 'How far is the village?'

They said, 'Just two miles.'

They moved two miles. Ananda became desperate. He said, 'Are these people absolute fools or are they knowingly deceiving us?—because we have again moved two miles and there is no village. Are they playing tricks? Why should they lie?'

Buddha said, 'You don't understand. They are like me. It is because of compassion that they say, "Just two miles," so you get courage. And you say, "Okay, so just two miles? Let two miles be passed." They help you. If they say, "It is a hundred miles," you will drop dead. You will be flat on the earth. You will lose courage.'

A master cannot do it for you. He cannot pass through the misery, through the chaos. If he could he would have done it, but that is not possible in the nature of things. But he can help you, he can give you courage, he can say, 'Come on, just a little more, and the night will pass. And when the night is the darkest the morning is nearest.' He will give you courage, and that is needed.

That's why without a master it is almost impossible to travel on the path, because who will help give you courage? Who will say, 'Just two miles more...'? Who will say that you are almost at the end of the journey, you have almost reached, just a little bit more...? And as Lao Tzu says, a thousand-league journey is completed by taking only one step at a time. You take one step, then another, then another, and a thousand-mile journey is completed.

Chaos is going to be there. When you enter inside, all diseases that you have suppressed will erupt to the surface. All the miseries that you have been avoiding—they are waiting for you there, restlessly waiting for you. They will surface. You will pass through hell. But nobody ever reaches heaven if he is not ready to pass through hell. Hell is the gateway. Hell is the way, heaven is the journey's end. But one has to pass through the hell. Through a dark night one has to pass to come to the morning. And you will have to encounter it.

Man is ignorant, and he resists any effort to break his ignorance because he is afraid a chaos is waiting. And you rightly suspect, the chaos *is* there. You will almost go mad. A master will be needed who can hold your hand while you are going mad, and take you out of the madness.

These are the implications. That's why the mind goes on playing games with you. It says, 'Yes, tomorrow I am going to meditate.' But it is afraid. Meditation is like death. And it is. You will have to die as you are; only then the new can be born.

This is a small story by Sheik Saadi, one of the great Sufi mystic poets. A very simple anecdote, but carrying much meaning. And all those who have known, they talk in the simplest words possible...because the truth itself is so complex. Why make it more complex by complex words and theories? The truth is itself so difficult to reach, why make the journey more difficult? They talk in parables, so that even a child can understand—and as far as that ultimate is concerned, everybody is a child, ignorant, playing with toys and wasting life.

Said Sheik Saadi:

'A man had an ugly daughter. He married her to a blind man because nobody else would have her.'

Yes, this is the case. Many things that you are embracing are such that no man with eyes would look at them. But you are blind. You can marry an ugly woman, you are already married to an ugly woman. This world is the ugly woman you are married to. Money is the ugly woman you are married to. Politics is the ugly woman you are married to. Ambition is the ugly woman you are married to. But you cannot see the ugliness.

Have you ever watched an ambitious man, how ugly he looks? He loses all grace, because with ambition grace is not possible. An ambitious man is violent, aggressive. An ambitious man is almost mad. And that's why only mad people succeed in this race of ambition: Hitler and Mao Zedong and Stalin—they reach the top because they are the maddest. They become powerful...because if you are a little sane you cannot be in the competition at all. You will feel foolish. The madder a person is the more he is competitive because the more aggression is in him. He is full of fever. He has to do something. He is so restless that he has to run in the race. Of course, he will win.

Those who win in politics in fact should be in madhouses; they should not be in the capitals. But they are in the capitals, unfortunately, and they create wars and they create suffering and they create misery all over the earth.... They are bound to create them—mad people in power.... You have given a sword to a madman: now he is going to cut many throats and many heads. Without a sword he was dangerous enough; now he is danger incarnate.

Watch yourself. Whenever you feel ambitious go and look in the mirror. You will see a certain ugliness spreading on your face, in your eyes; you will lose the grace that belongs naturally to a human being. You even lose the grace that belongs to animals. You lose the grace—even that which belongs to rocks.

Violence is ugliness. A man after money, a victim of money mania—look, how ugly! A miserly man, clinging to money—you cannot find more ugly a phenomenon in the world. Greed is like spiritual leprosy. Everything stinks. Saadi is right in writing this small anecdote.

'A man had an ugly daughter. He married her to a blind man because nobody else would have her.'

Who would have an ugly wife? If you were not blind you would not have been married to this world and all its uglinesses. And deep down, the suspicion comes to you also. How can it be otherwise? Howsoever unaware, a ray of awareness is in you. If the ray was not there, I could not help you. If the ray was not there, Buddha could not help you. If the ray was not there then nothing could be done. If the ray is there, then through that ray you can move towards the very source of light. That ray will become the bridge. You also suspect in your more silent moments, in your still moments you also become aware of the ugliness that you are doing, the ugliness that has become your life, the ugliness that is your ambition, aggression, violence, hatred.... You have become so ugly that even if you touch love it becomes ugly. You touch gold and immediately it is dust; no more gold is there.

> *'A doctor offered to restore the blind man's sight.*
> *But the father would not allow him for fear that*
> *he would then divorce his daughter.'*

Who is this father? Can you suspect and find this father within you? This is what we have been calling the ego. All your miseries, all that has happened to you and is happening— the ego is fathering it all. And the ego won't allow the physician to cure your eyes. I am here, ready to cure your eyes. Who is creating the resistance?

The ego says, 'No, don't surrender. Be an individual, and be free. If you surrender you become a slave! And why surrender? There is no need—one has to be oneself....' And the ego goes on rationalizing.

But the whole point is, it protects your blindness because once your eyes are open the ego will not have any possibility to exist. It will not have any place to exist inside you. It is like darkness; light comes in—it has to leave. That's why it is afraid. It is afraid to go nearer a buddha because buddhahood is infectious. The ego creates all sorts of barriers.

I have come across people who are dead against me. They have not seen me, they have not read a single book, they have not listened to me, they don't know what I am doing and they are dead against me. Sometimes it is surprising. Even to be against, one has to come a little nearer, to know, to watch, to judge. They have not even seen me. They will not recognize me if suddenly they come across me. But they would like to kill me.

What has happened to them? A deep fear—the volcano inside and the ego is sitting on top of it. And they are afraid to come near. Even to hear they are afraid; to read, they are afraid, because, who knows, you may be caught in the trap. So it is better to protect yourself and protect your ignorance. Create some idea. That becomes the barrier.

The father is not somewhere outside of you. It is within you, the ego.... He is fathering all your hell.

> *'A doctor offered to restore the blind man's sight.*
> *But the father would not allow him for fear that*
> *he would then divorce his daughter.'*

There is investment; the father is afraid, the ego is afraid.

Saadi concluded:
'The husband of an ugly woman is best blind.'

If you are the husband of an ugly woman you will have to protect your blindness—that is one way. The other way is: if you want to drop your blindness, you have to be ready to face all the ugliness that your ego, your blindness, your ignorance, has created in its wake. You have to encounter yourself.

Self-encounter is a suffering in the beginning, painful, deeply painful; it hurts, and hurts like hell. But only through suffering, bliss is achieved; there is no other way. One who has passed through all sufferings becomes capable of the ultimate ecstasy—what Abraham Maslow and the humanistic psychologists call the 'Aha!' experience.

When you have passed through a suffering it is like a long journey. Journey-tired you come, you cannot even move, and suddenly you see the goal—and your whole being feels: Aha!—an ecstasy, and all suffering disappears. And you are in a totally different dimension.

Self-encounter is the deepest suffering in the world; that's why you are avoiding it. Socrates goes on saying: Know thyself—but nobody listens, because to know thyself means to know thyself as suffering. Of course, bliss follows, but that is not in the beginning, that is in the end. The beginning is painful. It is like a birth. Birth *is* painful.

If a child becomes afraid in the womb of the mother, afraid to pass through the birth passage—it is very narrow, it is painful, suffocating, it is a trauma, it leaves a wound forever— if the child becomes afraid, then there will be no birth, and there will be no life. Then the child will die in the womb. If the bird in the egg becomes afraid to leave the protecting shell.... He is closed in, completely closed in, and protected from everything, and he has whatsoever he needs inside. If a seed becomes afraid to sprout...because as a seed there is no suffering, there is no death because there is no life. As a seed there is no danger; the seed can remain for millions of years.

In Mohenjo Daro, seeds have been found that are ten thousand years old. They are still alive, they can sprout. In a cave in China, seeds have been found which are one million years old. They are still alive. Put them in the soil, water them, care—and they will sprout. One million years a seed has remained inside!

And you are the same seed. Wherever you are, in the cave of China or in the cave of New York, it makes no difference: you have been a seed for millions of lives. You have been afraid to take the jump and become a plant. It is a great jump. It is a risk. The shell is torn asunder, the protection lost; the security disappears.

The plant comes out, so delicate, so tender, and such a difficult world!—where all sorts of hazards exist. Animals are there, and children are there—and nobody knows what will happen. And the plant is so tender, so soft, so feminine, and the seed was so masculine, so protective, so hard, so strong. And life *is* soft, death *is* hard. Life *is* tender.... For death there exists no hazard, because a dead person cannot die again. For life—millions of hazards. Hazards and hazards—it is an adventure into the unknown.

Watch a seed sprouting, breaking the hard shell, then the hard crust of the earth, then rising into the world—the unknown, unmapped, uncharted future. Nobody knows what is going to happen and all sorts of danger all around. If the plant becomes afraid and remains in the seed, then it will never taste what life is.

Don't be afraid. Come out of your ignorance, come out of your protective shell, come out of the ego. Ego is just like the egg: a shell which protects. Come out of your character, come out of your conscience. Take the challenge! Adventure into the unknown.

In the beginning much misery, much suffering will happen. But it is only in the beginning, I promise you; it is only in the beginning. And if you can pass through it—and the more totally you pass through it the sooner it passes away.... If you can be really total, in a single moment it passes away. But in the single moment you suffer all hell.

And that suffering, when it passes then you know what it has done to you. It cleanses you, it purifies you. It is like fire; you are like gold. It purifies you. It doesn't burn you, it doesn't destroy you. It destroys only all that is rubbish in you, all that is not gold. All that is just foreign to you is destroyed.

But your nature, your *tao*, is saved, purified, absolutely cleansed of all impurities. And in that pure heart happens that ecstasy which we call *moksha*, the absolute liberation. Or you can call it god. Purified, you become god. Purified, cleansed, you become divine.

That ultimate ecstasy is yours, but at a cost. And the cost is to pass through the suffering.

Enough for today.

Seven

A Man who Loved Seagulls

There was a man living by the seashore who loved seagulls. Every morning he went down to the sea to roam with the seagulls. More birds came to him than could be counted in hundreds.

His father said to him one day: 'I hear the seagulls all come roaming with you—bring me some to play with.'

Next day, when he went to the sea, the seagulls danced above him and would not come down.

THE GREATEST SECRET of life is—and remember it always—that life is a gift. You have not deserved it in the first place. It is not your right. It has been given to you, you have not earned it. Once you understand this, many things will become clear.

If life is a gift then all that belongs to life is going to be a gift. Happiness, love, meditation—all that is beautiful is going to be a gift from the holy, from the whole. You cannot deserve it in any way and you cannot force existence to make you happy, or to make you loving, or to make you meditative. That very effort is of the ego. That very effort creates misery. That very effort goes against you. That very effort has destroyed you—it is suicidal.

In the American constitution, they have given a right, a

basic right—and they call it the basic fundamental right—to pursue happiness. It is impossible to pursue happiness. Nobody has ever pursued it. One has to wait for it. And it is not a right at all. No law court can force you to be happy or force happiness to be with you. No government violence is capable of making you happy. No power can make you happy.

The founding fathers committed a very deep mistake. It seems Jefferson didn't know much about happiness. Politicians can't know—they are the unhappiest people on earth. Jefferson added this right to the American constitution, and you will be surprised that because of this, the very wording of it, America has become one of the unhappiest countries in the world, ever....Because the very idea that you can pursue happiness, that you can deserve it, that you can demand it, that you have the *right* to be happy, is foolish. Nobody has the right to be happy. You can be happy, but there is nothing like a right about it. And if you think that it is your right you will go on missing, because you have started to look in the wrong direction from the very beginning.

Why is it so? If life is a gift, all that belongs to and is intrinsic to life is going to be a gift. You can wait for it, you can be receptive to it, you can remain in a surrendered mood, waiting, patient, but you cannot demand, and you cannot force.

Emile Coue is more alert than Jefferson. Emile Coue has discovered a law he calls The Law of Reverse Effect. There are certain things which, if you try to do, you will undo. If you don't try to do them you may be able to do them. The very effort leads you to the reverse effect. For example, sleep. You want to go to sleep—what can you do? Everybody has a fundamental right to sleep, but what can you do? Can you ask the police to come and help? What can you do when you don't feel like going to sleep? Whatsoever you do is going to disturb you because the very effort works against sleep. Sleep is an effortlessness. When you simply relax, not doing anything, by and by you drift into sleep. You cannot *swim* towards it—you drift. You cannot make any conscious effort.

And this is the problem with all those people who suffer from sleeplessness, insomnia. All insomniacs have their rituals. They do certain things to cause sleep to come to them. And that is where they miss, that is where everything goes wrong. How can you force sleep? The more you force the more *you* will be there—aware, alert, conscious. Every effort will make you more aware, more alert, and sleep will be put off.

What do you do when you want to go to sleep? You don't do anything. You simply wait, in a restful mood. You simply allow sleep to come to you—you cannot force it. You cannot demand, you cannot say, 'Come!' With closed eyes, in a dark room, on your pillow, you simply wait...and waiting, you start drifting. Like a cloud glides, drifts, you drift by and by from the conscious mind to the unconscious.

You lose all control. You have to lose control; otherwise you cannot go to sleep, because the part that controls is the conscious mind. It has to allow. Control has to be left completely. Then—you don't know when and why and how—sleep comes to you. Only in the morning you become aware that you have been asleep, and you slept well. Ninety-nine percent of people who suffer from sleeplessness create their own trouble. I have not come across more than one percent of insomniacs who are really suffering from something in their body chemistry. Ninety-nine percent are simply suffering because they don't know Emile Coue's Law of Reverse Effect. They are followers of Jefferson; they think sleep is a right.

In life, only on the surface, in the marketplace, rights exist. As you move deeper, rights disappear. As you move deeper, gifts appear. This is one of the most basic things to remember always: you have not deserved life, and life is there! Absolutely undeserved, you are alive, with tremendous energy—alive!

How does it happen? And if life can happen without deserving it, without any right to it, why not happiness? why not love? why not ecstasy? They can all happen, but you have to understand the law. The law is: don't try directly. Happiness cannot be pursued. It can be persuaded. Persuasion is indirect. It is not an attack. You move, but not directly, because when you are direct you are aggressive. Nothing is as direct as violence. And nothing is as violent as directness.

Life moves in circles, not direct. The earth moves around the sun. The sun moves around some greater sun. Galaxies move, the whole universe moves, in rounds. Seasons move in a round. Childhood, youth, old age, move in a round. The whole of life is circular, it never goes direct. It is not like an arrow that goes direct to the target. An arrow is man's invention. In life there is nothing like an arrow. An arrow is man's violent mind. An arrow chooses the very shortest cut between two points. The arrow is in a great hurry, seems to be too time-conscious. But god is not in a hurry.

Just the other day, I was reading a small booklet from Jesus freaks—ninety-nine percent nonsense, but one percent really beautiful! And even if something is one percent beautiful it is so much, because if you go to the Christian theologians, they are one hundred percent nonsense. The one percent that was meaningful, I loved. That part says, 'Hurry kills! Haste is waste.' And god is not in a hurry. He moves with infinite patience. God is a loafer, he hangs around. In fact, god is not going anywhere—he is already there. So there is no goal. The arrow is dancing round and round and round. It is not going to any target—there is no target. Just *being* is the target. So god hangs around like the fragrance of a flower which hangs in a summer night—just around and around, nowhere to go.

And god has infinite patience. He works with care, and in very indirect ways. He creates a baby, and takes nine months—he doesn't seem to have any efficiency experts around him. This has been going on for millions of years, and he has not learned anything; otherwise he could have managed to create better instruments so that a baby could be created within nine minutes. Why nine months? And from the very beginning he has been doing the same thing; he has not learned anything. He should ask the experts, particularly the efficiency experts. They will show him how to produce, how to produce on a mass scale, and not waste so much time—nine months per baby!

But it is not only with babies—with flowers also he takes infinite care; with birds, even with a blade of grass he takes infinite care and time. He is not in a hurry. In fact, it seems he is not aware of time at all. He exists timelessly. If you want to be with him, don't be in a hurry; otherwise you will bypass him. He will be always loitering here and now, and you will always be going there and then. You will always be like an arrow, and he is not like an arrow.

And to be with god is to be happy, to be with god is to be alive, to be with god is to be in meditation.

But the whole training of man is how to do things fast. Speed in itself seems to be a value. It is not. In itself it can create only madness—and it *has* created madness.

Move indirectly. And what is indirectly?

I used to know an old man who was always complaining, always grumpy. Everything was wrong—he was a born critic. And of course as critics suffer, he suffered, because sometimes it was too hot, and sometimes it was too cold, and sometimes it rained too much, and sometimes it didn't rain at all. All seasons, all the year round, he was suffering. A negative mind, a negative attitude—and he was continuously in search of being happy, continuously making every effort to be contented and satisfied. But I have not seen a more discontented man than him; he was the very personification of suffering, dissatisfaction, discontent. In his eyes there was nothing but discontent. On his face many wrinkles of tension and discontent, all the grumblings of his whole life were written there.

But suddenly one day he changed. He had become sixty and the next day was his birthday; people came to greet him, and they could not believe their eyes—he had changed so suddenly, in the night. Somebody told me about it also, so I walked down to his house to inquire, because this was a revolution! The Russian Revolution was nothing compared to it. The Chinese Revolution, nothing compared to it. A revolution! For sixty years this man had trained himself for discontent. How, suddenly...? What had happened, what miracle? I could not believe that even Jesus could have done such a miracle, it was not possible, because you never hear in the Bible.... Jesus cured blind men, he cured the deaf and dumb, he cured even the dead, but you don't hear a single story of Jesus curing anybody of discontent. It is not possible.

I asked the old man—he was really happy, bubbling with happiness—I said, 'What has happened to you?'

He said, 'Enough is enough! For sixty years I tried to be

happy and could not, so last night I decided: Now forget about it; don't bother about happiness, just live. And here I am, happy.'

He *pursued* happiness for sixty years. If you pursue, you will become more and more unhappy. You are going direct, like an arrow, and god doesn't believe in shortcuts. You will attain to *your* target, but happiness will not be there.

Millions of people attain their targets: they wanted to be successful, they are successful—but unhappy. They wanted to be rich, they are rich—but unhappy. The richer they get, the unhappier they become, because now even the hope is lost. They were thinking that when they became rich they would be happy; now they are rich, and happiness—they cannot see any sign of it anywhere. Now, with unhappiness hopelessness also settles.

A poor man is never hopeless, a rich man always is. And if you find a rich man who is not yet hopeless it is certain he is not yet rich. Hopelessness is the symbol of being rich. A poor man can hope. Millions of things are there which he has not got. He can dream, he can hope that when these things are there he will have attained the target. Then everything will be okay, he will be happy.

This man pursued happiness for sixty years. At sixty death is coming nearer, and he must have felt it that night, because whenever a birthday comes a subtle feeling of death arises. To suppress that feeling we celebrate birthdays. Whenever a birthday comes, on that day it is impossible to forget death. To help you forget, friends come and greet you and they say, 'This is your birthday.' Every birthday is a death day, because one more year has gone, death is nearing. In fact a birthday is not a birthday, cannot be—death is approaching, death is coming nearer. Time is slipping fast through the fingers. The very earth on which you are standing is being pulled away. Soon you will be in the abyss. A birthday is a death day. To hide it, to suppress it, the society has created tricks. People will come with flowers and gifts to help you forget that death is coming nearer—and they call it a birthday.

He had become sixty. Next morning a new birthday was approaching. He must have felt, he must have heard the sounds, the footsteps, of death somewhere around...the shadow. And he decided: Enough is enough. I pursued long— almost my whole life has been wasted in trying to be contented, and I could not be, so now I will do without. The old man said, 'Now here I am. I have never been so contented as I am today, absolutely contented. There is no discontent, no unhappiness.'

In the very search you create unhappiness. When you don't search, happiness searches for you. When you search, you search alone and you will not find. Where will you seek? How will you search? Mind can never be happy. Mind is your accumulated discontent. Mind is your accumulated unhappy past, the whole suffering that you have passed through: it is a wound in your being. And the mind tries to seek, to pursue, and you miss.

When you forget about happiness, suddenly you are happy. When you forget about contentment, suddenly it is there. It has always been there around you, but *you* were not there. You were thinking: Somewhere in the future a target has to be achieved, happiness earned, contentment practised. You were in the future and happiness was just around you like the fragrance of a flower.

Yes, god is a loafer. He is always loitering somewhere around. And you have gone too far, seeking. Come back home! And just be. Don't bother about happiness. Life is there as a gift; happiness is also going to be there as a gift—a gift from the whole, a holy gift.

When you are seeking too much, you are closed; the very tension of seeking and searching closes you. When you are desiring too much, the very desire becomes such a tense state of affairs that happiness cannot penetrate you. Happiness penetrates you in the same way as sleep; contentment comes to you in the same way as sleep: when you are in a letgo, when you allow, when you simply wait, they come.

In fact, to say they come is not right: they are already there. In a letgo, you can see them and feel them, because you are relaxed. In relaxation you become more sensitive—and happiness is the subtlest thing possible, the most subtle, the very cream of life, the essence. When you are relaxed in a total letgo, not doing anything, not going anywhere, not thinking of any goals, no target, not like an arrow but like a bow, relaxing, without tension—it is there.

I have heard a story about a great mogul emperor, Babur, who conquered India. He became one of the greatest emperors in the world, ruled almost the biggest part of the world any man has ever ruled.

A man, a very wise man, came to see him, but the wise man was very disappointed because Babur was talking to his court people in such a profane way—vulgar, cracking jokes; ordinary, not refined even—and laughing a belly laugh. The wise man was disappointed. He said, 'I was thinking that you were a cultured man, and I have heard many stories that you love wisdom; that's why I am here. I have heard that in your court you have many wise men, learned men, scholars, musicians, philosophers, religious men, and what do I see here? A simple vulgarity. It is intolerable. I cannot be here in your court a single moment more!'

Babur said, 'Just one moment, then you can go. Look in that corner.' In that corner was a bow.

The wise man said, 'What has that to do with the situation?'

Babur said, 'I cannot be always tense. If the bow is always tense, and the arrow is always on it, soon the bow will be broken. It will lose its elasticity. It won't be flexible then, and a bow has to be flexible; only then is it alive...the more flexible, the more alive. That is my bow, and I am like my bow. Sometimes, yes, I am tense; the arrow is on it, the bow is stretched. But only sometimes. Then I rest and relax also.'

I don't know what happened to that wise man. I feel Babur was wiser than that wise man. A bow needs relaxation. You are also a bow. You also need relaxation.

For small matters, the world of the market, you can move like an arrow, because that is man-created. But for that which is not man-created, you cannot be like an arrow—you have to be like a relaxed bow.

God is total relaxation. Hence Patanjali says that perfect *samadhi* is like sleep, with only one difference—otherwise the quality is the same, the same flavour, the same taste— with just one difference: in sleep you are unconscious, in samadhi you are conscious. But the relaxation, the letgo, is the same. Everything untense, not going anywhere, not even a thought of going anywhere, just being here and now— suddenly everything starts happening.

You are not to do anything to be happy. In fact you have done too much to become unhappy. If you want to be unhappy, do too much. If you want to be happy, allow things, allow things to be. Rest, relax, and be in a letgo.

Letgo is the secret of life. Letgo is the secret of religion. Letgo is the greatest secret. When you are in a letgo, many things, millions of things, start happening. They were already happening but you were never aware. You could not be aware; you were engaged somewhere else, you were occupied.

The birds go on singing. The trees go on flowering. The rivers go on flowing. The whole is continuously happening, and the whole is very psychedelic, very colourful, with infinite celebrations going on. But you are so engaged, so occupied, so closed, with not even a single window open, no cross-ventilation in you. No sun rays can penetrate you, no breeze can blow through you, you are so solid, so closed, what Leibniz called monads. You are monads. Monad means something without any windows, with no opening, with every possibility of opening closed. How can you be happy? So closed, how can you participate in the mysteries all around? How can you participate in the divine? You will have to come out. You will have to drop this enclosure, this imprisonment.

Where are you going? And you think that somewhere in the future there is some target to be achieved? Life is already here! Why wait for the future? Why postpone it for the future? Postponement is suicidal. Life is slow; that's why you cannot feel it. It is very slow, and you are insensitive; otherwise postponement is the only poison. You kill yourself by and by. You go on postponing—and you go on missing the life that is here and now.

For those who have attained to the here and now, the whole life starts showering flowers on them. Many things start happening which they never dreamed of.

When for the first time you are really relaxed in a meditative state, you cannot believe that life is so beautiful, so euphoric, such infinite bliss, such a *sat-chit-anand*; you cannot believe it! It is unbelievable. When a Buddha reports, nobody believes. When a Jesus talks about his kingdom of god, nobody believes. Even those who follow, they also are not absolutely trusting.

There is a story that Thomas was Jesus' most beloved disciple, but even he was not an absolute believer, even he doubted; hence the phrase, Doubting Thomas. Thomas was the most beloved disciple, the closest—and yet he too was a doubting Thomas.

It happened that Jesus was moving from one shore of Lake Galilee to the other shore. He told his disciples to move ahead and he would be coming. So they moved off in a boat. Then suddenly, when they were just in the middle of the lake, they couldn't believe their eyes—Jesus was coming on the water, walking. They forgot everything about Jesus; they thought this must be a ghost. They had seen so many miracles, even the dead had been raised, but now they could not believe. They forgot everything in the moment of surprise, it was such an unbelievable phenomenon—Jesus walking on the water.

The disciples became so afraid and trembling, they started praying to God: 'Save us! Who is this man coming? It must be a ghost! We are in danger.' Even Thomas cried, 'Who are you?' when Jesus came near.

Jesus said, 'Can't you see me? Have you forgotten me completely? Can't you believe that I am Jesus, your master?' But still they were trembling.

Thomas said, 'If you are really Jesus and not a ghost, or the devil in disguise, if you are really Jesus, and if you are really walking on the water, then let me also walk on the water, master.' This was a trick to test.

Jesus said, 'Yes, you can come!' Then there was trouble. Thomas walked two, three steps. Yes, he could walk, but then the doubt arose: 'Maybe this is the devil playing a trick on me; otherwise how can I walk? It is impossible!' The thing was happening, he was walking on the water, but he couldn't believe it himself: a doubt arose and immediately he sank into the lake and Jesus had to run and bring him out.

And Jesus said, 'You man of little faith.' From that day the phrase doubting Thomas became prevalent. But he was the *most* beloved. The others were not even trusting enough to come out of the boat, even to *try*.

When Jesus brings the news, the good news of the kingdom of god, nobody believes him. When Buddha talks about the infinite emptiness within, nobody believes him. We cannot believe! How can we believe unless we know? At least a glimpse is needed.

We live in such a suffering, hell, the news about the kingdom of god seems to be just a dream, a poem maybe, but nothing more. Religion seems not more than literature: fictitious—great fiction, but nothing more. It has to be so, it is natural in a way, because you don't know where you are standing, what is happening all around you. You are so insensitive, closed....

Open the windows, break the doors open! And run out of this imprisonment, stand under the skies. Feel again! Thinking won't help. Thinking can go on and on inside you without opening a single window. Only feeling brings you out of yourself—and you are so afraid of feeling, so much at ease with thinking and so afraid of feeling, because feeling will bring you out. It will bring you again into the very current of life. You will be in the river, moving towards the ocean.

Feel more, think less, and by and by you will see that the more you can feel, the more relaxed you are. The more you can feel, the more you become aware of the secret of life—

that you need not do anything about it, you just have to be available. Just available, I say, and everything comes to you. Once the idea arises to catch hold, to cling, everything disappears. This is the meaning of this Sufi story.

> *There was a man living by the seashore who loved seagulls.*

Love is the very center of all feelings, love is the soul of all feelings. All feelings hang on love. If you don't love, by and by all feelings will disappear. If you love, all feelings will be revived. And remember, I say *all* feelings: negative, positive, all. When you love, you start hating also—immediately. When you love, you start feeling anger also—immediately. When you love, you feel sad, you feel happy. When you love, all feelings are again back to life.

This is the trouble. That's why no society allows love; because if it were the case that with love only good feelings, feelings that society decides are good, came up, there would be no trouble. But with love, the trouble is that not only heaven starts flowering, but hell also. They are together, they are two aspects of the same coin. They cannot be separated— and there is no need to separate them, because a heaven without a hell would be poorer. A love without anger would be impotent. A love without sadness would be shallow.

Life is a polarity, and through polarities life becomes richer and richer and more and more complex. Life is not like ordinary Aristotelian logic, life is more like Hegelian dialectics: thesis, antithesis. Two polarities meet and fight, and a third phenomenon arises: synthesis. A greater harmony arises out of two polarities; then that greater harmony again becomes thesis, a new antithesis arises, then again a higher rung of the ladder of synthesis is reached.

This is how life moves. Life is Hegelian dialectics, it is not Aristotelian logic. It is not simple duality. It again and again reaches to oneness through duality—and that oneness again becomes a pole. It creates another pole; the movement starts. This is how life is trying to reach higher and higher pinnacles of being.

When you love you become happy, and you become sad also. These are the thesis and antithesis. Love is a harmony, the synthesis. Life moves through opposites, just like a river moves through two banks. You cannot conceive of a river with one bank. If you conceive of this, then all rivers disappear. If you try to ensure that one shore will be better, then rivers cannot exist.

That's what has happened to human consciousness. In the very beginning man decided against hate, against anger, against all negative poles, that they are not good. They are not good if they are alone, they are very bad. If a man is simply angry without love, he is mad. This anger is a disease. But if a man is angry because of love, a father angry with his child, with love, then anger has a beauty of its own.

No child will ever feel bad towards a parent who was angry with love. But a parent who was simply angry without love cannot be forgiven. The child may forget him, but he cannot forgive. Just anger, with no love? It is illness. It is poisonous. But if you are angry with love, the child understands. He understands your love. And in that bigger whole of love, the anger fits. It is just love in action, nothing else; and the child immediately feels it, and loves you more for it.

A husband angry without love is just ego, trying to possess, dominate. A husband angry with love is not ego trying to possess, but love, trying to help. Even if anger is needed, love is ready to be angry.

When love arises, all feelings erupt; a volcano explodes and man becomes afraid. So it is better, man decided, not to touch this volcano. Let it be there, hidden, because it brings negatives also. But those who know, they say don't be afraid of the negative. The negative is bound to be there with the positive, like a shadow is bound to be with you. If you want no shadow, you will have to kill yourself. Then only can the shadow disappear. But nothing is wrong in a shadow. If you are there, nothing is wrong. If love is there, nothing is wrong.

Somebody asked Saint Augustine, 'Tell me in one sentence, in a simple sentence, the whole message of Christ, because I am an ignorant man, and I cannot understand the subtleties of theology. And I don't know much about morality, so don't give me complex disciplines I may not be able to follow. Give me a simple discipline, so simple that I can understand and follow.'

It is said Saint Augustine closed his eyes and meditated, and then he said, 'Then there is only one thing—love, and everything else will follow.'

Love is the greatest morality, because it brings the feeling part of you up, and the thinking part goes down. Nothing is wrong with the thinking part, but it is playing the role of the master, which is wrong. Reason is good if it helps feeling. Feeling should be the master and reason should be the servant. Feeling should guide and reason should manage. But if reason becomes the master and feeling has to follow, you will be dead…because how can you be alive only with reason? Life is feeling. Trees can exist without reason, but they cannot exist without feeling.

Now even scientists are becoming more and more aware

that trees feel, and feel tremendously. Stars, rocks, rivers—they cannot exist without feeling. Feeling is their very life. Birds, animals, the whole—exist with feeling. Except man. Man is upside down. The head has become the prominent thing, and the head has been suppressing feeling.

And it has happened all over life in that way. Politicians rule, dominate; in fact, poets should be the guides, not politicians. But as it happens in the atomic individual, so it happens on a vaster scale in society. If feeling rules the individual, then poets will rule life, then poets will rule nations. The world will be totally different. If the head rules, if reason rules the individual, then politicians will rule the world, and the world is going to be constantly in trouble, constantly at war, in constant conflict.

It is good to feel, and if feeling surrounds you, then there is nothing wrong in thinking. If thinking follows feeling—beautiful; it helps. It is like a radar. It opens the way for the feeling to move on. It protects the feeling from dangers. It helps the feeling to know what is going to happen next, to plan a little. It is good! But good only as a servant.

If you love, you will have a deep affinity with existence. Trees will talk to you. Birds will start coming nearer to you. Animals will not be afraid of you—there is no need. Man creates fear because of his head. With his heart he is again one with the universe.

There was a man living by the seashore who loved seagulls. Every morning he went down to the sea to roam with the seagulls. More birds came to him than could be counted in hundreds.

Thousands of seagulls gathered around him. They

jumped and hopped, and they flew and they danced, and they moved with him on the shore. The man was accepted by the seagulls, because feeling is everywhere accepted. That is the language of existence: feeling. Reason is the language of humanity, not of existence—a local phenomenon, not universal. Feeling is the language, the forgotten language. If you understand feeling, you understand the whole.

It is said of Lukman, one of the wisest men ever born— he is the founder of Yunani medicine—it is said about Lukman that he would go to plants, to bushes, trees, sit there, feel them, and ask them, 'What use can you be put to? What disease can you be helpful in?' And it is said that he discovered millions of herbs, just by feeling them. The herb would say, 'It will be good if you use me in tuberculosis; I can help.'

This looks like a myth, a fiction, but scientists have been at a loss: if this is a fiction, then how did Lukman come to know?...because whatsoever he knew has been proved by all scientific experiment to be right. And no laboratories existed then, like they exist today; not such refined instruments, not at all! If this is a fiction, then a greater problem arises: How did he come to know? And not one or two or a hundred herbs—millions! If he had been experimenting with crude implements then it would have taken at least ten to twenty thousand years for him to discover all that. That seems to be more fictitious. The first fiction seems to be nearer reality— that he asked.

And there is the same story in India also. Ayurveda, the Indian medicine, is based on the same secret. Those secrets were revealed by the plants themselves. But then a language is needed, a language which is universal and not local to humanity. Feeling is that language. Greek or Arabic or Sanskrit won't do. No language originating in the mind is divine language. No, the divine language originated in the heart. Feeling is the language.

If you start really feeling, and your heart starts really throbbing with feeling, you can ask a tree, and a tree is always ready to reveal its secret. You can ask a bird, and the bird is ready to reveal its secret. You can ask existence, and existence is ready to reveal its heart. That heart is god, the kingdom of god, the ecstasy, the final liberation, *moksha*, nirvana; whatsoever you want to call it, you can call it.

More birds came to him than could be counted in hundreds.

He knew the language of feeling. It is love. Nobody is afraid of love, not even birds. And they can certainly feel more than you because they have no thinking apparatus, no disturbance of the mind.

In the West now they are experimenting with plants. They say that if you come near a plant with the idea to pluck the flowers, just with the idea—you have not plucked the flowers yet—if just with the idea you come near the plant then the whole plant starts trembling. A fear arises: the enemy is coming.

Now they have made very refined instruments which can check what emotion the plant is going through. If it is fear, then just like a cardiogram, on the paper the instrument records fear. If you come with the idea to water the plant, the whole plant feels happy. This is recorded, the instrument goes on recording that the plant is very happy. You water the plant, the plant is satiated, very thankful; in fact, showing all gratefulness towards you.

It happened in one of the laboratories in New York, suddenly it happened: A scientist was working on insects, and a plant was in the room, a cactus plant. He was working with earthworms, experimenting in many ways—and scientists, in the name of experiment, are torturing many types of insects, animals; he threw one earthworm in hot boiling water. He was also working with plants, and the cactus plant was accidentally connected with the instrument that records the feelings of the plant. Suddenly the plant went through much anger, fear, a very violent state. An earthworm had just been thrown into hot water!

Life is dying: a plant feels it. You cut one plant—the whole garden feels it, because everything is surrounded by an ocean of feeling, all around. You create vibrations. When you are angry you create vibrations. When you are lustful you create vibrations. When you are loving you create vibrations. Those vibrations are the universal language—they are understood by the whole existence.

It is said that when Buddha attained to enlightenment, trees flowered out of season. It may not be a fiction, it may be true. And one day we may be able to prove it scientifically, because if an earthworm, not related to a plant at all, of a totally different species, is thrown into hot water, and the death, the torture, the violence, is felt by the plant and the plant goes through a turmoil, a terrible turmoil, shaken to the very roots, then the other thing also seems possible.

Buddha attains to nirvana, he becomes enlightened. One life has reached the goal: it does not seem too fictitious that the trees around him suddenly flower out of season, in celebration. If pain can be felt, celebration can also be felt. Just a few steps more and science will be saying, 'Yes, this is not a fiction.' Life sometimes is stranger than fiction. It is.

His father said to him one day: 'I hear the seagulls all come roaming with you—bring me some to play with.'

Now an idea had entered the man's head. He was no longer the same. Love was not there. The heart was not functioning that day. A desire had entered. He had a target now. He had come to the seashore now with a business. He was no more a friend to the seagulls—he was going to catch them—he was the enemy.

Next day, when he went down to the sea, the seagulls danced over him and would not come down.

The seagulls cannot understand what you are thinking in the mind but they can understand the vibes that you are creating around—and you are continuously creating vibes around you. You are a continuous broadcast of vibes, *continuous*. Whatsoever happens in your heart, it is just as if someone has thrown a stone in a lake: ripples arise, and they go on and on and on—they will go to the very end, to the very shore, all around. A feeling arises in you; immediately a stone has been thrown in the lake of your being. An idea arises in you—ripples arise. They go all around.

Those seagulls don't know exactly what the father has said to the son, because they don't understand the local language of man. They don't know what has really happened, but deep down they still know that this man is not the same. Somebody else has come, a stranger, not the old friend. Now he has come with an idea. The idea is not known, but throughout his whole body he is now not in a letgo. He has some idea to *do*, some plan, some desire. He is not the same relaxed man with whom seagulls could feel at home.

And this is the secret of the whole of life: not only seagulls but happiness, meditation, ecstasy—they all come to you when you are in a total letgo, in a deeply friendly mood, in a loving attitude towards existence. When you are at the heart, they come. When you are persuading them, and you think that happiness is something like a right, that you have to pursue it, suddenly the seagulls of happiness are not descending. They will dance above your head but they will never come down to play with you, to move with you, to jump and hop! No, they will never become one with you. They will not descend into your being.

Yes, happiness is a seagull. Meditation also is a seagull. Ecstasy is also a seagull. Existence understands only letgo. If you are in a letgo, you will attain. You will attain to whatsoever this existence can give you—and it can give you infinite blessings, infinite benediction. It can give you total satiety, contentment. You can become a buddha.

Existence is ready to give, but you are not ready to take it, because you are thinking in terms of how to snatch it. Existence gives to you as gifts; you cannot snatch, you cannot conquer, you cannot achieve. You surrender, please. Please, be in a letgo.

All that is beautiful is like seagulls. Remember this: nothing can be done. The feast is already ready—you have been invited. You can enter from the front door. But you are foolish, you are trying to enter from the back door, and in existence there is no back door. You are trying to enter like a thief. The front door is open for you, and the host is waiting on the steps to receive you, and you are trying to enter from the back door like a thief.

Life has no back doors. You cannot steal life. You cannot be a thief. Life gives, and gives infinitely and gives unconditionally. You please be just in a letgo. Let the seagulls descend and play with you, and loiter with you on the seashore. Everything is ready. The feast, the host—everything is ready, just waiting for you to come in from the front door. Effort is not needed. Effort is the back door. Effortlessness is needed.

Don't listen to Jefferson. Happiness is not a right, you cannot pursue it. You have to persuade it. It is like a shy woman: you have to court it, indirectly. You don't go to a woman and say, 'I would like to go to bed with you.' That is too direct, too insulting, too vulgar. Any worthwhile woman would slap your face. One has to be a little more subtle with a woman. One has to be a little more indirect.

Patience is needed. Poetry is needed. And even if you have the idea in your mind to go to bed, that will be a disturbance, that will create an unbridgeable gap. If the idea is not there then you simply enjoy being with this woman. One day you will go to bed with her, but that will happen. The seagulls will descend on you.

Let life happen, don't try to force it. Through doing, only worthless things are achieved; through nondoing—all that is beautiful, all that is sacred, all that is divine.

Enough for today.

Eight

Beyond Mother's Knees

Three men made their way to the circle of a Sufi, seeking admission to his teachings. Almost at once one of them detached himself from the group, angered by the erratic behavior of the master.

On the master's instructions, the second was told by a disciple that the sage was a fraud.

The third was allowed to stay, but he was offered no teaching for so long that he lost interest and left the circle.

When they had all gone away the teacher instructed his circle thus:

The first man was an illustration of the principle: Do not judge fundamental things by sight.

The second was an illustration of the injunction: Do not judge things of deep importance by hearing.

The third was an example of the dictum: Never judge by speech, or the lack of it.

When asked by a disciple why the applicants could not have been instructed in this matter, the sage retorted: 'I am here to give higher knowledge, not

*to teach what people pretend that they already
know at their mother's knees.'*

I AM TALKING to you, not *about* something, I am talking that
very something. And whether I am talking or not talking, I
am that very something. You may call it God, you may call
it X.

The unknown cannot be taught, the unknown has to be
learned. And even when you have learned it, it remains
unknown—that's the beauty of it. It never becomes the
known. God never becomes knowledge. On the contrary,
the more you know, the more he becomes mysterious. The
more you penetrate him, the more he is elusive. As you come
nearer to the centre you start feeling lost—all certainty gone,
all clinging disappeared. In fact *you* are disappearing.

And when you have really reached the centre, god is there
in his absolute grandeur. But you are not there; the seeker
has disappeared, the knower has disappeared. And when there
is no knower, how can you reduce the unknown to
knowledge? The unknown becomes knowledge through the
knower. If the knower has disappeared, there is no possibility
of knowledge. The abyss remains, the mystery remains. But,
in a very paradoxical way, the mystery is also revealed to
you. You know it, you feel it, because you *are* it.

A master is not there to impart knowledge, a master is
there to impart himself. A master is not communicating
something about god, he is communicating god himself. The
about does not interest a master; the about is lower
knowledge. If you have come to me to know about god, you
have come to a wrong person because I am not interested in
about. If you have come to know god, you have come to the
right person. But then, you have to be ready, ready to die for

it—nothing less will do. It is the greatest risk that one can take.

Unless you lose yourself you will not gain anything here. And if you have come to gain something, and you are not ready to lose yourself, then you are wasting your time—and a master will not allow that wastage, he will push you away. Subtle will be his ways. He will not push you away in such a way that you feel that you have been pushed; rather, he will give you the impression that you yourself have left him: he was not worth it, there was nothing to be got there. The master, even in rejecting you, will not give you the feeling of being rejected. That is his compassion. On the contrary, he will give you the impression that you have rejected the master.

Sufis have the essential religion with them. This story is a very fundamental one. Before we enter the story a few things have to be understood.

First, when you come to a master decide well that you will not judge him, because if you judge you cannot trust. It is better to leave. If you trust, you cannot judge. A disciple has to decide whether he is still continuing judging, or he has started trusting.

Trust is a totally different dimension from judgement. In judgement *you* remain the centre, and from *your* centre and from *your* mind, you judge. *You* remain the criterion, the touchstone. In trust, you are no more. You have no centre to judge from, no values to judge by.

When you surrender to a master you surrender your valuation. You say to him, 'Now, I will not be a judge. From now onwards I will be a shadow to you, a surrendered soul. Whatsoever you do, it is none of my business to judge.'

It happened: A king wanted to become a disciple of a Sufi master, Bayazid, Bayazid of Bistun, one of the greatest names amongst the Sufis. When the king approached it was difficult for Bayazid to say no—and the king was not ready at all. He was not worthy to become a disciple and to be accepted.

Bayazid asked, 'Why have you chosen me? There are other masters better than me. Why have you chosen me? I am nothing, just an ordinary master.'

The king said, 'I have chosen you because of your character, your behavior, your morality. You are a good man. About others I am not so certain; their behavior is a little erratic, and they confuse me. About you I am certain. You are a good man, a saintly man, that's why.'

Bayazid said, 'Then wait a little. Postpone a little, because you don't know me and my character. You wait a little and watch.'

One day the king had gone for some hunting in the forest. Suddenly he saw, near a lake, Bayazid sitting on the other shore—it was a small lake and the king could see to the other shore—and he was not alone, he was with a woman. What was he doing in the forest with a woman, with no disciples around? Whenever he had gone to see Bayazid in the town he was always surrounded by hundreds of disciples. What had happened? What was he doing with the woman? Suspicion arose: in this privacy with a woman...?

And not only that, as he watched, hiding himself behind a tree, the woman poured something into a glass. Maybe it was wine? The flask seemed to be of wine. Now he was absolutely certain that it was good he didn't surrender to this man. He seemed to be a debauchee.

He started moving from the shore but Bayazid called out loudly, 'Don't go. Come nearer, because a judgement from that far can be wrong.' And judgements are always from a distance. In fact if you judge, the distance cannot disappear. Just to remain a judge you have to be at a certain distance. If you move closer you will lose the capacity to judge, you will become so intimate you will get involved, you will be committed. You will lose the clarity of judgment.

Seeing that Bayazid had seen him, the king felt a little awkward and embarrassed, but when he had seen him and was calling him, it was difficult to go away. And there was also a lingering curiosity inside: What was happening here?

He came nearer. Bayazid said, 'Now what do you decide? The right moment has come for me to accept you. What do you say?'

The king laughed, and said, 'You are not even worthy to be my servant, so how can you pretend to be my master?'

Bayazid said, 'So you take back your idea of being initiated by me? If you take it back, then the reality can be revealed to you.' He threw back the screen under which the woman was hiding, the *burqa*, the cover, the veil Mohammedans use. The king could not believe his eyes: the woman was Bayazid's mother. And then Bayazid gave the flask of 'wine' to him and said, 'Taste it. It is nothing but pure, coloured water.'

The king fell at the feet of Bayazid and said, 'Accept me.'

Bayazid said, 'You have missed. If you judge, you cannot trust—and you can judge from that faraway distance? No, we are not made for each other.'

This situation Bayazid created so that he could show the king that judgement can never be trusting.

Trust is a blind leap.

It is not that you judge that the jump is worth it. No, if you have taken the jump with judgement you have not yet taken it. If you have taken it by your own values, mind, you have not taken it, because the jump is possible only when you stop judging.

Through judgement you can never be intimate with a master. Judgement creates barriers. Only through trust an intimacy arises, and that intimacy is deeper than any love; hence it is blind. But to see the other world you have to be blind in this world, because when these eyes are closed, your other eyes open. Blindness in spirituality is the capacity to see. Your eyes stop looking at the outside and you start a new journey inwards.

Remember, judgement can never lead you to trust, and if judgement has led you to trust, that trust is false, not rightly grounded. Underneath there is nothing but sand and foam. Your house is going to fall any moment. It is better to abandon it before it falls and destroys you.

The second thing to remember is: You may be inquiring but that doesn't mean you are ready to receive. There are curious people who go on inquiring about higher things, but they never mean it because they are not ready to take any risk. They are not ready to put themselves at stake. They are curious people, in a way childish, inquiring about each and every thing as if just by inquiry you can attain to truth.

Curiosity is not enough. You have to be ready. Sufis say that a master accepts you not because of your inquiry, he accepts you because of your preparation—and that is a totally different thing.

Just a few days ago a young man came and he said he would like to be initiated by me. I asked him, 'Have you really decided?'

He said, 'Fifty-fifty. Sometimes I feel like taking sannyas, and sometimes I don't feel like entering into it, and I am at a loss. So I leave it to you, whatsoever you say.'

I told him, 'You had better wait three days more. There is no hurry. Just wait for three days more, and let your mind come to a decision. But the decision must be a hundred percent.'

He came to a decision, and the decision must have been a hundred percent, because the next day he simply disappeared. He never came back, and I don't think that he is going to come back again.

He was ready to be initiated—he was thinking that he was ready to commit himself, to enter the path—and just a three days' postponement.... As I feel it, it is postponed for at least thirty lives. The man was not ready at all, not even a ray of light in him, not even a seed ever sown in his past lives, and he was ready to cut the crop, and he has never sown a single seed. But people remain in absolute unawareness. They don't know that you cannot cut the crop if you have not sown the seed.

But a master has to see within you whether the possibility exists. When I accept anybody I have to see whether the possibility exists in *this* life, because I am not going to come back again, and it is better not to start work on you if you don't have the potentiality to attain in this life.

You may not attain, you may miss, but I must be certain about the potentiality, the very possibility, because if I start a certain type of work in you, and I am no more there, it will be difficult for you to be adjusted with any other master. You will have a certain structure given by me, and that will create trouble. It is better not to start so that you are completely available for somebody else to work upon. When I am certain that this man can attain in *this* life, in this very life, only then I initiate. The man may not be aware of his possibilities. He may be completely oblivious of the type of work he has done in past lives.

You are very ancient ones, you are not new ones here. You have trodden the same earth thousands of times. The earth is new in comparison to you because you have been to other planets also. You have been eternally here. You have been millions of things. You are not a clean slate, much is written there. Many incomplete systems are alive there. I have to look: Is something possible in this life?—otherwise it will be more compassionate not to start the work, so that you remain open. Otherwise I can create trouble.

So when a master rejects somebody it is because of compassion. If he accepts, it is because of compassion. Nothing else is possible because a master is nothing else; he *is* compassion.

I know well that I cannot be here very long. In fact my ship has arrived, and has been waiting for almost two decades. I have to leave the shore any moment. Somehow I go on postponing. A little longer I can be here, and a little more I can help you.

Of course, I cannot accept people at random. Even when you think I am accepting people at random I am not accepting at random. You may not be aware—because you don't know who you are, what you are, what is possible with you. When I reject a certain person I reject because he has no possibility in this life, and he cannot take the risk. He is not prepared. He is asking for things which he is not ready to receive.

And the spiritual, the occult, is not like something that can be given to you whether you are ready or not. You can inherit riches from your father, but you cannot inherit spirituality from your master. It is not a simple inheritance. It cannot be transferred. You have to be absolutely ready for it; otherwise it can be given and it will never reach you. You will forget it somewhere or other.

Sufis say a master starts working only when he feels the potentiality exists, that the man is ready in many ways; a few strokes here and there and the painting will be complete. Otherwise he will not waste his time and your time. And a master is not there to teach you ordinary things. For that many teachers exist; you can go to them. A master is to give you something of the higher, of the extraordinary, of the invisible. You have to be very refined, very delicately prepared, because only then can the music of the unknown descend on you. A master cannot teach you if you already think that you know.

Many knowers come to me: pundits, scholars.... One old man I know has been coming to me for at least ten years. After every few months he comes again, and he talks about his knowledge, the Vedas, the Upanishads, and he talks about his yoga and what he has been doing, and what type of experiences he has attained. If he is right, he need not come to me. But he persists in coming. Whatsoever he says is just pretension, imagination. He thinks he has attained. And I can see that he has not attained anything, he has just learned from the scriptures. He has been moving in the spiritual circles, so he knows many rumours about *kundalini* and about *chakras* and about light and this and that, and every time he comes he wants me to say something to him, he wants my help. But he himself prohibits it. If he wants my help he has to stop pretending that he knows. He has to stop all this nonsense that he thinks is knowledge. And he goes on repeating that these things are not sayings from the scriptures, he has experienced them.

So I say, 'It is very beautiful that you have experienced— this is what I am here to help happen. But you have attained, so no need…. Why do you bother to come to me?' But then I see that his face becomes sad. He has not known anything. But he cannot drop the pretension either, he cannot say, 'I don't know.' Such a simple thing seems to be impossible for him. And unless he realizes that, nothing is possible.

If you think that you know without knowing, your doors are closed. You have to feel the ignorance, and feel it profoundly, feel deeply in the very depths of your being that you don't know. In that knowledge of ignorance, the door opens. You become available to a master, and then he can work.

Sufis are very choosy. Every master is, has to be, by necessity, otherwise the wrong people will surround him. I had to get rid of wrong people, in subtle ways. I was surrounded in the beginning by Jainas. Of course, because I am a born Jaina they were the first to come to me. But they were around me not because of me, they were around me for a wrong reason—that I am a Jaina. And I am *not* a Jaina. I am not a Christian, not a Hindu, not a Mohammedan…or I am all. I am nobody in particular.

They surrounded me by the thousands all over the country. They were not seekers. They were not in any way interested in any transformation. They wanted me to strengthen their beliefs that Jainism is right, that whatsoever Mahavira says is true. They were not interested in me, they were interested in Mahavira. They already knew that Mahavira is true; they simply wanted my support also.

I had to get rid of them. But how to get rid of them? I started talking about sex. They disappeared, because *brahmacharya*, celibacy, absolute celibacy, remains their foundational doctrine, and when I talked about sex, and I said that from sex you can go towards super-consciousness, that *samadhi* is possible through sex, they simply disappeared. Nothing else was needed. Then those who were left were the seekers. There was one left in a thousand. That crowd has never turned up again.

Then I found another group around me—of Gandhians. They had been in search of a mahatma. When Gandhi died, they had been left without a guru. I had to do simple things. I used to wear *khadi*. I loved it: it is so cool, and handmade— so aesthetic. But I had to stop using it, because there was a link: I was using khadi, and Gandhians were thinking that I was a Gandhian. I had to suffer. Now I am using terri-cotton. It is a suffering—but that was necessary, they made it necessary. The moment I stopped wearing khadi many of them left me. And then I criticized Gandhi—since then I have not seen those faces again. They were not seekers. Only one in a thousand has been left behind.

To the seeker—the real seeker who is really in inquiry, who does not bother whether I am for Gandhi or against Gandhi, or for Mahavira or against Mahavira, who is directly related to me and who is not in any way judging me, who trusts me—whatsoever I say does not make any difference.

A master has to be very very choosy; otherwise work becomes impossible. You can talk to the crowds, but you cannot convert them. They exist on a very low level of being. Only a man who is finished with this world, completely frustrated, has become hopeless, and has been able to feel that all this is not more than a dream—at the most a good dream, at the worst a nightmare—who is really frustrated and is in a situation where he starts thinking of committing suicide, is ready for a master....Because a man who starts thinking about suicide, finishing his life because life seems so meaningless, is ready to be transformed. He is ready to die in front of a master. And then the master can resurrect him.

When you are near a master you don't just listen to his words, you listen to him, his being, the symphony of his being, the subtle music of his being. You try to listen to that, not to what he says, because whatsoever he is cannot be said in words. Even in silence only a part of him is expressed. In words almost nothing is expressed, in silence only a part. You have to listen to his being. Whatsoever he is doing— talking, in silence, walking, sitting, not doing anything— you have to watch, and you have to be alert, and you have to become receptive to the subtle music that surrounds him, the subtle vibrations. It is there.

One has to be in an absolutely feminine mood to be near a master and to be profited by him. The male attitude won't help.

Just the other day one sannyasin, one woman sannyasin, told me that this is rare: Why is it happening that many male sannyasins have started leaning more towards the feminine side of their being? They have become feminine.

That's right, it happens, because to be a disciple is to be feminine. It is to be receptive, not aggressive. You cannot snatch, you cannot steal; you have to be receptive. A master has to be eaten, chewed, absorbed, so that he becomes your blood, your bones, your marrow.

The other night a sannyasin came and said that it is just unbelievable what is happening to him. He said, 'I start feeling, while I am doing meditation, I start feeling like a dog, and I bark—and not only that, sometimes I feel that I am eating your toe!'

Yes, a master has to be eaten, chewed, absorbed, digested. I told the sannyasin, 'Don't take it literally'—because once it happened, one sannyasin did exactly that. He jumped on me like a dog, and he started eating my toe. Blood came out, he hurt the toe very much. He took the vision in a literal way.

That vision is right. One of the American seekers—he is dead now—has written a beautiful book; I love the title. The name of the man was Rudi, and he has written a book the title of which is *Spiritual Cannibalism*. The title is good, the book not so much, but the title is really wonderful. One has to eat the master, one has to become a cannibal.

But don't take it literally. It is an inner vision, and an inner phenomenon. By and by you are replaced completely by the master. You no more exist, the master exists in you. Saint Paul has said, 'I don't exist. Christ exists in me.'

The master by and by replaces you. When you go in, you don't find yourself, you find the master there. When this has happened, the knowledge—knowledge that cannot be known—has been transferred. The master transfers himself.

It is a very subtle phenomenon. So people who have come just as curious people, childish inquirers, have to be rejected; they cannot be allowed. They exist in millions. If they are allowed, then the seekers will never be able to reach near the master.

I have heard: Mulla Nasruddin's father was dying, on his deathbed, and he wanted to give some advice to his son who was going in many ways astray. He had become the Don Juan of the town, and was chasing every woman. The old man said, 'Nasruddin, remember one thing: beauty is only skin-deep, and don't be mad for it—and this is my whole life's experience I am telling you. I have chased women, but this is how I feel now, at the end of my life, that beauty is nothing but a skin-deep phenomenon, an appearance.'

Nasruddin brooded over it and said, 'Dad, that much

will do—because I am no cannibal, I am not going to eat women. Skin-deep is enough for me. Who wants the inside of a woman?'

But if you are related to a master in a skin-deep way, with only the skin of the master, you are not related at all. With a master you have to be a cannibal. You have to eat him all, whole and all, all of him, in his totality. But that is possible only if *you* drop totally. You create the vacuum, you create the emptiness, and suddenly that emptiness sucks the master in. It is a transfer of being to being. It is not a transfer of knowledge but a transfer of life itself—just as if you bring an unlighted lamp near a lighted lamp and the flame jumps.

The master loses nothing, and you gain everything, because from the lamp that is already lighted nothing is lost. Another lamp is lit—it gains everything, and from the first lamp nothing is lost, it loses nothing. And you can light thousands of lamps from one lighted lamp, and the lighted lamp remains the same. Nothing is lost. Just the flame jumps.

A master is a lighted lamp. Come to him, be close to him.

Judgement won't allow you to be close, and then the flame cannot jump because the flame can jump only when both lamps have become so intimate that no distance exists.

Now, this beautiful story.

Three men made their way to the circle of a Sufi, seeking admission to his teachings. Almost at once one of them detached himself from the group, angered by the erratic behavior of the master.

Masters are difficult people. Never take them at their

face value, never take them by their appearance; their appearance can be deceptive.

It is said about Gurdjieff that whenever a new disciple would come who would like to enter into the inner circle, he would start behaving erratically, suddenly he would start being crazy. And the old disciples would know that again he was playing his old trick, but the new one would escape, looking at this madman, what he was doing.

Once it happened, a journalist came. He wanted an interview, and he was showing much interest in Gurdjieff's teachings. Gurdjieff looked around, saw an old disciple and asked, 'What day is it today?'

The disciple said, 'Today is Saturday.'

Gurdjieff said, 'How is it possible? Yesterday it was Friday, how is it possible that it is Saturday today? That is just mad— yesterday was Friday, how is it possible then that today is Saturday?'

The journalist stood up and he said, 'I am not in search of mad people. What's going on here?'

And Gurdjieff looked at him in such an angry way, such a penetrating way, that the journalist started perspiring with fear, feeling that this man can be dangerous. And Gurdjieff was a very strong man. If he jumped, he could kill you. The journalist simply escaped, never came back again. And Gurdjieff had a belly laugh.

Some disciple asked, 'But why did you behave in such a way? He could have been helpful. He could have written an article. And he has contacts, he is a very well known man. Why...?'

Gurdjieff said, 'It is better to finish from the very beginning, because once he starts coming he will be coming more and more, and he cannot understand; he is a superficial man. He just took the appearance, how can he understand deeper things?'

Almost at once one of them detached himself from the group, angered by the erratic behavior of the master.
On the master's instructions, the second was told by a disciple that the sage was a fraud.

On the master's instructions the second was told by a disciple, 'Don't be deceived by this man, he is a fraud.' And the second disappeared.

Man is really something! If somebody says that the master is a fraud, it is enough. You never see that maybe *this* man is a fraud, or this man is playing some game, or this man has some motive for saying it.

To believe in the master is difficult, but to believe in this man is so easy. You never ask about *his* credentials, *his* bona fides you never ask about—you simply believe. It seems that whenever somebody says that something is wrong you are always ready to trust. Whenever somebody says that something is good you are reluctant to. In the bad you trust, in the devil you believe. In god you have doubt.

In English we have the expression: Too good to be true. This shows the mind. You never say: Too *bad* to be true. No, there exists no expression like that. Too bad is never too bad, and it is almost always true. But too good cannot be believed. You distrust humanity so deeply that you are always ready to believe if something wrong is said about something or somebody.

If somebody comes and says, 'This man has attained to buddhahood,' you laugh, you say this is not possible; this is all fiction, it has never happened, and it will never happen. How can it happen that somebody else can become a buddha and you have not become a buddha yet? Impossible. If ever buddhahood is going to happen to anybody, it is *you* to whom it is going to happen. Nietzsche says somewhere: I cannot believe in god, because if he is already the god then what are the chances for me? I don't believe that there is any god. If there was, I would have been him.

You always believe negative things about people, you never believe the positive. Even if you don't show the doubt, the doubt is there. How foolish! Somebody says that this man is a fraud and immediately you accept. You don't go into it, you don't inquire. You don't say, 'I will postpone and I will inquire, and then I will decide.' Immediately trust comes to you. But even if a buddha comes to say to you, 'I have attained to perfect bliss,' you look at him with suspicion. How is this possible? It is too good to believe.

You believe in the devil. God may be dead, the devil is never dead. And I have seen people who are absolutely atheistic—they don't believe in god—but I have not seen a single person who does not believe in the devil. Everybody believes in the devil, even the atheist. Atheists have never brought any arguments against the devil. Against god they have thousands of arguments, but against the devil, no argument. Everybody seems to be the disciple of the devil! He seems worth believing.

When you come nearer to a master it is very difficult to judge. The master had instructed the disciple to say, 'This sage is a fraud.' This was under the instructions of the master. He was creating a situation.

Can you believe the devil easily? Then you are not for spiritual growth. Do you resist belief in the wrong? the negative? Then you have taken one step towards the right, the good, the divine. How can you trust a master if you trust so much what any ordinary man says?

There are thousands of people who have never reached me because somebody, just a taxi driver, or a *pan wallah*, or a coolie in the station, a porter, said, 'Where are you going? It is all fraud.' And they have stopped many reaching me. They may be my disciples under instruction! You never know.

The second man left.

The third was allowed to stay but he was offered no teaching for so long that he lost interest and left the circle.

The third was allowed to stay, but was offered no teaching for so long that he lost all interest and left the circle. A master knows well how to instruct you. You need not advise the master how he should instruct you. He knows well. One has to trust and wait. When the right moment comes he will say something.

The first man was an absolutely third-rate possibility. Nothing was possible. The master immediately disposed of him by his erratic behavior. The second must have had a little possibility. The master gave him a chance, but he failed. The third must have had the most potential of all three. The master allowed him to remain but wouldn't instruct him, wouldn't say anything—not that he was not saying, because a master is a constant message. Even while he is talking to others, he may be talking to you.

This has been my observation. Many times when I am talking to somebody else I am talking to you, because I feel that is the most appropriate way. When I am talking directly to you, you may miss, because your ego becomes too prominent. When I pay attention to you, your ego comes up to the surface, and the ego won't allow…. No, you are just sitting by the side, I am talking to somebody else; then you are listening more properly. Then the ego is not involved.

If I am telling somebody else how to drop anger, you are listening, and because you are not concerned you are a little detached, and when you are detached you listen better. When you are concerned, when it is *your* problem, you are so worried about it that there is a barrier. When I am talking to somebody else and talking on his problem, I may not be talking to him at all, I may be talking to somebody else really. And when I start talking to you I may be talking now to the other person, not to you.

That has to be decided by the master: what to do, how to do it. I had to stop personal interviews because of this, because I felt it took a longer time for the thing to reach you. If you are alone with me you become so nervous—and it is *your* problem, you cannot be detached, you cannot be an observer. And you are burdened so much by the problem that whatsoever I say, when I am saying it you know well it is impossible, because you think you have tried everything, and nothing happens.

I had to stop personal interviews completely. Now it is better: ten, twelve people are there in the interview. I talk to A, and I may be talking to B; I talk to C, and I may be hinting to A. Now it is simple. When I hit somebody else, the hit may be for you. And you can take it easily, because it seems not to be meant for you. But it works. It finds you unaware. It penetrates deeper in you. It moves into the subtle layers of your unconscious without any effort because you are sitting relaxed. It is somebody else's problem.

You may have observed that whenever somebody else is in difficulty you can be a wise counsellor, a good adviser—everybody is a good adviser, I have never seen anybody who is not a good adviser when others are in difficulty. Everybody is a good adviser. You can give such wise counsel that even Lao Tzu will feel jealous. Such a great wise man! But when the problem is yours, suddenly you become childish. Suddenly you lose your bearings, you lose balance.

Why does it happen?—because now it is too close a problem. You are already disturbed and you are expecting a miracle. You cannot give the same advice to yourself that you have given to others in the same situation. A detached feeling helps.

The third was allowed, but no particular instruction was given to him directly. Then he became uninterested. It seemed the master was not interested in him. And the master *was* interested; otherwise he would have disposed of him already, as he had disposed of the other two. He was interested, but he was waiting for the man to become a little more patient, become a little more settled. He may have been giving instructions, but the man was foolish. He was thinking that instruction is only instruction when it is given directly to you.

Subtle are the ways of masters. They know better how to give an instruction. Sometimes when they don't give you a message, that is the message: Wait. Wait a little more; you are not yet ready and ripe. But the man lost interest—he left the circle.

It may have been an interest, but it was not a thirst. An interest can be lost, but never a thirst. If you come to me through your intellectual interest, or even a bit of your spiritual interest, if it is only interest, sooner or later you will have to leave me because interest cannot be sustained for long. One gets fed up with one's own interest, it becomes heavy.

But if it is a thirst, a hunger, then the more you wait the more the hunger grows. The more you have to wait the more fiery becomes the thirst. In the beginning it was just a slight sensation. The master waits until the thirst becomes the totality of the man, because only then will the meeting be possible, only then can he be instructed. When the thirst is so much that the man is ready to stake anything for it, when for just one glass of water he is ready to pay with his life, when the thirst is so great that he is ready even to lose life for it, only then positive instruction, direct instruction, becomes possible—never before. Otherwise the master has to look at somebody else and talk to somebody else; as yet the thirst is not enough, it is just an interest.

If you are forced to wait, thirst will grow. A moment comes when your whole being is thirsty, every cell of it. It is not only in the throat—the whole body is burning with it. Only then the cool breeze from the heart of the master can penetrate you. And in deep thirst and hunger your trust is tested, whether you really trust.

It happened to Bayazid, with his master. For twelve years, the tradition has it, Bayazid had to wait. For twelve years the master didn't say anything to him. One day the master said, 'You go into the hall'—the hall that Bayazid had passed through every day, coming and going to the master—'and there in the hall there is a book. Bring me that book.'

Bayazid said, 'But I have never seen the book. In fact, I have never looked in the hall, because I was interested in you, not in any book, not in any hall. But I will go—if you say, I will go.'

The master said, 'No need. I was just trying to learn whether you are interested in anything else or not.' Such a total interest—thousands of times in twelve years coming and going to the master he passed through the hall and he never looked around. That was not his interest, his whole interest was the master. The master said, 'There is no need for the book. There is no book there. I was just trying to find out whether you are looking here and there also, or if you are completely focussed, arrowed.'

That very night the transfer happened. The master said, 'Don't go. Tonight you sleep here.' Bayazid slept just by the side of the master—but he could not sleep. It was such an intense moment. He could not dream, he could not think, it was such an intense moment, so expectant, so pregnant. His mind completely stopped in that intensity of thirst, hunger, and the flame jumped.

Next morning Bayazid was no more the same man. The old died, the new was born. And no instruction was ever given. He just had to wait for twelve years, that was the message, that was the method the master used for him. If he had left even one day before, the whole effort of twelve years would have been lost.

And he could have left, because one gets uninterested: twelve years—such a long phenomenon. And how long has one to wait? The mind goes on saying, 'Now what are you doing here? Now leave this man, because nothing is going to happen—twelve years have passed!' But even twelve lives are nothing, because when it happens then you know that you could have given twelve thousand lives for it. That too would not be costly; then too it would be cheap.

The third was allowed to stay, but he was offered

no teaching for so long that he lost interest and left the circle.

When they had all gone away the teacher instructed his circle thus: The first was an illustration of the principle: Do not judge fundamental things by sight.

...Because by sight you can see only the appearance, not the reality. The first judged by sight. Behaviour is just an appearance, the man is hidden deep down. Behaviour is just like the ripples on the surface of the ocean, the ocean is hidden deep down. You have to go in deep. Eyes cannot go in deep, they are meant to see only the appearance.

Sufis have it as a fundamental principle: Do not judge fundamental things by sight. The first man was an illustration of this principle; he judged by sight and missed. How can you see the depth with your eyes? You can see what I am doing; how can you see *me* with the eyes? You can listen with the ears to what I am saying; how can you listen to *me* with the ears? You can touch my body—how can you touch *me*? All senses are superficial. Never judge anything by sight, by the senses, because everything has an inside; everything, even a rock, has an inside. Don't judge it by sight.

And when you come to a master, a realized man, he is as deep as existence itself—that's why he is enlightened.

Never judge by sight; otherwise you will miss. You may have come many times near a buddha and missed, and you haven't even known. You must have missed because Buddha walked on this earth for forty years after his enlightenment, and thousands of buddhas before him, and hundreds after him. Jesus walked on it—you may have been somewhere in

Israel; Mahavira was here and you may have been somewhere in Bihar; and Krishna, and thousands of others....

It is impossible, almost impossible that you never came across a buddha. In millions of lives, many times it must have occurred that you passed a buddha, you touched a buddha, you listened to a buddha, and you missed. If you judge by sight, then that is going to happen. You can miss me also if you judge by your senses, if you judge by your mind, when you cannot penetrate to the depth that is talking to you.

The second man was an illustration of the injunction: Do not judge things of deep importance by hearing.

He simply heard a disciple say that this sage was a fraud, and he believed him—and the disciple was under instruction from the master.

People will say a thousand and one things. Don't be too trusting of your ears. Ears cannot penetrate to the depth. One has to be with a master to feel him, to feel him from the heart. A thousand and one things will be said—don't listen. Good and bad things will be said—don't listen, because how can you judge by the ears? It is not ordinary music, that can be judged by the ears; it is the eternal music. You can hear it, but not with your ears. You can hear it, but the ears are not enough.

And how foolish man is! Fundamental things he goes on judging by appearance, or somebody says something and he judges.

The third was an example of the dictum: Never judge by speech, or the lack of it.

...Because the truth cannot be said, and all that can be said cannot be true. Truth remains unsaid, so don't judge by speech or by the lack of it.

The third simply waited for the master to instruct him, in words, what is to be done and what is not to be done. He missed because of that. He should have listened to the very being of the master, to the miracle that had happened there in the master, to the unknown that was throbbing there in the master, to god that had descended in the master. He should have listened to that reality, not to the words.

And the master was continually giving messages, in thousands of ways—sometimes silent, sometimes talking to others.... But the man wanted attention to be paid to him, and a master never pays attention to you unless you stop asking for attention, because if he pays attention to you when you are demanding it, it will strengthen your ego more; he will not be a help, he will be a hindrance. A master gives you attention only when you have completely dropped the very idea.

Everybody asks for attention because attention is food for the ego. So whenever people pay attention to you, you feel very important. If more people pay attention to you, you feel very very important. When nobody pays attention to you, you feel already dead; people have forgotten you, you are worthless. You start feeling your uselessness.

And when you come to a master, of course that desire is there; it has to be. It is natural that he should pay attention to you—not only attention, but special attention. But he cannot do that, because he cannot give you poison. He will have to wait. And you will have to drop the very hunger for attention. The day you drop it, he will look at you.

The day you drop it he will become all attention towards

you, because only in that attention, when the ego is not demanding, can he help. That attention becomes a bridge. When ego is there, attention becomes food for the ego. When the ego is not there, attention becomes food for your being.

> *When asked by a disciple why the applicants could not have been instructed in this matter, the sage retorted: 'I am here to give higher knowledge, not to teach what people pretend that they already know at their mother's knees.'*

A master is to instruct you in the highest dimension of life and existence. That's not possible if you already think that you know. Then you are closed. The first man knew already what erratic behavior was. The first man knew already, he had decided what erratic behavior was.

The journalist who met Gurdjieff already knew that this was sheer insanity; this man was neurotic who was saying, 'How can today be Saturday when just yesterday it was Friday?' This man was either a fool or a madman. The journalist simply decided this, without looking at Gurdjieff. Such a light this man was! Such a tremendously wonderful phenomenon this man was! But just an ordinary trick, and the journalist was befooled.

How could he befooled so easily?—because he already knew that he knew how to define a neurotic man, a madman or a fool. He had definitions. The first man immediately knew that this man was not right. Without knowing what is right and what is wrong, without knowing what is good and what is bad, he had conclusions. A disciple should not have conclusions; otherwise conclusions will become the obstacles, and there will be no possibility to reach the master. By your conclusions you become surrounded and walled and imprisoned. If you have knowledge, you have conclusions. Drop all conclusions. Don't be the first man.

The second man simply believed somebody without even knowing the name of the man. Without knowing his past, without knowing anything of what he was saying, he believed him. If you believe in this way you will never reach a buddha, because on the way towards a buddha you will meet thousands of people, and they will say a thousand things, and you will believe them, and you will return to your home.

Buddha is not standing just in front of you, you will have to pass thousands of people before you reach a buddha. They can distract you. Anybody can distract you, and you never think how impotent you are. Anybody can distract you. Somebody you meet on the road says, 'Where are you going? Are you mad?' And suddenly you stop. Somebody has put an idea into you, and now you will follow this man. And you will never ask anybody who this man is. And you will think yourself very wise. You are simply gullible. And you have no strength of being. You can be led astray by anybody. Don't be the second man.

The third man waited. But he wanted attention to be paid to him, and special attention. Because of that, he missed. Don't be the third man also.

And right was the master. He said:

'I am here to give higher knowledge, not to teach what people pretend that they already know at their mother's knees.'

Enough for today.

Nine

When Shibli is Absent

Shibli went to visit another great sage, Junnaid.
The wife of Junnaid was about to conceal herself
modestly behind a screen.
Junnaid said: 'Stay where you are—Shibli is
absent.'
At that moment Shibli began to weep.
Junnaid said to his wife: 'You must now be absent,
for Shibli has returned.'

WHY DOES MAN go on missing that which is always present, that which is everywhere present, that which has always been, is, and will be, within and without? Why does man go on missing that? It should be the easiest thing to be realized. But something functions as a barrier.

Why can't you see it? Why are your eyes closed? You cannot see it because you are too full of yourself, too much filled with the 'I'.

Just a few days ago a man came to see me and he said, 'I am a humble man. I am just like the dust on your feet. I have been trying for almost twenty years to achieve higher consciousness, but I have been a failure. Why can't I attain?'

And on and on he went. Every sentence started with I. If the grammar allowed, every sentence would have ended with I. And if everything was allowed, every sentence would have consisted only of I's. 'I et cetera, I et cetera, I et cetera,' it went on and on.

You are filled too much. There is no room, no space for god to enter in you. You are too crowded. A thousand I's milling inside—they don't leave any space for anything to enter in you. That's why you go on missing that which is always present.

This is the arithmetic of spirituality: If *you* are present, you will miss the divine. If *you* are absent, only the divine is, nothing else exists. God may be absent if you are present. God will be present if you are absent.

So the whole effort of a seeker is how to be not present, how to become an absence. Absence is meditation. That space where you exist but not as an I, not focussed in the ego, unfocussed, not centred anywhere...you exist without a centre, an empty house, a temple, not even the worshipper inside—suddenly, god is there! god has always been there, not even for a single moment was he absent. But you were too much present. Your presence is the barrier.

Self-consciousness is the barrier. Self-unconsciousness is the gate. And remember, self-unconsciousness means unself-consciousness. Self-unconsciousness is the highest form of consciousness. It is unself-consciousness: consciousness exists, but there is nobody in it. The self has disappeared, melted away, has been absorbed. You are and yet you are not.

It looks paradoxical, but the whole existence is paradoxical. When you are not, it can be said that for the first time you are, because now you are divine. Now you don't exist separately. Now you exist as an organic part—not even like a mechanical part, because a mechanical part, howsoever joined, still remains separate. It functions with the whole but it is still a part. An organic unity—you are not even a mechanical part. You have become the whole, and the whole has become you.

I have heard: Once a great Sufi saint, Hassan, had a dream. For years he was seeking and seeking, and suddenly that night in the dream he found god himself standing in front of him, and in his hand god was holding an onion. Hassan was surprised: Why an onion? And god said to him, 'Now you choose. Now you have become able to choose. Would you like a slice of onion or the whole onion? The alternatives are open, and whatsoever you want you can have—you choose.'

Hassan started meditating in his dream. He was at a loss to choose. He could have chosen the part if the ego was there; he could have chosen the part because the ego always chooses the part. It cannot choose the whole because in the whole is fear. It will have to disappear. Or, he could have chosen the whole, because ego is greedy; not knowing that in the whole it will have to disappear, it may choose the whole.

But he opened his eyes in the dream and said to god, 'It is difficult. I cannot choose because if I choose the part there will always be conflict. If I choose the part there will always be fear and death. The part has to die, it cannot live forever; only the whole can live. If I choose the part I am choosing struggle, conflict, disharmony; I am choosing limitation, bondage, because I am choosing the finite. No, I cannot choose the part.'

God laughed and said, 'Then why don't you choose the whole?'

Hassan said, 'I cannot choose the whole because a whole without the parts won't be much alive.'

God blessed Hassan and said, 'You did well. It is right.'

If you choose the part there will always be conflict, struggle to survive—because the part is always on the verge of dying, it is always near death. In fact it is already dead. If you choose the whole against the part you again choose a dead thing. A whole without parts won't be alive. It will be monotonous. It will have no inner tension in it to make it alive. It won't throb. It cannot dance, it cannot walk. It will be like a dead rock, with no music coming out of it. Music needs tension, a throbbing, expectant tension.

With the part and the whole there is continuously a tension—and that tension is the very life. Between the part and the whole the river of life flows as between two banks. Between the part and the whole, god exists, as the subtlest, delicatemost tension. Between the duality, the oneness exists. The duality is like two banks and the oneness is the river between the two. It doesn't belong to either, and it belongs to both; hence the paradox.

A part is always going separate and coming nearer together again. A part is moving away from the whole and still is rooted in the whole—just like a plant moving towards the sky, away from the earth, and still rooted in the earth; trying to be a bird, but rooted, trying to reach the sky, but rooted in the earth. Only then the tree can exist. It is a subtle tension between the earth and the sky.

A part is continuously marrying the whole and continuously divorcing it. And there is the whole beauty of it: moving away and coming nearer, falling in love and fighting—and this goes on simultaneously. The oneness is not against duality; in fact the oneness is between the duality, and hence it is so alive.

God is not a dead concept. If god is simply one, the whole, it will be a dead concept. That's why the Hegelian absolute is a dead concept—it is the god of the philosophers.

Soren Kierkegaard, one of the great Danish philosophers,

has said a very beautiful thing. He said, 'My god, I pray to you, but you are not the god of the philosophers. I don't pray to the god of the philosophers,' says Kierkegaard. 'I pray to the god of Abraham, Jacob and Jesus. The god of philosophers is dead. The god of Abraham, Jesus, Jacob, is totally different.'

The god of the lover, the god of the poet, the god of the devotee, is different. The god of the lover is alive. It has all the contradictions in it, and still the harmony exists.

God is harmony in contradiction. God is relaxation in tension. God is one in the many. God is formless in the form, nameless in all names.

Hindus have a very beautiful scripture. The name of the scripture is Vishnu Sahasra Nam, one thousand names of God. Hindus continuously say that god has no name, and then they write a book in which they compile simply the names, nothing else. The whole scripture consists only of one thousand names of god. Almost all the names have been compiled. God is nameless, and yet all names belong to him, because to whom can they belong? Your name is also god's name; otherwise is not possible, because to whom will it belong?

Only god exists. So the sinner is god, and the saint is also god. In fact, between the sinner and the saint, remember, *between* the sinner and the saint exists the harmony. Without sinners, god will be impoverished, infinitely impoverished. Without saints, god will not be so rich. Sinners alone—and the whole harmony will be lost; saints alone, and you cannot find more boring a phenomenon, more monotonous. There will be no music.

The whole music throbs between tense notes, contradicting and yet not contradicting, going apart, and still coming together. If you understand this, then Hassan's dream is really tremendous. God said, 'Hassan, you did well. Had you chosen one, you would have missed an opportunity. I will give you both. I will give you the part in the whole, and the whole in the part.'

The whole exists in the part. The part exists in the whole. In fact part and whole are not two things. You cannot draw a dividing boundary. The part melts into the whole and the whole melts into the part.

But you have become too much of the part; you have chosen, you have become a self. And you have completely forgotten the no-self. You have become too much of a presence, and you don't have absence; hence, you have lost the music. You have become a discord. The same notes can become a disharmony—only a new arrangement is needed.

Everything you have; you don't lack anything. I have not come across a single man in my thousands of lives who lacks anything. Maybe a little mismanagement, but you are not lacking anything. Maybe things are not in their right places, but you are not lacking anything. Maybe you have put A in the place of B, and C in the place of D, but the whole alphabet exists in you. It may not be in order, maybe there is a disorder, but you lack nothing.

And the clue exists within you. The clue is: Become as much absent as you are present. Exist in a deep contradiction. You may have never thought about it. You have been trying to exist very consistently. You are trying to be consistent, never in contradiction. Then, either you choose the part—as you have chosen, as many have chosen—and then there is conflict, continuously, because the part feels it is against the whole. If you choose it, if you get identified with the part...that is what I mean when I say 'I,' the ego: it is an identification with the part.

You are vast, as vast as the universe, and you are trying to get into a small hole. For a mouse, okay, but for you—too narrow. Misery follows. You feel in bondage. You feel from everywhere walled in, imprisoned. You become angry, you get irritated. You start fighting, you start being destructive, because life seems to be a narrowing, a continuous narrowing.

A child is born—and the narrowing starts. A child is born and he comes through a very narrow passage, from the mother's womb. From the very first moment of life narrowing has started, and then the whole life, until death releases you—for entry into another hole—you feel yourself being narrowed continuously, you don't feel the expansion. And the further ahead you look, the more the hole seems to be like a tunnel. Have you ever stood in front of a tunnel and looked in? The far end looks very small.

Once I was travelling with a villager in a bullock cart, and we had to enter a tunnel to pass over a river. The villager refused completely. He said, 'It is okay from this end, we can enter, but look at that end: how can we get out?' He had never been in a tunnel, and I tried and tried…but he said, 'Whatsoever you say, I can see the hole here is big enough—we can enter, but then it goes on narrowing. What will happen at the other end? You will kill my bullocks! And it may be difficult even to come back if once we are caught.'

Death looks like the other end. The passage of the mother's womb is the beginning, and then life goes on narrowing, and then one day somebody simply disappears. That means the whole process has become so narrow you cannot find the man again.

The whole process of narrowing, why is it so?—because

you get identified, and when you start getting identified with the part, then it is a natural process that you will be getting identified with smaller and smaller parts. In the end only a very small thing, the narrowest thing in the world, the ego, is left. To be too much present, to be too much in the I, to be too much the I, is an identification with the part.

Hassan did well. He said, 'I cannot choose the part, because that is the foolishness I have been doing all along. Now I cannot choose the part.' But he must have been a very perceptive man, because it ordinarily happens that if you have been too much identified with the part, you are too prone to choose the whole. Simple logic. One moves to the other extreme.

Many have done that also. Then they try destroying their egos. The monks in the monasteries, the traditional sannyasins in India, you go to them, they have been trying to kill the ego, to destroy the part. But they don't know: if the part is destroyed, the very path to the whole is destroyed.

It is a delicate affair. Life is very very subtle and mysterious.

You should not get identified with the part, that's right, but you should not destroy it, because then the very base is destroyed.

That's why monks live a very monotonous life—that is my definition of a monk: one who lives a monotonous life. He may not be living in a monastery, but he lives in monotony. Monotony is his monastery. He lives a life of a single note, he has no other notes. He cannot create a harmony, because he is afraid of the conflict. He is trying to destroy the part. If you destroy the part, in the destruction of the part the very possibility to move to the whole is lost.

But fortunately nobody can destroy the part, you can

only think that you have destroyed it: it always remains hidden in you. At the most you can suppress it, that's all. You cannot destroy it.

Destruction is not possible in this world. You can neither create anything nor can you destroy anything, because destruction means something was there and now it has become nothing. Something cannot become nothing, there is no way to reduce something to nothing. And there is no way to create anything, because creation means to bring something out of nothing. There is no way. Something can change into something else, but there is no creation and no destruction.

You cannot destroy the part, because in fact the part never belonged to you—who are you to destroy it? The part belongs to the whole, how can you destroy it? You never created it. Can you create the ego? If you cannot create the ego, how can you destroy it? Don't be stupid.

All that you can do is to create a gestalt or to destroy a gestalt. This German word is beautiful. Out of this word a whole attitude towards life has arisen—gestalt psychology. It is meaningful, tremendously meaningful. There is no way to translate this word into English or into any other language. Gestalt means: the relationship between the figure and the ground.

Gestalts change. For example, I am talking to you. Then everything else that is going on around—the airplane, the constant singing of the birds, chirping, the movement of the wind in the trees, the traffic noise—everything has become the background, the field. You are listening to me, attentive to me—my words have become the focus. You are focussed on my words, on me. That has become the figure.

But if I stop, suddenly the gestalt disappears. You start

listening to the birds, to the noise around. The gestalt has disappeared. Gestalt means: when you pay attention to something it becomes important, and everything else becomes just the background. It does not disappear, it is there; the chirping of the birds is there even while I am talking. Even while you are listening, it is there, it has just gone a little back, stepped a little back to the boundary. It has become the very background. You are concentrated towards me. This has become the gestalt.

Gestalts go on changing. A child has a different gestalt of the world. If you give him a flower and a one hundred rupee note, he will take the flower.

I used to know a beggar in my town who was always sitting under a tree near the river. And it had become a joke, not only in the town but all around in the surrounding towns, that people would offer him one *anna* or a one *rupee* note, and he would always choose the one *anna*, he would never choose the one rupee note. Even if you offered a hundred rupee note and one anna, and gave him the choice— 'Whatsoever you want between the two you can take'—he would take the one *anna* piece. It had been going on for years.

Once I asked that old man, 'You must know the difference by now, and you don't seem so foolish—why don't you choose the hundred rupee note if somebody is offering it?'

He said, 'Then the whole game will be lost. Then they won't give me even one *anna*. They enjoy my foolishness, but I am not so foolish. Don't tell me that I should choose the hundred rupee note. I can choose it, but only once; then nobody is going to play the game. They enjoy my foolishness and my emotions. I am not so foolish as they think. For twenty years I have been living on the game. I always choose the smallest coin they offer, and they enjoy and they laugh at my foolishness. But I am not a foolish man.'

A child will choose the flower. He is not foolish, his gestalt is different. A hundred rupee note doesn't mean anything, he has not yet come to the world of the market where a hundred rupee note means something. But if you offer him a plain paper or a hundred rupee note, he may choose the hundred rupee note, not because it is a hundred rupee note, but because it is painted, coloured. He has a different gestalt.

A young man has a different gestalt, an old man has a different gestalt. That's why there is the gap between generations—they have different gestalts, and gestalts go on changing. They not only change over the years, every moment they go on changing. This morning you were so loving, and now you are so angry, your gestalt was different. When you were loving anger disappeared into the background, love came into focus. Now you are angry, love has gone to the background and anger has come into focus.

But nothing disappears, remember. Everything remains, always remains. Only gestalts change. Something comes up, something goes down; something surfaces, something goes to the bottom. But nothing disappears, nothing *can* disappear. Everything is everlasting and eternally everlasting. Everything always is. That's what Hindus call *nama-rupa*. This Hindi word, *nama-rupa*, can give a little feeling and nuance of gestalt. Hindus say only name and form change; otherwise reality remains the same.

So don't try to kill the ego—you cannot. If you try to kill the ego you will become a very, very humble man, but remember, 'very, very' is important. You cannot be an ordinary humble man but very, very humble—and that will be the hiding place of your ego. Then you will claim that you are the humblest man on earth.

I was reading an anecdote: Three monks belonging to three Christian monasteries met at a crossroad. Of course they started bragging. One said, 'You will have to concede that our monastery has produced the greatest saints. Your monasteries are nothing in that matter. Look at our legendary past—how many saints we have produced!'

The second said, 'You are right. But you will have to concede that all the great theologians have come from our monastery—the great philosophers, the great knowers, systematizers. You cannot boast even a single theologian of the calibre that we have produced in thousands.'

Both looked at the third, and they said, 'We feel sorry for you because you have nothing to claim.'

The third said, 'No, we have not produced great saints, that's right. And we have not produced great thinkers, theologians, that too is right. But as far as humility is concerned we are at the top.' Concerning humility we are at the top! What type of humility is this, when you are at the top?

The gestalt has changed. The ego has gone to the bottom, but starts functioning from there. Now you are humble, but at the top. A humble man has to be last, how can he be at the top? But a humble man always claims that he is at the top. The ego is not dead, cannot be dead. It has only gone to the deeper layers of the unconscious and functions from there and controls from there. Humility on the surface and ego deep down, controlling humility. Humbleness is controlled by the ego.

Look at people who say and think that they are humble,

look in their eyes: you will not find any humbleness there, but a very subtle pride. Pious egoists they are, holy egoists they are. And when ego becomes holy it becomes more poisonous. Poison in itself is bad, but when poison becomes holy then it is very dangerous.

You cannot kill the ego. If you try to kill it, two things will happen. One, your life will become monotonous, it will lose the tension of the opposites. It will lose the music. That's why monks are so monotonous.

Once it was asked of a great American actor—somebody interviewed him and asked him, 'Can you say what has been the greatest disappointment in your life?' The interviewer must have been thinking that in the life of an actor there are many failures: when people don't respond, don't clap, then whatsoever the actor is doing goes flat.

The actor said, 'The greatest disappointment in my life, you ask? Yes, it happened.... I was a child, a small kid, and I was passing down a road, and near the road I saw a big tent. I thought there must be a circus going on, but I had no money, so I tried to enter the tent from somewhere other than the main entrance, and somehow I sneaked in. And when I entered, it was not a circus but a priest was giving a sermon—and that was the greatest disappointment in my life.'

Priests, monks, are so monotonous, so deadly monotonous, with no music, with no harmony, because they have been trying to walk with one leg, or to fly with one wing. They have been trying to improve upon god himself. Even god cannot be without two, and they have been trying that. Of course, they can hop on one leg a little—that is what their sermons are. Or they can try to fly on one wing— just an ugly effort, and they fall to the ground. Or they can go on producing the same note on their *veena*....

I have heard, Mulla Nasruddin's wife was very very irritated one night and she said to Mulla, 'Enough is enough—now you stop! Why do you go on playing the same note on your veena continuously for hours together? I have seen many people playing but they never do this. They change, they change notes, they move their hands. You go on playing on the same spot!'

Nasruddin said, 'Stop! You don't know, I have been playing for twenty years. The others have to move their hands because they have not yet found the right spot. I have found it, so why bother? I go on playing the same note.'

That is the note of the monks, the priests, the religious people. They are so sad, so serious, so sombre and solemn—dead graves, no music of life arises out of them. They have killed religion everywhere. They have captured all the temples and all the churches.

And temples are meant to be places of celebration. Temples are meant to be places of thanksgiving. Temples are meant to be places where one learns how to love and how to live, and how to pray and how to be blissful. They have turned all those places into very serious, deathlike places. They are more like cemeteries than temples. And in those temples only a dead god is worshipped.

God is alive, near, in the trees, in the clouds, in the birds chirping! God *is* life, and life depends on duality. Of course it is not only duality, it is a deep harmony between the two, between the many. It is one manifesting as many.

Don't try to kill the ego; otherwise you will suppress it, and you will miss the whole point of being alive here. You will miss the whole opportunity.

Then what to do? Just change the gestalt. Don't be

identified with the part—because you are also the whole. And don't be identified with the whole—because you are also the part.

To cut it short: Don't be identified at all.

You are both and neither, and that is transcendence. Then suddenly you are absent, and everything is present. Nothing is lost. But when you lose identification the feeling of 'I' is lost. You remain, you remain more than ever, you are more than ever, your being is infinitely rich. Without identification, the I disappears. But the I is getting identified either with the part—that is the I of the worldly man—or getting identified with the whole; that is the I of the so-called religious man.

Real, authentic religion is born when you are not identified at all. You move in the part and you move in the whole also. You are both: part in the whole, whole in the part, a harmony in discord, a continuous marriage and a continuous divorce, a continuum of coming together and falling apart. Then there is flow, then there is movement— and then there is grace.

Now this small anecdote.

Shibli went to visit another great sage, Junnaid.

This must have happened before Shibli became an enlightened man himself. Junnaid was already a perfect master, but Shibli was still on the path, still moving towards the perfect illumination of being. He was not a beginner, that's right, he was already an adept. But the journey had not ended yet—far advanced on the path, but the journey not yet complete.

Shibli went to visit another great sage, Junnaid.

The wife of Junnaid was about to conceal herself modestly behind a screen.

As is the custom with Mohammedans, the wife tried to conceal herself behind a screen as she should do for ordinary mortals.

Junnaid said: 'Stay where you are—Shibli is absent.'

There is no need to hide yourself, because nobody has come. When I say nobody has come, I mean two things. One, *nobody* has come, he who is a nobody; and second, nobody has come—Shibli has come but there is nobody like Shibli in him.

'Stay where you are—Shibli is absent.'

Nothing has happened, as if Junnaid is sitting with his wife and nobody has entered. What do you do when a breeze enters the room and passes by? You don't hide behind a screen. Or if a sun ray penetrates, you don't hide. 'No need to hide,' said Junnaid. 'Shibli is coming, but he is deeply absent inside.'

At that moment when Shibli entered, he was not identified with himself; a nonidentifiable being without any gestalt coming in like a breeze comes in—unobtrusively. Not even giving a feeling: What is happening? As if a drunk man comes in, drifts in, rather, because there is nobody who is coming in. It may be better to say, Shibli *drifted* into the room of Junnaid. The wife started hiding herself.

Said Junnaid: *'Stay where you are—Shibli is absent.'* At

that moment Shibli began to weep.

The identification entered immediately. A gestalt formed; he is no more the same. Just this being said, that Shibli is absent, must have brought the ego back. So much appreciation from the mouth of a great sage like Junnaid. Even a look from Junnaid would have gratified you tremendously. And a man like Junnaid said, 'Stay—Shibli is absent.'

This is the highest appreciation that can be given for people who are on the path. This is the greatest achievement—when a man is absent. Nothing more is there then, because when you are absent, god is present. In fact Junnaid said, 'Don't be worried. Shibli is not coming, god is entering.' It is the same. To say that Shibli is absent is to say that god is present. And where can you hide from god? And what is the need to hide from him?—because god is nothing but your purest being.

Immediately the gestalt came in.

At that moment Shibli began to weep.

Why did he begin to weep? Immediately, when he was appreciated by Junnaid, the ego came back. Immediately he felt: Yes, I am absent—and the I was there. god disappeared.

He was moving dazed, filled with the grace of the divine. An aura was surrounding him—not *his* aura, but the aura of the very centre of existence. He was filled with unknown bliss. He was like a flower, with a divine fragrance. Suddenly, in a single moment, or even in a particle of a single moment, in a split second, a gestalt formed.

The gestalt takes no time to form. Just a look and the gestalt forms. It is constantly being created and being destroyed. That is the only thing you can create and destroy, you can do nothing else. It is just like waves coming high and falling down.

At the peak was Shibli, at the peak of absence. The moment he heard Junnaid saying, 'Shibli is absent,' and, 'Shibli has not come, nobody has entered. It is god, look. Where are you hiding?'—hearing this, the ego entered, jumped back in. A gestalt formed: 'So I have achieved? So I have entered? So Junnaid has certified, recognized me?' Everything is lost.

Junnaid played a trick. In fact, the wife was not the concern. He tried a trick on Shibli and helped him to see what was happening to him.

From the peak Shibli has fallen into the abyss. Just a second before he was the divine; now he is just a worm on the earth, an ordinary mortal, fallen from immortality. Just a moment before he was in the garden of Eden, and just a moment afterwards he is thrown out, expelled. The peak has gone far away. Even to dream about it will be difficult now.

The valley and the darkness...the fall. This is the fall all religions talk about. It is not something that happened in the past. It happens to every individual and it happens many times. The fall is not something that happened to Adam and Eve. It happens to every Adam and every Eve. And the snake in the parable is nothing but the ego, that rises, persuades you. Why has the symbol of a snake been chosen?—because a snake seems to be the most cunning animal in the world, very clever and cunning. Ego IS cunning and clever. The snake persuaded Eve to eat the forbidden fruit. This is not something which happened in the past, somewhere one day, and then the doors of the garden of Eden were closed. No, it happens to every man. Whenever you are at a peak, you are again in the garden—

and immediately, if the ego arises, you have fallen back.

It happened in that moment to Shibli. He was floating in a different world; altogether different was the quality of his being, a different dimension. He was not part of this world; he was floating high like clouds, and suddenly he has fallen. A cloud has fallen into the dust—a sudden fall. The ego has arisen.

Junnaid did well. And he has not even uttered a single word to Shibli—he was talking to his wife—but he created a situation. This is how Sufis work. They create situations very deliberately.

At that moment Shibli began to weep.

Seeing that he had fallen he began to weep. Adam must have wept, wept bitterly, when he was being expelled from the garden of Eden. What else could he have done? Tears must have been flowing down...his whole heart in a turmoil.

It is the greatest misery that happens—when one comes out of bliss into the darker realms of suffering. Up to now he was innocent. Now, suddenly, all innocence is lost. The child has suddenly become old. In a single moment the flower of innocence is dead.

Shibli began to weep.

Why is he weeping? He is weeping for his own fall. He became aware of what Junnaid had done: not even uttering a single word to him, he had penetrated him so deeply. He provoked his ego. Shibli started weeping. Again he is present and god is missed. No more is he a child, no more in ecstasy. The samadhi has disappeared.

Junnaid said to his wife: 'You must now be absent, for Shibli has returned.'

Don't come out. Now there comes an ordinary man, just an ordinary man, filled with lust and greed and sex, filled with anger, jealousy, ego. Here comes an ordinary mortal. Now you hide yourself, don't come out.

You are both; that's why this can happen. You are both the peak and the valley; that's why this can happen. You are the expelled Adam, and the father who expelled him. You are both; that's why it can happen. Otherwise, how is it possible to come from the peak to the valley so suddenly and so immediately in a single moment? How is it possible if you are not both?

Both these extremes are yours: the devil and the divine. You will weep when you get identified with the devil, because you cannot be blissful with the devil. With the part you will weep. With the whole, if you get identified, you may feel happier, but that identification also cannot last forever—a Junnaid can bring it immediately back. A man who knows the art can throw you back. No, don't get identified.

Where did Shibli miss? What was the point of his misfortune? He was getting identified with the idea of his liberation, freedom, enlightenment. He had forgotten completely that the ego existed; it had just moved into the background, but it was there. And you can be a victim again. Just a slight provocation and the gestalt will change: the figure will become the background and the background will become the figure. A small change, just a slight change. This man Junnaid must have been the greatest gestalt psychologist.

I have been doing it every day. Just a slight device and

you are suffering no more; you are flowing high, moving in the skies, no gravitation. You have become weightless, you are not walking on the earth. Just another sentence, and you fall—and you fall so fast, as if no time is needed, and you are back in hell.

You have been moving between heaven and hell continuously. And wherever you are you get identified, that is the problem. You have suffered. You have seen the downs, the blues, but you get identified; you say, 'I am suffering.' You become one with the valley and the darkness.

And then, someday suddenly, a woman laughs at you, smiles, and you are high and the doors of heaven are open. Again you get identified. You are in love, not walking on the earth. In fact not walking, flying—no gravitation exists for you. You have completely forgotten the valley, the darkness, that existed just a minute before. It has moved into the background—the gestalt changed. And the woman is not laughing now. She has turned her face away. She is looking at somebody else. And the doors of the garden are closed, you are expelled, weeping bitterly, weeping and crying. The valley, the darkness—you are again identified with it.

Pain comes, pleasure comes—but you go on missing the thing. You should not get identified, you should remain transcendental.

In the valley, yes, but you are not the valley. At the peak, yes, but you are not the peak. The peak is the situation around you. You are in it, but not of it. In the world? Okay, move in the world—but you are in the world, the world is not in you. Go to the Himalayas—nothing wrong with it—but you are in the Himalayas, the Himalayas are not in you. Remain transcendental. Pain and pleasure, suffering and bliss, day and night, summer and winter—remain unidentified.

Disidentification, remaining unidentified, is the way of transcendence. Then you remain always far away: in, and yet away. Then life becomes a beautiful game. Hindus call it *leela*, a game, a play.

Then you neither suffer nor do you become blissful. You simply move through all the shades and nuances—and millions are the shades and millions are the nuances. God has taken thousands of names and thousands of forms. Everywhere is his mark. If you are transcendental, even in the valley you are in him. Then you never lose contact with him, because god means: that which transcends duality yet lives in it, yet surrounds it, yet enjoys it. God is the greatest paradox, the mystery.

Once you understand the art of nonidentification, you have learned all that Sufis can teach you. Gurdjieff introduced Sufi essentials into the West. He was the man who brought to the West the secrets of the Sufis. His whole teaching depends on one word, and that is nonidentification. Don't get identified with anything because consciousness is always transcendental. It cannot be reduced to anything.

Seasons come and go, consciousness remains. Childhood comes and goes, youth comes and goes, health and disease; consciousness remains. That which remains always is god. That which passes is the world. That which comes and goes is not you.

You are the witness, to whom things happen but who remains a witness. Witnessing is the art of nonidentification, and nonidentification is all. Nonidentification is all there is to meditation. It is the whole meditation.

It is said that this situation created by Junnaid helped Shibli, and after a few days, just after a few days, he himself became enlightened.

Someone asked Shibli when he became enlightened, 'Who have been your teachers?'

He counted many. A dog—because the dog was thirsty and tried to jump into the river and drink to his heart's desire, but as he looked into the river he would see another dog and he was afraid. But the thirst was too much. Finally he overcame his fear and jumped into the river—and the reflection disappeared. There was no other dog, it was just a reflection. The river was just mirroring himself.

And Shibli said, 'That dog was my first teacher...because there is nobody else—only I am, and everybody else is just mirroring my face, and I am unnecessarily afraid. Once I understood the art of jumping into the river, I jumped, and reflections disappeared and only the river was there—the river of god, the river of existence. And since then I have never been thirsty. I live in the river.'

He counted many. He said, 'The second master was a thief, because I was lost in a town one night, and all the doors of all the serais were closed and I was at a loss to find some shelter for the night. Then I found a thief. In a dark street, he was trying to enter a house, and I asked him: 'Where can I stay for the night? I am tired, and I am hungry.' He said, 'You can stay at my house, but I must be frank with you because you look like a saint—I don't know whether you are or not because I never believe in appearances—but for me it will be bad if I don't tell you that I am a thief. And I am *really* a thief. You may not be a real sage but I am a real thief. So if you are ready to be a guest in a thief's house, you are welcome. Come!"

Shibli hesitated a little—to go to a thief's house and stay there, and people would come to know and what would happen to his respectability? He was an honoured man....

The thief stopped immediately and he said, 'You are afraid, and a real sage is never afraid. Why are you afraid? Are you afraid that the thief can convert you to an atheist? I am not afraid of *you*. I don't care—you cannot change me a little bit. I am a perfect thief, but you don't look a perfect sage.'

And Shibli said, 'He was my second teacher. I stayed in his home for one month. He was really a lovely person, and very true and authentic. Every night he would go out and by the morning he would return. I would open the door and I would ask, 'Have you been successful?' And he would say, 'Not today. But tomorrow....' He was always happy—and for one month he was never successful. Every night he would go out and every morning he would come back empty-handed. But he was always laughing and happy, and he was never miserable. He could live with failure, and he could hope. His hope was great.'

And Shibli said, 'When I was seeking god, many times the moment came to me when it seemed to be absolutely futile, the whole search nonsense. Many times I was just on the brink of stopping the whole nonsense and going to the world to enjoy and indulge a bit while life lasts. I had been doing everything that I had been told to do and there seemed to be no god appearing, not a sign. I had not even heard a footfall, not even seen a footprint. The whole thing seemed to be imaginary, a great deception. But immediately, whenever I was ready to drop the search, I would see that thief in my vision, standing at the door and saying, 'Tomorrow...' and I would again hope, and I would say, 'Okay, one day more.' That is how one day I attained. I am very much obliged to that thief. He was my second teacher.'

And he said, 'My last teacher was the wife of Junnaid—because she tried to hide behind a screen. That became a situation. And Junnaid brought me down from my high flight to the earth, I crashed to the earth, shattered. Junnaid was cruel—but he helped. And the wife was just helping the device. When I started crying, she started laughing behind the screen. I was shattered, completely shattered and destroyed. But that became the destruction of my identification. Since then I have been in the valleys, and I have been to the peaks, but I remain aloof. I can still hear—whenever I go to the peak I can still hear the laughter of Junnaid's wife behind the screen. She is still laughing. I never get identified.' Soon after this situation Shibli became an enlightened man.

What is enlightenment? It is to live in transcendence.

Enough for today.

Ten

Just a Small Coin

*Uwais Al-Qarni was offered some money. He said:
'I do not need it as I already have a coin.'
The other said: 'How long will that last you?—it
is nothing.'
Uwais answered: 'Guarantee me that I shall live
longer than this sum will suffice me and I will
accept your gift.'*

LIFE IS ALWAYS in the now. There is no other moment to it. Only one moment exists—this moment—all else is just a projection of the mind. Only today is, and only today remains. Tomorrow never comes, it cannot come because it doesn't belong to reality. Only today comes, goes on coming, because today belongs to reality.

Tomorrow is your dream. And you need a dream because you are not rooted in reality. This has to be understood. Why are dreams needed? When reality is available, why do you dream?

A man fasts. The whole day the body suffers; the hunger is there. He suppresses the hunger because he is on some religious fast, a religious ritual. To satisfy the ego he makes the body hungry—so that the ego can feel that he is religious, something special, not an ordinary man, a saint, a sage, not an ordinary sinner.

To feed the ego you make the body hungry. You starve the body. Ego is a dream—the body is the reality. The whole day you have been fasting; in the night you cannot sleep because the body goes on asking for food. It is a need, it is a necessity. You feel restless, you turn from one side to another, you cannot go to sleep. Food is a need, but rest also is a need. So the mind creates a dream: You are an honoured guest in a great feast given by the king; you are eating delicious food, you go on eating.... Of course the body doesn't get nourishment, but there is a false notion that you have eaten well; now you can go to sleep. In the morning you will be hungry, more than ever, but at least the dream helped you to rest and relax. One need, the need for food, could not be fulfilled, but another need, the need for rest, could be fulfilled through the dream.

If you are tense you will need dreams, because they help you to relax. If you are not *here*, you will need a dream of being *there*, because you have to be somewhere. If you cannot be here then you will feel suspended in the sky, uprooted, unanchored, just hanging in the middle. That will give you a very restless, uncomfortable feeling. So...a dream: 'I may not be here, but I am going to be there.' The dream helps you to rest and relax.

If you cannot be now, then you create a future. The future is needed. The future gives you a consoling sleep, it relaxes you. Millions of things are there which you cannot fulfil right now, and if there is no future you will be too much burdened by unfulfilled desires. A future is needed so you can at least say to yourself: 'If things are not as they should be, there is tomorrow. Don't get panicky, things will be better tomorrow.' You can hope, because there is time.

Hope needs space, desire needs space, ambition needs space to move.

Look at the trees—they don't dream. They don't need to, they are already here, in the now—fulfilled, flowering. Listen to the birds—they are singing *now*, they are not preparing to sing tomorrow. Except man, nobody is preparing for tomorrow. This day is so beautiful, who bothers for tomorrow?

If this day is ugly and it is inconvenient to live with it, a beautiful dream of the future is needed as a substitute for reality. Otherwise you will feel so much anguish—intolerable. You will not be able to live! The more desire you have, the more future you need, the more ambitions the more future you need. For needs, this moment is more than enough. Today is enough. Jesus said to his disciples, 'Look at the lilies. Look in the field—the flowers are flowering, and they are so beautiful that even Solomon in all his grandeur was not so beautiful.'

Solomon is the greatest king in the mythology of Jews— the richest man ever on earth, and the wisest man also. The wisest, the richest, the greatest emperor in the world was not so beautiful as these ordinary lilies in the field. 'Look!' said Jesus to his disciples. 'These lilies must be carrying a secret within their hearts.' What is the secret? The secret is, lilies are here and now. Solomon may have been very very wise but he was not here and now.

All beauty is here, and all life is now.

Tomorrow is death, tomorrow is no life. But why do we live in the tomorrow? It looks absurd: How can you live in the tomorrow?—but you live there. You never live here; that's why you look so dead. How can one live in the tomorrow? Jesus said to his disciples, 'Take care of this moment. Live today, and tomorrow will take care of itself. Don't worry for the morrow because the moment you are losing in worrying about tomorrow is the real moment. And tomorrow is never going to be there.'

For dreams you are losing life. Needs don't need them, but desires need them. For example, if you are hungry, you can eat; if you are thirsty, you can drink. There is not much trouble about it. There would have been no trouble and there would have been nothing like poverty in the world if man remained true to his needs. Then everybody has more than enough. The earth has plenty. The sky is not poor, the rivers are rich, the oceans vast—life has tremendous treasures. Not a single bird sleeps without food, not a single tree remains thirsty. Everything is more than is needed. Life is affluent, very luxuriant—if you stick to the needs. But if you start desiring, then life becomes poor.

If you are hungry you can eat and feel satiated—and there is nothing like satiated hunger. It is a deep prayer, a gratefulness. I tell you, not by fasting will you become religious, but when hunger is satisfied. In that moment of satisfaction a gratefulness, a gratitude arises, a prayer. You feel fulfilled. You can thank god. Never by fasting do you become religious. How can you become religious by destroying your body and being violent towards it? That is the way of the murderer, the torturer, the sadist, the masochist, the somehow perverted.

When you have eaten well, eaten rightly and the food suits you, in that moment a prayer arises, not only from your mind but from your body also. Satiety is a prayer. You were thirsty and you have drunk to the full. Now suddenly nothing is needed. You are absolutely perfect in that moment. You are a god, a fulfilled god. No thirst...what else is lacking?

If you stick to the needs—and this is my message, that a religious man sticks to his needs. He is never against needs and never for desires. Desires are false needs. For example, if you are hungry you can eat right now, but if you are desiring a Rolls Royce, how can you get it right now? If you are ambitious for a big palace—Rome is not built in one day, a big palace will need time. You will have to exploit money. You will not only have to exploit others you will have to exploit your own needs also, because you will have to accumulate money. You will sleep hungry, because tomorrow—the palace, and when the palace is ready, then you are going to eat. How can you eat without a palace? Tomorrow comes the Rolls Royce, and there is nothing wrong in being a little hungry for a few days, starving your needs; otherwise how are you going to have a Rolls Royce?

A Rolls Royce is neither a thirst nor a hunger, it is simply a foolish desire. When it is not there you will be waiting for it and destroying your life, and when it comes you will feel nothing has come. And you waited so long, and you killed yourself so much. The Rolls Royce is there, but you are already dead. There is no real need for it; that's why it can never satisfy. Satisfaction comes out of real dissatisfaction.

Contentment comes out of real hunger, real thirst. You were dying, you could not do without it; only then contentment happens. Desires need the future; they cannot be fulfilled right now. If you want to be the president of a country, how can you be the president right now? You will have to pass long ladders of ambition, much time will be needed. By the time you reach, if death has not reached before, you will be already dead. People become presidents when they are already senile, past their sixties, becoming seventy, just ready for the grave. Then they enter the presidential house.

And the whole life wasted,—for nothing. Even if your picture is in all the newspapers, what does it matter? How does it satisfy? Birds are happy without newspapers, trees are happy without the radio and the television. If trees are happy and birds are happy, and they don't bother a bit for the tomorrow, why can't man be happy right now?

The whole of religion, real religion, is the message to drop desires and to fulfill needs. And needs are simple and beautiful. Thirst is beautiful—it comes out of nature—and then being satisfied is also beautiful. It gives a balance, a subtle tranquillity. A silence happens to your whole existence. You are at rest; no dream is needed.

A man who lives true to his needs will live here and now; he has no tomorrow. But look, the bigger the need for desires, the bigger the ambition, the bigger the future you will need. But worldly people don't really need a big future because their desires, howsoever big, can be fulfilled in one lifetime. If you need a Rolls Royce, you feel you need it, okay—you put your life at stake and you will get a Rolls Royce. If you want to be a president you can, because people just as stupid as you have already become presidents. You are not lacking anything. You can also become one, there is not much of a problem about it; you need to go a little madly after it, that's all. One only has to go madly after something, and he will attain. Others have attained, you can attain.

If you have not attained, that means only that you are not so stupid and so mad. A desire comes but it is a vagrant desire. You are not ready to stake your whole life for it. A dream comes, but it is a very superficial dream. If somebody makes you a president you will become one, but you are not going to stake your whole life for it.

One day I saw Mulla Nasruddin on the road, smoking. I

was surprised. I asked him, 'Nasruddin, just the other day you told me that you have stopped smoking.'

He said, 'Yes, I have stopped purchasing cigarettes, but if somebody offers me one, it's okay.' He said, 'One has to go by and by, in steps. I have stopped purchasing—that is my first step towards no smoking—but if somebody offers me one, it's okay. Later on I am going to drop that also.'

If you have not become a president of a country or a prime minister, you have just a superficial dream about it, that's all. If you become obsessed by it, nobody can prevent you. You have to be mad. An ambitious man is mad, crazy!—obsessed by one idea. Unless that idea is fulfilled he himself is not going to rest, and he is not going to allow anybody else to rest.

Worldly desires can be fulfilled in a mere lifetime, but what about *moksha*? What about god? What about nirvana, enlightenment? A mere one life seems to be not enough. There are so many things to do, and for nirvana there seems to be no time.

If you live for seventy years…. Life has an inner pattern, it is good to understand it. Every seven years, physiologists say, the body and mind go through a crisis and a change. Every seven years all the cells of the body change, are completely renewed. In fact, if you live seventy years, the average limit, your body dies ten times. Each seventh year everything changes. It is just like changing seasons. In seventy years the circle is complete. The line that moves from birth comes to death. The circle is complete in seventy years. It has ten divisions.

In fact, man's life should not be divided into childhood, youth, old age—that is not very scientific, because every seven years a new age, a new step is taken.

For the first seven years a child is self-centred, as if he is the centre of the whole world. The whole family moves around him. Whatsoever are his needs they are to be fulfilled immediately, otherwise he will go into a tantrum: anger, rage…. He lives like an emperor, a real emperor. The mother, the father—all are servants, and the whole family just exists for him. And of course he thinks the same is true for the wider world. The moon rises for him, the sun rises for him, the seasons change for him. A child for seven years remains absolutely egoistic, self-centred. If you ask psychologists they will say a child for seven years remains masturbatory, satisfied with himself. He does not need anything, anybody. He feels complete.

After seven years—a breakthrough. The child is no more self-centred; he becomes eccentric, literally. Eccentric—the word means going out of the centre. He moves towards others. The other becomes the important phenomenon—friends, gangs…. Now he is not so much interested in himself; he is interested in the other, the bigger world. He enters into an adventure to know who is this 'other.' Inquiry starts.

After the seventh year, the child becomes a great questioner. He questions everything. He becomes a great skeptic, because inquiry is there. He asks millions of questions. He bores the parents to death, he becomes a nuisance. He is interested in the other, and everything of the world is his interest. Why are the trees green? Why did god create the world? Why is this so? He starts becoming more and more philosophic; inquiry, skepticism—he insists on going into things.

He kills a butterfly to see what is inside, destroys a toy just to see how it works, throws a clock just to look into it, how it goes on ticking and chiming—what is the matter inside? He becomes interested in the other, but the other remains of the same sex. He is not interested in girls. If other boys are interested in girls he will think they are sissy. Girls are not interested in boys. If some girl is interested in boys and plays with them, she is a tomboy, not normal, average; something is wrong. This second stage psychoanalysts and psychologists will say is homosexual.

After the fourteenth year a third door opens. He is no more interested in boys, girls are no more interested in girls. They are polite, but not interested. That's why any friendship that happens between the seventh year and the fourteenth is the deepest, because the mind is homosexual, and no more in life will such friendship happen again. Those friends remain friends forever; it was such a deep tie. You will become friendly with people but that will remain acquaintance, not that deep phenomenon that happened between the seventh and the fourteenth year.

But after the fourteenth year a boy is not interested in boys. If everything goes normal, if he is not stuck somewhere, he will be interested in girls. Now he is becoming heterosexual—not only interested in the others, but really *the other*, because when a boy is interested in boys, the boy may be other but he is still a boy just like himself, not exactly the other. When a boy becomes interested in girls, now he is really interested in the opposite, the real other. When a girl becomes interested in a boy, now the world enters.

The fourteenth year is a great revolutionary year. Sex becomes mature, one starts thinking in terms of sex, sex fantasies become prominent in the dreams. The boy becomes a great Don Juan, starts courting. Poetry arises, romance. He is entering into the world.

By the twenty-first year—if everything goes normally, and

a child is not forced by the society to do something which is not natural—by the twenty-first year a child becomes interested more in ambition than in love. He wants a Rolls Royce, a great palace. He wants to be a success, a Rockefeller, a prime minister. Ambitions become prominent; desiring for the future, being a success. How to succeed, how to compete, how to move in the struggle is his whole concern.

Now he is not only entering the world of nature, he is entering the world of humanity, the marketplace. Now he is entering the world of madness. Now the market becomes the most prominent thing. His whole being goes towards the market: money, power, prestige.

If everything goes right—as it never goes, I am talking of the absolutely natural phenomenon—by the twenty-eighth year a man is not in any way trying to enter into an adventurous life. From twenty-one to twenty-eight one lives in adventure; by the twenty-eighth year one becomes more alert that all desires cannot be fulfilled. There is more understanding that many desires are impossible. If you are a fool, you can go after them. But people who are intelligent, by the twenty-eighth year enter another door. They become more interested in security and comfort, less in adventure and ambition. They start settling. The twenty-eighth year is the end of hippiedom.

At twenty-eight hippies become squares, revolutionaries are no more revolutionaries; they start settling, they seek a comfortable life, a little bank balance. They don't want to be Rockefellers; finished, that urge is no more there. They want a small house, but established, a cozy place to live in, security—so at least this much they can always have; a little bank balance. They go to the insurance company nearabout the age of twenty-eight. They start settling. Now the vagabond is no more the vagabond. He purchases a house, starts living...he becomes civilized. The word civilization comes from the word *civis*, citizen. Now he becomes part of a town, a city, an establishment. He is no more a vagabond, not a wanderer. Now he is not going to Kathmandu and Goa. He is not going anywhere—finished, travelled enough, known enough; now he wants to settle and rest a little.

By the thirty-fifth year life energy reaches its omega point. The circle is half complete and energies start declining. Now the man is not only interested in security and comfort, he becomes a Tory, orthodox. He becomes not only not interested in revolution, he becomes an antirevolutionary. Now he is against all change. He is a conformist. He is against all revolutions; he wants the status quo because now he has settled, and if anything changes the whole thing will unsettle. Now he is talking against hippies, against rebels; now he has become really a part of the establishment.

And this is natural. Unless something goes wrong a man is not going to remain a hippie forever. That was a phase, good to pass through, but bad to be stuck in. That means you remain stuck at a certain stage. It was good to be homosexual between seven and fourteen, but if one remains homosexual for his whole life that means he has not grown up, he is not adult. A woman has to be contacted, that is part of life. The other sex has to become important because only then will you be able to know the harmony of the opposites, the conflict, the misery, and the ecstasy: agony and ecstasy both. That is a training, a necessary training.

By the thirty-fifth year one has to become part of the conventional world. One starts believing in tradition, in the past, in the Vedas, the Koran, the Bible. One is absolutely against change because every change means your own life will be disturbed; now you have much to lose. You cannot be for revolution—you want to protect.... One is for the law and the courts and the government. One is no more an anarchist; one is all for the government, rules, regulations, discipline.

By the forty-second year all sorts of physical and mental illnesses erupt, because now life is declining. Energy is moving towards death.

As in the beginning energies were coming up and you were becoming more and more vital, energetic, you were becoming more and more strong—now just the opposite happens, you become weaker every day.

But your habits persist. You have been eating enough up to the age of thirty-five; now you continue your habit. You will start gathering fat. Now that much food is not needed. It was needed but now it is not needed because life is moving towards death, it does not need that much food. If you go on filling your belly as you were doing before, then all sorts of illnesses will happen: high blood pressure, heart attack, insomnia, ulcers—they all happen near about forty-two. Forty-two is one of the most dangerous points. Hair starts falling out, becoming gray. Life is turning into death.

And near the age of forty-two religion starts becoming important for the first time. You may have dabbled a little here and there in religion before, but now religion starts becoming for the first time important—because religion is deeply concerned with death. Now death is approaching and the first desire for religion arises.

Carl Gustav Jung has written that in his whole life he has been observing that people who come to him at the age of forty or thereabout are always in need of religion. If they go mad, neurotic, psychotic, they cannot be helped unless they become deeply rooted in religion. They need religion; their basic need is religion. And if the society is secular and you have never been taught religion, the greatest difficulty comes neara the age of forty-two, because the society does not give you any avenue, any door, any dimension.

The society was good when you were fourteen, because the society gives enough of sex—the whole society is sexual; sex seems to be the only commodity hidden in every commodity. If you want to sell a ten-ton truck then too you have to use a naked woman, or toothpaste—then too. Truck or toothpaste, it makes no difference: a naked woman is always smiling there behind. Really the *woman* is sold. The truck is not sold, the toothpaste is not sold; the woman is sold. And because the woman comes, the smile of the woman comes with the toothpaste, you have to purchase the toothpaste also. Everywhere sex is sold.

So this society, a secular society, is good for young people. But they are not going to remain young forever. When they become forty-two suddenly the society leaves them in limbo. They don't know what to do now. They go neurotic, because they don't know, they have never been trained, no discipline has been given them to face death. The society has made them ready for life, but nobody has taught them to become ready for death. They need as much education for death as they need education for life.

If I was allowed my way then I would divide universities into two parts: one for young people, another part for old people. Young people would come to learn the art of life— sex, ambition, struggle. Then when they became old and they reached the forty-two mark, they would again come back to the university to learn about death, god, meditation—because now the old universities wouldn't be of any help to them.

They would again need a new training, a new discipline, so that they can become anchored with the new phase that is happening to them.

This society leaves them in limbo; that's why in the West there is so much mental illness. It is not so much in the East. Why?—because the East still gives a little training in religion. It has not disappeared completely; howsoever false, pseudo, it is still there, it exists, just by the corner. No more in the marketplace, no more in the thick of life, just by the side, but there is a temple. Out of the way of life, but still it is there. You have to walk a few steps and you can go there. It still exists.

In the West religion is no more, part of life. Neara about the age of forty-two, every Westerner is going through psychic problems. Thousands of types of neuroses happen—and ulcers. Ulcers are the footprints of ambition. An ambitious man is bound to have ulcers in the stomach: ambition bites, it eats itself. An ulcer is nothing but eating yourself. You are so tense that you have started eating your own stomach lining. You are so tense, your stomach is so tense, it never relaxes. Whenever the mind is tense the stomach is tense. Ulcers are the footprints of ambition. If you have ulcers, that shows you are a very successful man.

If you have no ulcers you are a poor man: your life has been a failure, you failed utterly. If you have your first heart attack atabout forty-two you are a great success: you must be at least a cabinet minister, or a rich industrialist, or a famous actor; otherwise, how will you explain the heart attack? A heart attack is the definition of success. All successful people will have heart attacks. They have to.

The whole system is burdened with toxic elements: ambition, desire, future, tomorrow—which is never there.

You lived in dreams. Now your system cannot tolerate it anymore. And you remain so tense for the future that tension has become your very style of life. Now it is a deep-rooted habit.

At forty-two, again a breakthrough comes. One starts thinking about religion, the other world. Then life seems to be very much. Little time is left. How can you achieve God, nirvana, enlightenment? Hence the theory of reincarnation: don't be afraid, again you will be born, again and again, and the wheel of life will go on moving and moving. Don't be afraid: there is enough time, there is enough eternity left—you can attain.

That's why in India three religions were born—Jainism, Buddhism and Hinduism—and they don't agree on any other point except reincarnation. They don't agree on any other point. Even about such an important theory as god there is not an agreement. Jainas say there is no god, Buddhists say there is no god…. Even about a more important theory than god, the theory of the soul, *atman*—Buddhists say there is no atman, no soul. Such divergent theories!—not even agreeing on the basic foundations: God, self…. But they all three agree on the theory of reincarnation. There must be something to it.

They all need time, because to attain *Brahman*—Hindus call it Brahman—much time is needed. It is such a great ambition, and at the age of forty-two you become interested. Only twenty-eight years are left.

And this is just the beginning of the interest. In fact, at the age of forty-two, you become again a child in the world of religion. And only twenty-eight years are left. Time seems too short, not enough at all to attain such great heights—Brahman, Hindus call it. Jainas call it moksha, absolute freedom from all past karmas. But thousands and millions of lives have been there in the past; within twenty-eight years how are you going to cope? How will you undo the whole past? Such a vast past is there—bad and good karmas. How are you going to clean your sins completely within twenty-eight years? It seems unjust. God is demanding too much, it is not possible. You will feel frustrated if only twenty-eight years are given to you.

And Buddhists, who don't believe in god, don't believe in the soul—they also believe in reincarnation, nirvana, the final emptiness, the total emptiness. When you have remained filled with so much rubbish for so many lives, how are you going to unburden within twenty-eight years? It is too much, seems an impossible task. They all agree on one thing, that more future is needed, more time is needed.

Whenever you have ambition time is needed. And to me a religious person is one who does not need time. He is liberated here and now, he achieves to the Brahman here and now, he is *mukta*, liberated, enlightened here and now. A religious man does not need time at all because religion happens in a timeless moment. It happens now, it always happens now. It has never happened otherwise, in no other way has it ever happened.

At the age of forty-two the first urge arises, vague, not clear, confused. You are not even aware of what is happening, but you start looking at the temple with keen interest. Sometimes, by the way, as a casual visitor, you come to the church also. Sometimes, having time, not doing anything, you start looking in the Bible which has always been gathering dust on the table. Vague, not exactly clear, just like the small child who is vague about sex starts playing with his own sex organ, not knowing what he is doing. A vague urge....

Sometimes one sits alone silently, suddenly feels peaceful, not knowing what he is doing. Sometimes one starts a mantra heard in childhood. The old grandmother used to do it; feeling tense, one starts repeating it. One starts seeking, searching for a guru, somebody to guide you. One takes initiation, starts learning a mantra, repeats it sometimes, then again forgets for a few days, again repeats.... A vague search, groping....

By the forty-ninth year the search becomes clear; seven years it takes for the search to become clear. Now a determination arises. You are no more interested in the others, particularly if everything has gone right—and I have to repeat this again and again because it never goes right—at the age of forty-nine one becomes uninterested in women. A woman becomes uninterested in man—the menopause, the forty-ninth year.... The man doesn't feel like being sexual. The whole thing looks a little juvenile, the whole thing looks a little immature.

But the society can force.... In the East they have been against sex and they have suppressed sex. When the boy is fourteen they are suppressing sex, and they want to believe that the boy is still a child: he doesn't think about girls. Other boys maybe—these always belong to the neighborhood, never your boy; he is innocent, like a child, like an angel. And he *looks* very innocent, but that's not true: he fantasizes. The girl has entered his consciousness, has to enter—it is natural—and he has to hide it. He starts masturbating, and he has to hide it. He has wet dreams and he has to hide it.

In the East, a boy of fourteen becomes guilty. Something wrong is happening—only to him, because he cannot know that everybody everywhere is doing the same. And much is expected of him—that he should remain an angel, a virgin, not thinking about girls, not even dreaming about girls. But he has become interested—the society is suppressing.

In the West this suppression has disappeared, but another suppression has come—and this has to be understood, because this is my feeling, that society can never be non-suppressive. If it changes one suppression, immediately it starts another. Now the suppression is near the age of forty-nine in the West: people are forced to remain in sex, because the whole teaching says, 'What are you doing?—a man can be sexually potent up to the age of ninety!' Great authorities are saying it. And if you are not potent, and you are not interested, you start feeling guilty. At the age of forty-nine a man starts feeling guilty that he is not making as much love as he should.

And there are teachers who go on teaching: This is nonsense. You can make love, you can make love up to the age of ninety. Go on making love. And they say if you don't make love you will lose potency. If you continue, then your organs continue functioning. If you stop, then they will stop. And once you stop sex, life energy will drop down, you will die soon.

If the husband stops, the wife is after him: What are you doing? If the wife stops the husband is after her: This is against the psychologists, and this may create some perversion!

In the East we did one stupidity, and in the West also in the ancient days they did the same stupidity. It was against religion for a child of fourteen to become sexually potent— and he becomes so naturally. The child cannot do anything, it is beyond his control. What can he do? How can he do it? And all teaching about *brahmacharya* at the age of fourteen is stupid. You are suppressing. But the old authorities, traditions, gurus, *rishis*, old psychologists and religious people—they were all against, the whole authority was against. A child was suppressed. A guilt was created. Nature was not allowed.

Now just the opposite is happening at the other end. At the age of forty-nine psychologists are forcing people to continue to make love; otherwise you will lose life. And at the age of forty-nine...as at the age of fourteen sex naturally arises, so at the age of forty-nine it naturally subsides. It has to, because every circle has to be complete.

That's why in India we had decided that at the age of fifty man should start becoming a *vanprasth*, his eyes should move towards the forest, his back towards the marketplace. Vanprasth is a beautiful word; it means one who starts looking towards the Himalayas, towards the forest. Now his back is towards life and ambitions and desires and all that. Finished. He starts moving towards aloneness, towards being himself.

Before this, life was too much and he could not be alone; there were responsibilities to be fulfilled, children to be raised. Now they have become grown up. They are married—by the time you are forty-nine your children are getting married, settling. They are no more hippies, they must be reaching the age of twenty-eight. They will settle—now you can unsettle. Now you can move beyond the home—you can become homeless. At the age of forty-nine one should start looking towards the forest, moving inwards, becoming introvert, becoming more and more meditative and prayerful.

At the age of fifty-six, again a change comes, a revolution. Now it is not enough to look towards the Himalayas, one has to really travel, one has to go. Life is ending, death is coming nearer. At the age of forty-nine one becomes uninterested in the other sex. At the age of fifty-six, one should become uninterested in others, the society, the social formalities, the club—Rotary and Lions. At the age of fifty-six one should resign from all Rotaries, all Lions; it looks foolish now, childish. Go to some Rotary Club or Lions Club and see people, tip-top with their ties and everything. It looks juvenile, childish; what are they doing? Lions—the very name looks foolish. For a small child, good. Now they have for small children Cub clubs, and for women Lioness clubs. For cubs, perfectly right, but for lions and lionesses…? It shows that the minds are mediocre. They have no intelligence, nothing at all.

At the age of fifty-six, one should be so mature as to come out of all social entanglements. Finished! One lived enough, learned enough; now one gives thanks to everybody and comes out of it. Fifty-six is the time one should naturally become a sannyasin. One should take sannyas, one should renounce. It is natural—as you enter, so you should renounce. Life should have an entrance and it should also have an exit; otherwise it will be suffocating. You enter and you never come out and then you say you are suffocated, in agony.

There *is* an exit, and that is sannyas. You come out. You are not even interested in others by the age of fifty-six.

By the age of sixty-three you again become like a child, only interested in yourself. That is what meditation is—to be moving inwards, as if everything has fallen away. Only you exist. Again you have become a child—of course, very much enriched by life, very mature, understanding, with great intelligence. Now you again become innocent. You start moving inwards. Only seven years are left, and you have to prepare for death. You have to be ready to die. And what is the readiness to die?

To die celebrating is the readiness to die. To die happy, joyfully, to die willingly, welcomingly, is to be ready. God gave you an opportunity to learn, and be, and you learned. Now you would like to rest. Now you would like to go to the ultimate home.

It was a sojourn. You wandered in a strange land, you lived with strange people, you loved strangers, and you learned much. Now the time has come: the prince must return to his own kingdom.

Sixty-three is the time when one becomes completely enclosed in one's self. The whole energy moves in and in and in, turning in. You become a circle of energy, not moving anywhere. No reading, not much talking. More and more silent, more and more with one's self, remaining totally independent of all that is around you. The energy by and by subsides.

By the age of seventy, you are ready. And if you have followed this natural pattern, just before your death, nine months before your death, you will become aware of your death. As a child has to pass nine months in the mother's womb, the same circle is totally repeated, completely repeated, utterly repeated. By the time death comes, nine months before, you will become aware. Now you are entering the womb again. This womb is no more outside in the mother, this womb is inside you.

Indians call the innermost shrine of a temple the *garbha*, the womb. When you go to a temple the innermost part of the temple is called the womb. It is very symbolically called so, very consideredly; that is the womb one has to enter. In the last phase—nine months—one enters into oneself, one's own body becomes the womb. One moves to the innermost shrine where the flame has always been burning, where the light has always been, where the temple is, where the god has always been living.

This is the natural process. For this natural process no future is needed. You have to be living naturally *this* moment. The next moment will come out of it on its own accord—as a child grows and becomes a youth. There is no need to plan for it, one simply becomes; it is natural, it happens. As a river flows and comes to the ocean the same way, you flow, and you come to the final, the ocean. But one should remain natural, floating, and in the moment. Once you start thinking about the future and ambition and desire, you are missing this moment. And this moment missed will create perversion because you will always lack something; a gap will be there.

If a child has not lived his childhood well, then that unlived childhood will enter into his youth—because where will it go? It has to be lived. And when a child is at the age of four and dances and jumps and runs around, butterfly-catching, it is beautiful. But when a young man of twenty runs after butterflies he is crazy. Then you have to admit him to the hospital; he is a mental case. Nothing was wrong with it at the age of four; it was just natural, it was the thing to do. It was the *right* thing to do; if the child was not running after butterflies something was wrong, he had to be taken to the psychoanalyst.

Then it was okay; but when he is twenty and running after butterflies then you should suspect something has gone wrong, he has not grown up. The body has grown, the mind is lagging behind. It must be somewhere in his childhood—he was not allowed to live it completely. If he lives the childhood completely he will become a young man: beautiful, fresh, uncontaminated by the childhood. He will shed the childhood as a snake sheds its old skin. He will come out of it fresh. He will have the intelligence of a young man, and he won't look retarded.

Live youth completely. Don't listen to the Eastern and ancient authorities. Just drop them out of the way. If you meet them on the way, kill them immediately. Don't listen to them because they have killed youth, they are suppressive of youth. They are against sex, and if some society is against sex, sex will spread all over your life. It will become poison. Live it! Enjoy it!

Between the fourteenth and twenty-first years a boy is at his highest peak of sexuality. In fact, near the age of seventeen or eighteen he reaches the peak of sexuality. Never will he be so potent. And if those moments are missed he will never achieve the beautiful orgasm that could have been achieved near the age of seventeen or eighteen.

I am in a difficulty continuously, because the society forces you to remain celibate, at least up to the twenty-first year. That means the greatest possibility of achieving sex, learning sex, entering sex, will be missed. By the time you reach twenty-one, twenty-two, you are already old as far as sex is concerned! Near the age of seventeen you were at the peak—so potent, so powerful, that the orgasm, the sexual orgasm, would have spread to your very cells. Your whole body would have taken a bath of eternal bliss.

And when I say sex can become *samadhi*, I don't say it for people who are seventy, remember. I am saying it for people who are seventeen. About From Sex to Super-consciousness…old men come to me and they say, 'We have read your book but we never achieve anything like this.'

How can you? you have missed the time, and it cannot be replaced. And I am not responsible; your society is responsible, and you listened to it.

If between the ages of fourteen and twenty-one a child is allowed to have free sex, absolutely free sex, he will never bother about sex. He will be completely free. He will not look at the magazines *Playboy* and *Playgirl*. He will not hide nude, ugly, obscene pictures in the cupboard or in the Bible. He will not go out of his way to throw things at women. He will not become a bottom-pincher. These things are ugly, simply ugly, but you go on tolerating them and not feeling what is happening, why everybody is neurotic.

Once you find a chance to rub against a woman's body you never miss it. What ugliness!—rubbing against a body. Something has remained unfulfilled in you. And when an old man looks with lustful eyes, there is nothing like that; it is the most ugly thing in the world when an old man looks with lust in his eyes. His eyes should be innocent now, he must be finished by now. Not that sex is something ugly; remember, I am not saying sex is ugly. Sex is beautiful at its own time and season, and sex is ugly out of season, out of time. Sex is a disease when it is in a ninety-year-old man. That's why people say 'dirty old man.' It *is* dirty.

A young man is beautiful, sexual. He shows vitality, life. An old man, sexual, shows unlived life, an empty life, immature. He missed the opportunity and now he cannot do anything, but he goes on thinking, rambling in the mind about sex, fantasizing.

Remember, between the fourteenth and the twenty-first year a right society will allow absolute freedom for sex. And then society will become less sexual automatically. Beyond this time there will be no sex; the disease will not be there. Live it when the moment is ripe and forget it when the moment has gone. But that you can do only if you have lived; otherwise you cannot forget and you cannot forgive. You will cling, it will become a wound inside.

In the East, don't listen to the authorities, whatsoever

they say. Listen to nature. When nature says it is time to love, love. When nature says it is time to renounce, renounce. And don't listen to the foolish psychoanalysts and psychologists in the West. Howsoever refined instruments they have—Masters and Johnson and others—and however many vaginas they have been testing and examining, they don't know life.

In fact I suspect that these Masterses and Johnsons and Kinseys in the West, that they are voyeurs. They themselves are ill about sex; otherwise who bothers to watch one thousand vaginas with instruments—watching what is happening inside when a woman makes love? Who bothers? What nonsense! But when things go perverted then these types of things happen. Now the Masterses and Johnsons—they have become the experts, the final authorities. If you are having any sexual problem then they are the final authority to go to. And I suspect they have missed their youth, they have not lived their sex life rightly. Somewhere something is lacking and they are fulfilling it through such tricks.

And when a thing is in the garb of science you can do anything. Now they have made false, electric penises, and those electric penises go on throbbing in the real vaginas, and they go on trying to find what is happening inside, whether orgasm is clitoral or vaginal, or what hormones are flowing, what hormones are not flowing, and how long a woman can make love. They say: to the very end. On the deathbed a woman can make love.

In fact their suggestion is that after the menopause a woman can make better love than ever—that means after the forty-ninth year. Why do they say that?—because, they say, before the forty-ninth a woman is always afraid of getting pregnant. Even if she is on the pill, no pill is a hundred percent proof; there is a fear. By the forty-ninth year, when the menopause comes and the period stops, then there is no fear; a woman is completely free.

If their teaching spreads, women are going to become vampires, and old women will chase men because they are unafraid now and the authority sanctions it. In fact they say that then it is the right time to enjoy—without any responsibility. And for men also they go on saying the same. And they have come across men—so now they say there is no average—they have come across a man who in his sixtieth year can make love five times a day. This man seems to be a freak. Something is wrong with his hormones and his body....And at the age of sixty! He is not natural, because as I see it—and this I am saying out of my own experience in many lives, I can remember them—by the forty-ninth year a natural man is not interested in women; the interest goes. As it comes, it goes!

Everything that comes has to go. Everything that arises has to fall. Every wave that arises has to disappear. There must be a time when it goes. At fourteen it comes; at forty-nine or nearabout it goes.

But a man making love five times a day at the age of sixty—something is wrong, something is very very wrong. His body is not functioning rightly. It is the other end of impotence, the other extreme. When a boy of fourteen does not feel any sex, a young man of eighteen has no desire, something is wrong—he has to be treated. When a man of sixty needs to make love five times a day, something is wrong. His body has gone berserk. It is not functioning rightly, naturally.

If you live in the moment totally, then there is no need to worry for the future. A rightly lived childhood brings you to a right, ripe youth—flowing, vital, alive, a wild ocean of energy. A rightly lived youth brings you to a very settled calm and quiet life. A calm and quiet life brings you to a religious inquiry: What is life? Living is not enough, one has to penetrate the mystery. A calm and quiet life brings you to meditative moments. Meditation brings you to renounce all that is useless now, just junk, garbage. The whole life becomes garbage; only one thing remains always eternally valuable, and that is your awareness.

By the time of the seventieth year, when you are ready to die—if you lived everything rightly, in the moment, never postponing for the future, never dreaming for the future, you lived it totally in the moment whatsoever it was—nine months before your death you will become aware...you have attained that much awareness, you can see: now death is coming.

Many saints have declared their deaths, but I have not come across a single instance when the death was declared before nine months. Exactly nine months before, a man of awareness, uncluttered with the past...because one who never thinks of the future will never think of the past. They are together, the past and future are together, joined together. When you think of the future it is nothing but the projection of the past; when you think of the past it is nothing but trying to plan for the future. They are together. The present is out of them. A man who lives in this moment now and here is not cluttered with the past and not cluttered with the future. He remains unburdened. He has no burden to carry, he moves without weight. Gravitation doesn't affect him. In fact, he doesn't walk, he flies. He has wings....

Before he dies, exactly nine months before, he will become aware that death is coming. And he will enjoy and he will celebrate and he will say to people, 'My ship is coming, and

I am only for a little while more on this bank. Soon I will be going to my home. This life has been beautiful, a strange experience. I loved, learned, lived much, I am enriched. I had come here with nothing and I am going with much experience, much maturity.'

He will be thankful to all that has happened—good and bad both, right and wrong both, because from *every*thing he learned, not only from right, from wrong also. Sages that he came across, he learned from them; and sinners, yes, from them also—they all helped. People who robbed him helped, people who helped him helped, people who were friends helped, people who were enemies helped. Everything helped. Summer and winter, satiety and hunger, everything helped. One can be thankful to all.

When one is thankful to all and ready to die celebrating for this opportunity that was there, death becomes beautiful. Then death is not the enemy, it is the greatest friend, because it is the crescendo of life. It is the highest peak that life achieves. It is not the end of life, it is the climax. It looks like the end because you have never known life. To one who has known life it appears as the very crescendo, the very peak, the highest peak.

Death is the culmination, the fulfilment. Life does not end in it; in fact life flowers in it, it *is* the flower. But to know the beauty of death one has to be ready for it, one has to learn the art. That's why I go on saying that I am here to teach you how to die. A master is a death. He allows you to die in him. He helps you to die every moment to the past, and he helps you to live an uncluttered moment—this moment.

This small parable is beautiful. It says:

Uwais Al-Qarni was offered some money...

Money is a symbol of the future. Why do you accumulate money?—for the future. Money is future, money is hidden future; that's why people who don't live in the present will always cling to money. They can afford to lose love but they cannot afford to lose money, because love is not a promise for the future. It may be good right now but what will you do in your old age? Be miserly, accumulate money, because in the future money will be helpful.

Why are people so mad after money? It is a symbol of the future. Money is future. Money is condensed future in a coin, in a note. It is a promise for the future. Every note says, 'I promise that this much amount of money whenever demanded will be given to you.' It is a promise for the future.

Misers never live here, they cannot. They live in their money. Uwais is an enlightened master. He was offered some money. It is a symbol, a symbol for the future. He was offered some future—let me put it that way.

He said: 'I do not need it as I already have a coin.'

Already I have a coin, I don't need it. Right now I am living, he said. And right now it is enough. I have a coin. What coin? This moment is the coin. It is a single coin, a very small coin. You can live it here now, it is not of much use for the future. It is such a small coin, you will look foolish if you gather it for the future. A moment is so small, it is a coin. Time is a promissory note, a thousand rupee note, a one lakh rupee note, a one crore rupee note. Time is big money. A moment—it is just a drop, a small coin.

'I do *not* need it as I already have a coin,' said Uwais.

The other must not have understood. Difficult, difficult when you talk to a man like Uwais. He has a different language, you have a different language; communication becomes impossible.

The other said: 'How long will that last you?—it is nothing.'

And he was looking at the coin, thinking of the coin; he did not understand what Uwais is saying. He said, 'How long will it last you?' The present moment, how long can it last? It is such a small coin. It will be finished.

'Don't think of the moment,' say the wiser ones. They say, 'Think of the future.' Say the wiser ones: 'Don't think of the immediate, how long will it last you? Think of the future.' And I tell you, these 'wiser' ones are the poisoners of humanity. They have poisoned your mind completely... because the immediate is all that is there. The immediate moment is the only reality that is there. Howsoever small, it is the only reality. And your promissory notes, howsoever big amounts they promise in the future, are simply promissory notes. The future never comes. No governor of the reserve bank can give you the guarantee for the future. Future?— who can guarantee it? who can predict it? How long will it last you? It is nothing, just a moment.

The wiser ones say, 'Don't live the momentary life.' They say, 'Think of the future.' They say, 'Don't live just here and now, look ahead! Think of the long range—not only of this world, of the other world also. Think of heaven and hell, moksha, Brahman, nirvana.' And I say to you, these wiser ones are poisoners. The real wisdom consists in being here and now because for the real wisdom that is the only existence, there is no other existence. It is the only existence there is.

> *Uwais answered: 'Guarantee me that I shall live longer than this sum will suffice me and I will accept your gift.'*

It is a beautiful dialogue. Uwais said: Guarantee me that I shall live longer, longer than this moment, this small coin. Can you guarantee me that I will live the next moment? Can you guarantee me that I will live tomorrow? If you cannot guarantee me that then please let me live today. If you cannot guarantee the next moment, then howsoever small this moment is please let me live it right now. Once lost, it is lost forever, and you cannot guarantee the next. So why should I waste my small coin for bigger coins which cannot be guaranteed?

Future is never; only this moment is. Don't listen to so-called wise ones who are really foolish. Listen to life! And listen to existence. It is better to go to the trees and listen how they live, go to the animals and watch how they live. Look all around, except at man. Man is perverted. Look at existence and see how existence lives—it lives moment to moment, with no planning for the future. That's why it is so beautiful, it is so ecstatic. Its ecstasy knows no boundaries. From one moment it flows into the other, but it never thinks of the other. One moment lived totally automatically brings another moment, with more possibilities—because the other moment is not coming from somewhere else, it grows out of you as leaves grow out of trees.

If the tree has been healthy, lived really, then out of beautiful trees come beautiful leaves, beautiful flowers and fruits. It need not worry about them. Have you seen any tree sitting like Rodin's statue of 'The Thinker' with the hand under the chin, wrinkles on the forehead, thinking how to bring fruits, how to flower this season again? where to go? who are the experts to ask? where to find a guru? It doesn't bother. Even if gurus come to them and talk to them they won't listen. They will say, 'Go somewhere else, find some stupid human being. Here no gurus are needed. We are already okay, absolutely okay. '

When the time comes, the tree flowers. When the time comes, it is laden with fruits. When the time comes, fruits are ripe, ready to fall, die into the earth, create new seeds, new trees—and the circle goes on and on and on. It is eternal. From each moment is born another moment—it comes out of it. Live it as totally as possible, because through that totality another will be born.

Uwais said: *'Guarantee that I shall live longer than this sum will suffice me.'*

This small coin of the moment seems to be enough for me because who can guarantee that there is going to be another moment for me to live? If you can guarantee it, I will accept your gift.

Nobody can guarantee the future. Only the present is. Live it as deeply, as ecstatically, as dancingly as possible, because from it will come the next....

I don't talk to you about the next life because I don't talk about even the next moment. The next life will come, I know. It comes, it always comes, why bother...? You live this life totally and the next will come out of this. If this has been beautiful the next is going to be better than this.

This moment will decide the fate of the next moment that is going to follow. There is no other way. Death is the only guarantee. This moment lived well is the only guarantee for the next moment which is going to follow it, because it is not following really, it is coming out of it, it is an outcome. You are growing each moment. Don't leave gaps, otherwise those gaps will hang around you. They will be holes in your being. In those holes will be wounds, and they will colour your whole life to come.

Die to the past. Die to the future and live in the present.

Death is the only message that I would like to give to you—and if you can allow, millions of things will become possible to you. Let me repeat the Sufi saying: Simply trust. Do not the petals flutter down just like that? Trust life. Trust this moment here and now and allow things to take their own shape. You need not worry, there is no need to worry. Trust life, simply trust.

Do not the petals flutter down just like that?

Go and see a rose, and by the evening the petals are fluttering down towards the earth, going to rest. They lived their day. They enjoyed, they enjoyed the strong wind, they took the challenge, they rose high in the sky. They have spread their fragrance to the four winds—the winds have taken it already to the corners of the earth. They loved the sun, they played with it a little while. Their day is over. Now they don't cling. Now they don't hesitate to fall. They are ready.

A beautiful life creates a beautiful death, because death is nothing but the whole life condensed again in a seed.

Now the petals are falling. Evening has come. The sun has set, the night will take over. The death has come, the petals are falling towards the earth. They don't hesitate. They don't know where they are going, they don't know whether there is any earth down there or not—maybe it is a bottomless abyss—but they don't doubt, they don't hesitate.

When you have lived your life, trust arises. It arises—it is an afterglow of a lived life.

Petals falling, fluttering down towards the earth. Simply trust—do not the petals flutter down just like that? And everything—god, moksha, nirvana—everything, I say to you, becomes possible.

Just trust. Just like that.

Enough for today.

OSHO INTERNATIONAL MEDITATION RESORT

Every year the OSHO International Meditation Resort welcomes thousands of people from over 100 countries who come to enjoy and participate in its unique atmosphere of meditation and celebration. The 40-acre meditation resort is located about 100 miles southeast of Mumbai (Bombay), in Pune, India, in a tree-lined residential area set against a backdrop of bamboo groves and wild jasmine, peacocks and waterfalls.

The basic approach of the meditation resort is that of Zorba the Buddha: living in awareness, with a capacity to celebrate everything in life. Many visitors come to just be, to allow themselves the luxury of doing nothing. Others choose to participate in a wide variety of courses and sessions that support moving toward a more joyous and less stressful life by combining methods of self-understanding with awareness techniques. These courses are offered through OSHO Multiversity and take place in a pyramid complex next to the famous OSHO Teerth Park.

You can choose to practise various meditation methods, both active and passive, from a daily schedule that begins at six o'clock in the morning. Each evening there is a meditation event that moves from dance to silent sitting, using Osho's recorded talks as an opportunity to experience inner silence without effort.

Facilities include tennis courts, a gym, sauna, Jacuzzi, a nature-shaped Olympic-sized swimming pool, classes in zen archery, tai chi, chi gong, yoga and a multitude of bodywork sessions.

The kitchen serves international gourmet vegetarian meals, made with organically grown produce. The nightlife is alive with friends dining under the stars, with music and dancing.

Make online bookings for accommodation at the new OSHO Guesthouse inside the meditation resort through the website below or drop us an email at guesthouse@osho.com

Take an online tour of the meditation resort, and access travel and programme information at: www.osho.com/resort

FOR MORE INFORMATION

www.OSHO.com

A comprehensive multi-language website including OSHO
Books, talks (audio and video), a magazine, the OSHO
Library text archive in English and Hindi with a searchable
facility, and extensive information about OSHO Meditation
techniques.
You will also find the programme schedule of the OSHO
Multiversity and information about the OSHO International
Meditation Resort.
The original recordings of the talks/interviews in this book
can be downloaded from www.osho.com/audiobooks

To contact **OSHO International Foundation** go to:
www.osho.com/oshointernational

OSHO International Meditation Resort
17 Koregaon Park
Pune 411001 MS, India
resortinfo@osho.net